The Modern Brazilian Stage

The Modern Brazilian Stage

By David George

University of Texas Press
Austin

Photo on page i: Eles Não Usam Black-Tie, *by G. Guarnieri. Teatro de Arena, 1958. Dir.: José Renato. Oduvaldo Vianna Filho and Xandó Batista. Photo: Hejo.*

Photo on page iii: Arena Conta Zumbi, *by Guarnieri and Boal. Teatro de Arena, 1965. Dir.: Boal. Dina Sfat, Marilia Medalha, Lima Duarte, Vanya Sant'Anna, Chant Dessian, Guarnieri. Photo: Derly Marques.*

Photographs from Arquivo Multimeios, Divisão de Pesquisas, Centro Cultural São Paulo, Secretaria Municipal de Cultura–PMSP.

Copyright © 1992 by the University of Texas Press

Printed in the United States of America

First edition, 1992

10001 69634

Requests for permission to reproduce material from this work should be sent to Permissions, University of Texas Press, Box 7819, Austin, TX 78713-7819.

♾ The paper used in this publication meets the minimum requirements of American National Standard for Information Sciences—Permanence of Paper for Printed Library Materials, ANSI Z39.48-1984.

Grateful acknowledgment is made to Editora Perspectiva, São Paulo, Brazil, for permission to use previously published materials from *Grupo Macunaíma: Carnavalização e Mito* by David George, Copyright © 1990.

Material from "Towards a Poor Theatre in Brazil," by David George, originally published in *Theatre Research International* 14, no. 2 (1989): 152–164, reprinted by permission of Oxford University Press.

Material from "Os Comediantes and Bridal Gown" and "Nelson 2 Rodrigues," originally published in *Latin American Literary Review*, Fall 1987 and Spring 1988, reprinted by permission of Center of Latin American Studies, University of Kansas.

Library of Congress Cataloging-in-Publication Data

George, David Sanderson.
    The modern Brazilian stage / by David George. — 1st ed.
        p.   cm.
    Includes bibliographical references and index.
    ISBN 0-292-75129-X
    1. Theater—Brazil—History—20th century.   2. Brazilian drama—20th century—History and criticism.   3. Rodrigues, Nelson—Dramatic production.   I. Title.
PN2471.G46   1992
792'.0981—dc20   91-579
                                                   CIP

For Bill and Laverne George

Contents

Right: O Rei da Vela, *by Oswald de Andrade. Teatro Oficina, 1967. Dir.: José Celso M. Corrêa. Edgard G. Aranha, Etty Fraser, and Renato Borghi. Photo: Fredi Kleemann.*

Acknowledgments

This book was written with a National Endowment for the Humanities Fellowship for College Teachers.

Acknowledgments: Sábato Magaldi, Alex Severino, Décio de Almeida Prado, and Merlin Foster, with a special debt of gratitude to George Woodyard.

Arsenic and Old Lace, by J. Kesselring.
*TBC, 1949. Dir.: Adolfo Celi. A. C.
Carvalho, Ruy Affonso Machado,
and Maurício Barroso. Photo: Fredi
Kleemann.*

Introduction

Overview

Teachers and critics in the arts and humanities have begun to look beyond the confines of their specializations and to view the traditional objects of their studies in the context of other disciplines. Among the best examples of this interdisciplinary interpretive strategy is the examination of relationships between dramatic literature and theatrical praxis, the performance-related approach. Scholars of American and European theatre have been in the forefront of a critical revolution, whose central thesis is that *dramatic texts are scripts that come to life on the stage.* This apparently simple idea flies in the face of the traditional approach, which has focused solely on scrutiny of the dramatic text. In the new scholarship, studies of performance and stagecraft are wedded to textual analyses in order to reexamine theatre from the perspective of its practitioners, to encompass a total theatrical language. The school of criticism to which I adhere has attempted to bring to Latin American theatre criticism this performance-related approach.

The Modern Brazilian Stage is a study of the theatrical companies and productions that have had the greatest impact on the development of Brazil's stagecraft, from the 1940s to the present. Utilizing the performance-related approach, the book scrutinizes a total theatrical language: the interrelationships of dramatic texts, stagecraft, and theatre groups. That is, it examines the history of several companies and their unique contributions to Brazilian stagecraft. I chose three of the groups for inclusion in the book because, among other reasons, each mounted at least one production whose impact on Brazilian theatre has been so great that by itself it points the way toward the future and by which all subsequent stagings would have to be measured. The chapters on specific stagings begin with a structural and thematic scrutiny of each playtext, utilizing a variety of analytical methods, depending on the work. The central issue in

Above: Eles Não Usam Black-Tie, *by*
G. Guarnieri. Teatro de Arena, 1958.
Dir.: José Renato. Guarnieri and Miriam
Mehler. Photo: Hejo.

Right above: Romeo and Juliet, *by*
W. Shakespeare. Centro de Pesquisa
Teatral/SESC–Grupo de Teatro
Macunaima, 1984. Dir.: Antunes Filho.
Giulia Gam and Marco Antonio Pamio.
Photo: João Caldas.

Right below: Summer and Smoke, *by*
Tennessee Williams. TBC, 1950. Dir.:
Luciano Salce. Sérgio Cardoso and
Cacilda Becker. Photo: Fredi Kleemann.

those chapters, however, is an in-depth analysis of the total language
of stagecraft; in other words, how does the playtext translate to the
boards? I examine the process of collaborative revision by which the
script is transformed by the director, actors, and designers into a visual and auditory "text." That means taking into account directorial
vision; mise-en-scène; acting styles and techniques; collaborative
rehearsal methods; light and set design; forms of blocking, movement, and choreography; use of special sound and visual effects and
music; and critical and audience response. This book is not primarily about dramaturgy, but it does discuss many of Brazil's most
significant modern playwrights, whose works were staged by the
companies in question, such as Oswald de Andrade, Augusto Boal,
Gianfrancesco Guarnieri, and most importantly, Nelson Rodrigues.

In assessing how and why I consider each troupe a key link in a forty-year national aesthetic evolution, I place it within a theatrical milieu, by comparing the company to contemporaneous Brazilian groups and by considering the influences of American and European theatre in each period. The study also weighs the influence of socio-historical context: (*a*) Getúlio Vargas's revolution, Corporatist New State, incipient populism, and repression (1930–1945); (*b*) developmentalism, populism, and nationalist euphoria (1946–1964); (*c*) military coup, state of siege, and reign of terror (1964–1975); and (*d*) gradual redemocratization and the end of military rule (1976–1988). The book considers theatrical response to the historical period, whether engagé social consciousness, in the case of Teatro de Arena, or countercultural *épater les bourgeois*, in the case of Teatro Oficina; it assesses the effects of the political climate on the companies by examining such issues as paramilitary terrorism and censorship.

Chapters 1 and 2 deal with Os Comediantes, the first *modern* company whose revolutionary 1943 staging of Nelson Rodrigues's *Vestido de Noiva* (*Bridal Gown*) broke with the outmoded comedy-of-manners formula that had dominated the national stage since the nineteenth century. The work, about a voyage through the unconscious, includes an examination of the play in the light of Jungian archetypes and their translation into visual images on the stage. Chapter 3 examines three companies: the Teatro Brasileiro de Comédia, which in the 1950s established a tradition of stagecraft with solid production values, based on Italian models; Teatro de Arena, which spearheaded the new engagé theatre of the 1960s and attempted to "Brazilianize" certain Brechtian principles; and Teatro Oficina, which introduced original Brazilian forms of stagecraft, based on both international avant-garde modes and popular Brazilian forms. Chapter 4 deals with Oficina's most notable production, the 1967 *O Rei da Vela* (*The Candle King*). I examine the play and the staging principally in terms of the application of the nationalist aesthetic of Anthropophagy and avant-garde techniques. Chapter 5 deals with the transition from the wasteland of the 1970s, in which a repressive military dictatorship muzzled artistic expression, to theatrical rebirth in the form of the Grupo Macunaíma and its 1979 stage adaptation of the seminal Modernist work of the same name—*Macunaíma*—while chapter 6 analyzes the company's continuing revolution in stagecraft, its 1984 production *Nelson 2 Rodrigues*. The book therefore begins and ends with stagings by Brazil's greatest modern playwright, Nelson Rodrigues.

Above: **Nelson 2 Rodrigues,** *by Nelson Rodrigues. Centro de Pesquisa Teatral/ SESC–Grupo de Teatro Macunaima, 1984. Dir.: Antunes Filho. Giulia Gam, Cissa Carvalho, Marlene Fortuna, Flávia Steward, and Lúcia de Souza. Photo: João Caldas.*

Right: **Macunaima,** *by Mário de Andrade. Grupo Pau Brasil, 1978. Dir.: Antunes Filho. Isa Kopelman, Deivi Rose, Teodora Ribeiro, Salma Buzzar, Mirtes Mesquita, Whalmyr Barros, Jair Assumpção, and Walter Portella. Photo: Ruth A. Toldeo.*

Above: **Nelson 2 Rodrigues,** *by Nelson Rodrigues. Centro de Pesquisa Teatral/ SESC–Grupo de Teatro Macunaima, 1984. Dir.: Antunes Filho. Marcos Oliveira. Photo: João Caldas.*

Right: O Rei da Vela, *by Oswald de Andrade. Teatro Oficina, 1967. Dir.: José Celso M. Corrêa. Renato Borghi. Photo: Fredi Kleemann.*

Nationalism and the Foreign Model

Central to my discussion of the Brazilian stage is the notion that the companies studied were driven by the desire to establish a national aesthetic, but their initial sources of inspiration came from Europe and the United States. That conflict, between cultural nationalism and foreign influence, produced a creative tension in part responsible for the groups' extraordinary successes. Each troupe examined in *The Modern Brazilian Stage*, while charting a course for an independent national theatre, owes a great debt to a foreign mode, theorist, director, or company: Os Comediantes to European Expressionism; Teatro Brasileiro de Comédia, the Italian stage of the 1940s and 1950s; Teatro de Arena, Brecht; Teatro Oficina, the Berliner Ensemble and the Living Theater; and Grupo Macunaíma, Robert Wilson and Jerzy Grotowski. The question of the foreign model—artistic, philosophical, economic—is fundamental to the concepts, consciousness, and ideologies of Brazilian national identity. Since the late nineteenth century, Brazilian thinkers and artists have become increasingly aware of the profound impact of imported forms on the national culture, and they have consequently experienced what amounts to a manic-depressive swing. The task of creating a national cultural identity has seemed at times hopeless; at other times writers and artists have proclaimed gleefully—or stridently— a new ideology of Brazilian culture. But the foreign model, whether rejected or embraced, has remained at the starting gate of every new direction.

Research

The writing of *The Modern Brazilian Stage* was funded by a fellowship from the National Endowment for the Humanities. The book brings to fruition a decade of research and publication on Brazilian theatre, on which I have brought to bear an extensive background as a theatre director, actor, and designer. I have conducted ongoing field research in Brazil since 1977, have led numerous theatre workshops in that country, and in 1984 I taught and directed in the University of São Paulo's theatre program. The book's broad scope and detailed analysis required a vast amount of data gathering for reconstruction of stagings and the companies' complex histories. I have relied on such material as interviews, books, articles, reviews, playscripts, programs, directors' notes, films, videotapes, photographs, and in the case of Grupo Macunaíma, because I have worked with the group and have seen its productions several times, my firsthand observations.

Right: L'Invitation au chateau, *by Jean Anouilh. TBC, 1951. Dir.: Luciano Salce. Eugênio Kusnet and Ziembinski. Photo: Fredi Kleemann.*

The Modern Brazilian Stage

1. Rio Theatre in the 1940s:
Os Comediantes

Rio de Janeiro was surely one of the most beautiful capitals in the world in the 1930s—the new capital in Brasília would not be built for decades—before pollution marred its beaches, smog dirtied its air, and population pressure and real estate speculation destroyed much of its architectural legacy. Rio was also the center of theatrical activity in Brazil and had been for more than a century.

The nation during the period was undergoing profound political changes. The continual coffee crises of the 1920s and the 1929 world economic collapse brought to power Getúlio Vargas, from the southern state of Rio Grande do Sul, whose 1930 Revolution put an end to the hegemony in national politics of the coffee-growing states, São Paulo and Minas Gerais. Ideology became polarized between Left and Right during the decade, and in 1937 Vargas assumed dictatorial powers and set up the Estado Novo, or New State, modeled after Mussolini's Corporatist State.

Brazilian artistic activity reflected and in some cases foreshadowed political and economic changes. The 1922 Modern Art Week (Semana de Arte Moderna), held in São Paulo in conjunction with the centennial independence celebration, launched the first Modernist generation, which revolutionized literary language through the assimilation of European avant-garde modes and their fusion with native forms and unique aspects of Brazilian Portuguese. The arts focused increasingly on national themes: Modernism attempted to "Brazilianize" literature, music, and painting. If the first phase of the revolution was exclusively aesthetic, succeeding generations produced significant engagé works, such as the novels of northeastern writers Jorge Amado, Graciliano Ramos, and Rachel de Queiroz in the 1930s. The year 1945 marks the end of the last phase of Modernism, but its influence is pervasive even today. There was one art form, however, that the artistic revolution failed to change in the twenties and thirties: theatre. The modern Brazilian stage was waiting to be born.

The national stage had been dominated since the nineteenth century by the comedy of manners, or *comédia de costumes,* which along with melodrama, operetta, and vaudeville (*revista*) still held sway in the 1930s and to some degree into the 1940s. The comedy of manners had once been a breakthrough in theatre art and constituted an autochthonous, popular genre. Martins Pena (1815–1848) "is the founder of our *comédia de costumes,* a rich vein . . . of Brazilian theatrical literature" (Magaldi, *Panorama* 40). He "extended the model of the Portuguese farce and created a typically Brazilian genre of light comedy" (Cacciaglia, *História* 3). To lighten the mood of the ponderous Romantic dramas, "a farce was served up as dessert. In Brazil, these farces were almost all Portuguese and were quite brief, just long enough to get a few laughs. . . . Martins Pena broadened the scope of the farce and introduced characters and situations from the *carioca* reality of the period. . . . His characters were stock types and his stories were thin [because] his main concern was to construct clever devices to provoke the public to raucous laughter" (47). The comedy-of-manners genre proved to be a rich source of inspiration for successive generations of comic authors, but by the 1930s what was once innovative and satirical had become tired and merely formulaic. Most artists and intellectuals—but few theatre reviewers—considered the comedy of manners an outdated form that had to be replaced, and many scorned the national stage as nothing more than a popular entertainment whose sole purpose was to get laughs. Modernist critic Antônio de Alcântara Machado summed up the comedy of manners in this exasperated fashion: "Give us no more stupid Portuguese; pretentious mulatto women who mix French and Portuguese . . . ; meddlesome servants; truculent mothers-in-law who verbally torture carousing sons-in-law . . . and stop filling comedies with screaming faints, much running about, conjugal betrayal, family quarrels . . ." (Alcântara Machado, "Terra" 141–142).[1]

The theatres themselves were located in the center of Rio and doubled as cinemas. As did the comedies they produced, the buildings followed nineteenth-century models. The stage was wide and high, so that cardboard or cloth backdrops could be raised and lowered easily. An orchestra pit was necessary for operettas and vaudeville. Seating was divided into main floor, balcony (box seats), and gallery, corresponding to social hierarchy.

Professional troupes had exclusive control over theatrical activity. The public favored particularly the Procópio Ferreira Company, which specialized in Brazilian comedies of manners and German and Spanish light comedies; the Jaime Costa, which staged mainly

Brazilian comedies of manners and an occasional drama; and the Eva Tudor and Dulcina-Odilon companies, both of which would eventually develop a more serious and artistic repertoire. The companies in turn were controlled by a single comic actor–impresario, the most famous of whom were Leopoldo Fróes (1882–1932) and Procópio Ferreira (1898–1979). Their success was based on a comic persona rather than on technical or artistic skill. Audiences expected them to play always the same character. The comic actors were Rio's, and therefore Brazil's, theatrical essence. In addition, there were many satellites revolving around the star. Most important were the character actors who played stock types and were applauded for their versatility. Some actors specialized in specific roles: male and female romantic characters, ingenue, old maid, devoted mother, and so on. Playscripts rarely strayed from these stock characters; they differed only according to minor plot variations.

Although there was no director in the modern sense, indispensable to production was a general coordinator known as the *ensaiador*. He was responsible for blocking, which he had to do quickly and efficiently, since companies often changed plays on a weekly basis. The *ensaiador* was in charge of the set, usually representing a drawing room. Lighting was simple and purely functional, so the role of lighting designer did not exist. There were no costume designers: each company had a wardrobe for occasional period pieces, but most plays had a modern setting and actors furnished their own costumes.

The *ensaiador* conducted rehearsals, which the lead actor did not attend with any regularity, for his real work was onstage in front of the audience, improvising and ad-libbing, using his imagination to improve inferior texts. The written word did not have the "sacred" respect it receives on the modern stage. In fact, authors were flattered by the comic actor's ad-libs. It was him audiences came to see; his single aim was to extract from them as many laughs as possible. Stagings were tentative and sloppy, and the comic actor had to be prompted constantly. The role of the prompter was therefore essential to avoid total chaos; he worked in the traditional box beneath the proscenium arch and was in general control of the show, aiding actors with lines and blocking cues, pressing buttons to signal light and curtain changes, and producing sound effects.

Theatre was a closed circle with built-in defects; it was a nineteenth-century relic. Careless stagecraft, the predominance of one comic star, and eternal type-casting reinforced, and were reinforced by, comedies without artistic merit or social concerns. By the late 1930s the Brazilian stage was sagging and change was urgent.

During that decade, a few professional companies made tentative steps to change the outmoded system, to put drama on an equal footing with comedy and to express social concerns on the stage. Three plays foreshadowed the transformation that would take place in the 1940s. The most famous, one that is occasionally included in anthologies even today, was Joracy Camargo's *Deus Lhe Pague*,[2] produced in 1932. The play deals with social problems aggravated by the 1929 economic crisis and had Marxist revolutionary overtones, but was highly successful mainly for its witticisms, bombastic language, and clever plot. Some critics believed the work was a harbinger of a genuine national theatre, and so it appeared. Renato Vianna's 1932 *Sexo* introduced the Freudian revolution to the stage and denounced masculine sexual tyranny. The 1933 production of *Amor* by Oduvaldo Vianna, whose son would become one of contemporary Brazil's most distinguished playwrights, railed against archaic legal and social strictures that prohibited divorce. The three works, however, were essentially thesis plays cast from a nineteenth-century mold and offered few innovations in terms of stagecraft. The thematic changes they promised were cut short by the rigorous censorship imposed by Vargas's New State.

Once censorship was imposed, Brazilian dramaturgy avoided controversial subjects, but a few theatres attempted to elevate the technical level of their stagings and depart from the comedy-of-manners formula; they began to produce historical comedies, epic dramas, and historical-sentimental plays, full of pomp and splendor. One innovative production was *Tiradentes*, staged in 1939 by the Olga Delorges Company. Tiradentes was the father of Brazilian independence and has long been a national symbol of struggle against tyranny. One can only speculate whether the Olga Delorges Company used the theme to criticize implicitly the Estado Novo, thereby circumventing censorship. São Paulo's Teatro de Arena would return to the subject in 1967, with a play entitled *Arena Conta Tiradentes* (Arena Narrates Tiradentes): in this case the historical metaphor unquestionably served as a means to denounce the military dictatorship and to skirt the barriers of censorship. The 1930s historical dramas brought some limited progress to stagecraft by making the spectacle broader and more flexible. The Dulcina-Odilon was the most daring of the professional companies, with productions of French boulevard comedies and American plays. Attempts to modernize the Brazilian stage, however, fell far short of the changes taking place in the other arts.

Modernist aesthetics did not revolutionize the stage; theatrical transformation would not take place until two decades after the 1922 Modern Art Week. And its most radical avant-garde precepts would only appear for the first time on the stage in Teatro Oficina's 1967 production of Oswald de Andrade's *O Rei da Vela* (*The Candle King*), composed three decades earlier. However, several Modernists attempted seriously, albeit unsuccessfully, to change Brazilian theatre. The only company that purported to bring innovative concepts to the stage was Eugênia and Álvaro Moreyra's Teatro de Brinquedo, or Game Theatre, which presented occasional works for Rio's intellectual elite in the late 1920s. The company's name derives from the Modernists' love of aesthetic games and jokes. Its one noteworthy production was Álvaro Moreyra's play *Adão e Eva, e Outros Membros da Família* (Adam and Eve, and Other Members of the Family). The group's efforts were frustrated, partly because neither the public nor the commercial theatre was ready for innovation, but also because the Moreyras were literati with little experience in stagecraft. Their productions were intelligent, well intentioned, but very amateurish diversions. They had no impact beyond a small circle of Modernist devotees.

First-generation Modernism's principal literary figures belatedly tried their hand at dramaturgy. Mário de Andrade wrote an operetta, *O Café*, in 1934. The work, more of a libretto than a play and never staged, deals with the coffee crises and rural poverty of the 1920s. Oswald de Andrade wrote three plays in quick succession during the 1930s: *O Rei da Vela*, *O Homem e o Cavalo* (The Man and the Horse), and *A Morta* (The Dead Woman). Those works were ignored at the time and fell into oblivion until Teatro Oficina's explosive production. Modernist drama critics, on the other hand, were influential in their own time.

Modernist criticism called for a theatre that would incorporate European modes, such as Expressionism, but most of all national themes and characters that had never appeared on the Brazilian stage. Critics were interested in what was most popular and authentic, such as the circus. Oswald de Andrade, Mário de Andrade, and others propagated the concept of native primitivism, which meant that Brazilian literature, including theatre, had to start from scratch with the simplest elements, the common denominators of national culture. The foremost Modernist writer on theatre, Antônio de Alcântara Machado, foresaw to a surprising degree the evolution that would take place during the following decades. The universalism he viewed as necessary to renew theatrical language would be later effected by Os Comediantes. His vision of a theatre informed by popular culture would be fulfilled in the 1960s by Teatro de Arena and Teatro Oficina. What he did not envision was that renovation would come first to stagecraft and only much later to dramaturgy.

The thirties, in sum, present an unfavorable picture of Brazilian theatre. "Commercial theatre, on its most ambitious level, failed to carry out any of its aesthetic goals or historical obligations. It was unable to withstand the impact of the cinema, continually losing ground as popular entertainment. It had nothing fundamental to say about Brazilian life and failed to carry through, as it once yearned to do, the messages of Marx and Freud. Most important, it was unable to incorporate the new literary tendencies [cultivated by] poetry and the novel" (Almeida Prado, *História* 540).

The problem was twofold: professional theatre depended exclusively on the box office and the expectations of the audience for entertainment and for the tried-and-true (Oswald de Andrade called it *o teatro, esse corpo gangrenado,* "the theatre, that gangrenous corpse"). It needed less, not more "professionalism." The necessary changes could not be effected within the context of commercial theatre. The amateurs would have to fill that need.

Amateur theatre has often been a source of renewal for the Western stage. Several examples come immediately to mind: Stanislavsky and the Moscow Art Players, O'Neill's Provincetown Players, and such avant-garde groups of the 1960s as the Living Theatre and the Open Theatre. Amateur theatre can play this role because it does not have to depend for survival on the box office, can hold its focus tightly on aesthetic and social values and form a new, younger, and more open audience. Professionalism can then reappear with a new artistic, social, and even economic purpose. That is precisely what happened in Brazil during the 1940s.

If Rio's professional companies in the 1930s were unimportant to the Modernist revolution, amateur theatre held no significance whatsoever until late in the decade. Its productions failed to attract wide audiences, functioning only within the context of clubs and other social organizations, putting on productions that represented amateurism at its worst. But at the turn of the decade things began to change.

A number of nonprofessional troupes were formed in the late 1930s and early 1940s, in both Rio and São Paulo, with aspirations to transform the theatre, to raise it to the level of the other arts, and to bring it into the mainstream of aesthetic renovation begun in 1922. But they lacked the technical know-how; that would have to come from Europe. In the end a few of them distinguished themselves and gained the support of the intellectuals, writers, and artists. They became a source of renovation and high aesthetic standards and had a profound influence on professional companies. Two amateur companies that contributed enormously to the advancement of the Brazilian stage were the Teatro do Estudante do Brasil, and the most influential, Os Comediantes.

Teatro do Estudante do Brasil

The Teatro do Estudante do Brasil (TEB) was founded in 1938 by Paschoal Carlos Magno (1906–1980). Diplomat, former member of Teatro de Brinquedo, critic, playwright, artistic director, and festival organizer, his enthusiasm and energy were legendary. Intimately familiar with European theatrical know-how, his influence spread throughout Brazil. In the late 1950s and early 1960s, he organized a series of national student theatre festivals that helped launch the careers of countless actors, playwrights, directors, and companies, the most important of which was Teatro Oficina.

Paschoal Carlos Magno formed the TEB when, upon his return from a diplomatic post in England, he found Brazilian theatre in a state of decadence: professional companies proliferated while audiences dwindled, actors had no training, and theatres lacked technical orientation. It was his objective to help transform the national stage, and he contributed to the renovation that was to take place in the 1940s.

TEB's first production was *Romeo and Juliet,* directed by Itália Fausta. Breaking with the tradition of drawing room and backdrop, the production included several changes of set. It featured a large cast, dance, and music. The TEB staged Western classics, as well as works by Brazilian authors, including nineteenth-century Romantics José de Alencar and Gonçalves Dias. Among the foreign authors whose works the TEB staged were Euripedes, Camões, Gil Vicente, Molière, Marivaux, and Ibsen. The company continued to present Shakespeare—*Macbeth, Midsummer Night's Dream*—and held a Shakespeare festival in 1949. Its most illustrious staging was the 1948 *Hamlet,* according to drama historians one of Brazil's most significant theatrical productions.

Poet Cecília Meireles translated Shakespeare's text, and Sérgio Cardoso, who would become one of Brazil's most highly regarded actors, played the lead role. He was twenty-two at the time. During the rehearsal period, the whole cast went into seclusion to study voice, movement, fencing, and Elizabethan culture, an intensive method of preparation that would characterize the groups of later decades. *Hamlet* was directed by Wolfgang Hoffman Harnish, who lent to the production a strong element of German Romanticism. By opening night the production was becoming a thing of legend. There was much ballyhoo and promotion in the press. "To stage *Hamlet* in Rio de Janeiro in 1948 was risky business, possible only for an amateur group . . . , considering the probable cost of an adequate production. . . . *Hamlet* simply took over the city, it became the main topic of conversation, it even influenced fashion" (Heliodora, "Hamlet" 42). The play was sold out for its entire run, and many young women attended every performance, forming a sort of cult following. *Hamlet* spawned jokes in the street: "Something is rotten in Rio." Sérgio Cardoso was responsible for much of the success. His delivery of lines was impeccable, he had tremendous energy, and he was willing to take terrifying—for the audience—physical risks. All of his monologues received standing ovations, and one audience carried the actor out on its shoulders. The TEB continued to present plays and tour the country until 1955, but it would never repeat the success of its staging of *Hamlet*. In the end, the TEB and Paschoal Carlos Magno influenced a transformation in Brazilian theatre that Os Comediantes brought to fruition.

Os Comediantes

Os Comediantes went from modest amateur beginnings to professional distinction. The company fulfilled the promise of the revolution begun by the TEB by placing the Brazilian stage in contact with the novel, poetry, painting, and architecture and situating it in the mainstream of universal theatre. Most scholars agree today that because of its scope, continuity, repercussion, and broad influence on the stage, the company's work marks the beginning of theatre with the aesthetic qualities of the other arts. Theatre as a phenomenon, artistic and social, had never been so important in Brazil, capable of capturing the collective imagination. Os Comediantes laid the groundwork for all the significant companies of subsequent decades: Teatro Brasileiro de Comédia, Teatro de Arena, Teatro Oficina, Grupo Macunaíma, and others. Its most important contribution was to renovate the language of the stage. Os Comediantes was a laboratory where experiments in stagecraft took place, a school, as it were, of the dramatic arts, a training ground for those who would carry on and improve upon those experiments.

The company grew initially out of an amateur theatre contest sponsored in 1938 by the Rio de Janeiro Association of Brazilian Artists. Although some of the members of that original group—then called Os Independentes—had participated in Teatro de Brinquedo, most of them, including noted artist Tomás Santa Rosa, worked in other professions, such as journalism, architecture, and painting. They were very much inspired by the TEB production of *Romeo and Juliet*, as well as the work of visiting French companies. The first step was to seek funding, which the company obtained from the Ministry of Education and Culture. The group was quite fortunate in that regard. Contrary to the rest of Vargas's Estado Novo apparatus, the ministry, headed by Gustavo Capanema, supported what was modern and even revolutionary in the arts: Os Comediantes, the work of Portinari in painting, and that of Oscar Niemeyer—who two decades later would design the new capital Brasília—in architecture. In spite of funding, Os Comediantes was entirely amateur in the beginning, and neither actors, directors, nor administrative staff were paid. Company members, in fact, often had to help with finances. Due to organizational and financial problems, but mainly because there were no precedents in Brazil for their ambitious goals, it took nearly two years of planning sessions and intermittent rehearsals before they could mount their first productions. Finally, in January 1940, Os Comediantes, as they now called themselves, staged Pirandello's *A Verdade de Cada Um* (*Right You Are*) and Marcel Achard's *Voulez-Vous Jouer Avec Moi?*, (*Uma Mulher e Tres Palhaços* [A Woman and Three Clowns]). Pirandello would be a mainstay of the early years of Teatro de Arena, and Achard's *Palhaços* would be its first successful production. The Pirandello play featured painter Santa Rosa's set design, which the audience greeted with an ovation as soon as the curtain opened, disconcerting the actors. The audience's response to the set was no fluke: Tomás Santa Rosa would become the father of modern Brazilian set design in Brazil, which he subjected to the aesthetic standards set by the Modernist revolution. Both of the company's first plays represented something new for the Brazilian stage: the possibility of a theatre approximating European models. As one of the original Os Comediantes members wrote, Santa Rosa "insisted, and there was general agreement about this, that our program should be a Brazilian interpretation of the [theatrical] movement in France" (Doria, *Teatro* 74).

The productions were greeted with enthusiasm by intellectuals previously alienated from the theatrical milieu. Among Os Comediantes's initial supporters were novelist José Lins do Rego and poets Carlos Drummond de Andrade and Manuel Bandeira. Members of the professional theatre community, on the other hand, were hostile. They accused Os Comediantes of having the gall to try and teach how theatre should be done. The theatrical status quo attacked company members as "adventurers," people without ethics attempting to destroy that which had already been established and proposing quixotically things that the public would never accept. Ironically, there was some truth in the latter point; audiences accustomed to the comedy of manners and melodrama did not support Os Comediantes,[3] but the company created new audiences, attracted to stagings of artistic quality. The older drama critics also had negative reactions to the renovations of the new company, or they paid no attention whatsoever. They were used to and defended the comedy-of-manners form and had never seen productions of visiting companies that had inspired new directions. Furthermore, critics did not review amateur stagings. In short order, however, several members of the critical community would come to the defense of the fledgling troupe.

The company had planned to stage a third production, Molière's *A Escola de Maridos* (*School for Husbands*)—later staged by Teatro de Arena—but it ran out of funds. To raise more money it planned a restaging of the Pirandello piece. Such revivals to avert financial crisis would characterize such groups as Teatro de Arena and Teatro Oficina in the following decades. It was not until late 1941 that the restaging would take place. Nevertheless, Os Comediantes continued to evolve.

The group's first director was Adacto Filho, singer and professor of diction. He was intelligent and enthusiastic but limited as a director, and his stagings were amateuristic in spite of laudable efforts to renovate production values. Company members read a great deal on directing and staging, but they lacked technical expertise. Santa Rosa was the initial driving force behind Os Comediantes who saw the need for training in the applied and practical aspects of the stage in order to go beyond the company's early intuitive phase. Those changes would come about through the efforts of Zbigniew Ziembinski, a man of the stage through and through.

The arrival of the renowned Polish actor and of other Europeans, mainly war refugees, was providential for Brazilian theatre. The Polish contingent was instrumental in revolutionizing the stage in Rio, and the Italians made a valuable contribution in São Paulo through the Teatro Brasileiro de Comédia. The Polish theatre in which Ziembinski had worked was in the mainstream of the European Expressionist theatre of Mayacovski, Rheinhardt, and Meierhold. Zbigniew Mariam Ziembinski was born in 1908, in a small town in Poland. In 1931 he became the director of the National Polish Theatre. "'When the war broke out [in 1939] I left Poland . . . and went to Rumania [and then] to Italy and France, where [I spent] two years doing theatre'" (*Nosso Século no. 49* 91).[4] On 6 July 1941, speaking no Por-

tuguese, Ziembinski arrived in Rio de Janeiro, and became immediately interested in the work of Os Comediantes, whose members
invited him to design the lighting for a restaging of *Right You Are.*
Although Adacto Filho was officially director of the production,
Ziembinski provided indispensable behind-the-scenes suggestions.
The group was fascinated with his ideas and asked him to stay. Although Ziembinski went to work elsewhere for a time due to financial considerations—the group had no money to pay him—he would
eventually devote himself entirely to Os Comediantes and transform it into his own laboratory.

The Polish director was the central force in bringing about revolutionary changes. He paved the way for elimination of the star system
by shifting the emphasis to the ensemble. He showed Brazilians
fully and for the first time the meaning of mise-en-scène. He introduced acting styles, both nonnaturalistic and nonhistrionic, based
on the imaginary and the hallucinatory, being especially versed in
Expressionist techniques. But he and other Polish emigrés also
brought the Stanislavsky method to Brazil. The latter fact is little
recognized by students of Brazilian theatre. Conventional wisdom
has it that Teatro de Arena's Augusto Boal introduced the Stanislavsky method in the late 1950s. In spite of his training in the Expressionist school, Ziembinski mastered many theatrical styles and introduced them to Brazil. Os Comediantes member Miroel Silveira
would say several decades later: "Ziembinski was classified by Décio
[de Almeida Prado] as a retrograde . . . director because he worked in
Expressionism, [which] is an injustice, because in fact Ziembinski
brought Expressionism with *Vestido de Noiva,* he brought Symbolism with *Pelléas et Mèlisande.* . . . He encompassed several styles.
Ziembinski did Greek Tragedy in a marvellous, violent, powerful
way, which today would be linked with modern forms of staging"
(*Depoimentos II* 122). Almeida Prado, however, had often defended
Ziembinski's work in his writings:

> We have frequently heard the criticism . . . that the actors di-
> rected by Ziembinski are not natural. [But] if they wanted to copy
> life, reproducing it exactly as we observe it every day, we could
> then correctly denounce their anti-naturalism as a flaw. . . . But
> it so happens that the "Comediantes" are aiming toward some-
> thing else. On the basis of one of modern theatre's most charac-
> teristic ideas, that theatre is theatre and not life, it is inevitable
> that the actors directed by Ziembinski would create an anti-
> naturalistic theatre, which would theatricalize and not merely
> reproduce events by deforming—or interpreting—them artis-

tically. To accuse them of being anti-natural is tantamount to criticizing a ballerina for dancing on point. (Almeida Prado, *Apresentação* 157)

Ziembinski was the first to use stage lighting dramatically and poetically, and he instituted a system focused on the director, who became the coordinator of all elements of stagecraft. No one in Brazil had ever seen a director dissect a text the way the visionary Pole did. Under Ziembinski's direction, production values gained equal footing with the text, and on occasion they would submerge the text, a characteristic—viewed unfavorably by many—of experimental theatres in the 1960s and 1970s. His interference in the script and the innovative and idiosyncratic nature of his stagings produced resounding successes and dismal failures.

Ziembinski began to work in earnest with Os Comediantes in 1943. The company had been unable to mount a production since the 1941 restaging of *Right You Are*, but with the help of the Polish director the group planned new stagings. The results would be subsequently characterized as the Great Season of 1944, the year that marks the beginning of the modern Brazilian stage. The first of those productions, which actually started in November 1943, were Molière's *School for Husbands*, Lúcio Cardoso's *O Escravo* (The Slave), and Sheriff's *Journey's End* (*Fim de Jornada*). Ironically, the latter staging, directed by Ziembinski, was unsuccessful. The play is a wartime psychological drama that should run two hours; Ziembinski stretched it to four. The agonizingly slow pacing, which he felt was commensurate to the play's psychological climate, produced tedium in the audiences. In January 1944, Os Comediantes opened Maeterlink's *Pelleas and Melisanda*, which Ziembinski directed and in which he acted. Although he continued to work in the style of slow subjective or psychological rhythm, audiences and critics responded positively to the production. Later the same month, the company presented Adacto Filho's staging of Goldoni's *O Leque* (*The Fan*), another success.

Although support for the group was growing strong—even in the press some reviewers began to perceive the glimmering of a theatrical revolution—many in the professional ranks continued to look askance. An assembly was held in which the professional theatre community requested government aid. Among its demands: that amateur theatres receive no aid whatsoever from official sources. In spite of those demands, the government did continue to provide financial support for Os Comediantes. The production *Bridal Gown* (*Vestido de Noiva*) would bring the company to the center of national attention and cause many Brazilians to view theatre as an art form for the first time.

The staging of Nelson Rodrigues's work was a fortuitous circumstance that brought together a play requiring the most modern techniques of stagecraft and the only director in Brazil in full command of those techniques. During the planning stage in 1943, company members asked for advice on repertoire from another war refugee, French director Louis Jouvet, who along with his company visited Rio and São Paulo in the early 1940s. He had been part of the French *cartel*, an innovative group that had modernized theatre in France prior to the Nazi occupation. He had originally been sent to Latin America on a cultural mission, but the occupation prevented him from returning home. Consequently, he staged a series of plays under the auspices of the Brazilian government. He had a marked influence on the burgeoning amateur theatre in both Rio and São Paulo. His counsel to Os Comediantes: a Brazilian theatre of genuine quality would have to mount Brazilian plays. If they did not exist, the group should stimulate national authors to write them.

Ziembinski found the answer. He discovered a play, *Bridal Gown*, written by a young journalist, Nelson Rodrigues, about a woman on her deathbed, the victim of an automobile accident. The play is a montage of short scenes that correspond to the dying woman's hallucinations and memories. Ziembinski was attracted to the play because of its nonlinear, Expressionist style, which would provide him the opportunity to demonstrate fully his directorial skills. Painter Santa Rosa would design the set.

Bridal Gown opened on 28 December 1943, in Rio's Municipal Theatre, and was an immediate and resounding success. Audiences sensed intuitively that they were witnessing something new and significant. A frequently heard comment was: "I don't understand anything, but it's wonderful!" The Rio theatregoing public had never seen a stage production of such complexity, with its myriad light changes and stage divided into three levels. For the first time in Brazilian theatrical history there was a barrage of articles and interviews, in newspapers and literary supplements, outside the context of the play-review format. Most drama critics remained loyal to the commercial theatres, others came to understand the changes that were taking place, but artists and intellectuals from outside the world of the stage had a clearer view of what had happened. One critic maintained that the production was a culminating point for Brazilian theatre (Lins, "Notas" 61–68), an intuition that would be borne out by history. The production aimed in many new directions: it encouraged national playwrights and put on display modern techniques of stagecraft. Moreover, its thematic treatment often violated social and moral taboos.

Bridal Gown ran concurrently with the other productions of the Great Season of 1944 and went through several revivals during the existence of Os Comediantes. The 1945 production featured renowned Polish emigré actress Irene Stipinska, and two of Brazil's finest actresses, Maria Della Costa and Cacilda Becker, played the leading roles in 1947.

In addition to *Bridal Gown*, Os Comediantes staged another Nelson Rodrigues play in 1945, *A Mulher sem Pecado* (Woman without Sin), which had debuted unsuccessfully with another company in 1942. The director, Polish emigré Ziegmunt Turkow, was more traditional than Ziembinski but equally sure of his métier. *Woman without Sin* ran for a month and a half, an unusually long time for the period. Ziembinski directed the final production of 1945, Anouilh's *Once There Was a Prisoner* (*Era uma Vez um Preso*), which closed after only a few weeks.

The following year, 1946, marked the company's professionalization, as well as a change of name: Os V Comediantes. There was a schism in the group, and the name was altered to avoid legal problems while preserving the company's identity. A critic of the time, Roberto Brandão, deemed the professional step extremely important because it would create a commercial foundation and provide financial stability and independence. It would remove the company's "character of adventure . . . of exception, of chance happening, of activity among friends, . . . the air of high school end-of-the-year party" ("Comediantes" 53). It would, maintained Brandão, open up the theatre to the general public, not just to friends and supporters. Unfortunately, professionalization meant the beginning of the end for Os Comediantes.

The first professional production was O'Neill's *Desire under the Elms* (*Desejo*), directed by Ziembinski and featuring celebrated actress Olga Navarro. Also appearing in his first professional role was Jardel Filho, later to become a leading screen actor. The staging, which had a running time of four hours, produced an impact approaching that of *Bridal Gown*. It had six months of performances and made a considerable profit. It appeared that professionalization was a wise step. The second production in this phase was Montherlant's *La Reine Morte* (*A Rainha Morta* [The Dead Queen]), directed by Ziembinski. The play's verbosity doomed it to failure. Expensive to mount, it drained the profits earned by *Desire under the Elms*.

In 1947, company members entered their third and final phase. They reorganized into a cooperative, now calling themselves Os Comediantes Associados. In August of that year they staged an adaptation of Jorge Amado's novel *Terras do Sem Fim* (*The Violent Lands*), directed by Turkow. The play received mixed reviews and did not do well at the box office. In early November, the company presented another failure, *Não Sou Eu* (I Am Not Myself), by Brazilian author Edgar Rocha Miranda. Late that month Os Comediantes presented its last performance, *Bridal Gown* with Cacilda Becker and Maria Della Costa. The principal reasons for the group's collapse were financial, although internal division contributed to its demise. With the final restaging of *Bridal Gown*, "one of the most important movements in the history of Brazilian theatre came to a close. It produced authors, actors, and directors who later joined other groups that appeared in Rio and São Paulo. Mainly, however, it elevated Brazilian theatrical production to a level known previously only through foreign troupes or through reports we received from the outside" (Doria, *Teatro* 100).

Os Comediantes and a few other pioneering companies were responsible for manifold changes that gave birth to the modern Brazilian stage. As a result of perhaps the most profound of these changes, the *ensaiador* was eliminated, replaced by a director who controlled the artistic unity of the spectacle and whose aesthetic and ideological vision determined all phases of production. Directors now imposed respect for the integrity of the dramatic text. The designers worked closely with them, and lighting, set, and costumes corresponded to the climate of the text and the production. The director oriented the actors and trained them in modern acting techniques and styles. As Os Comediantes actor Jardel Filho recalled many years later: "Ziembinski always said to me, as my professor, as my theatrical father—Jardel, you have talent, you have emotion, but you have to control that emotion of yours. You need to acquire something called technique. [Because] I always went on stage like a wild bull . . ." (*Depoimentos IV* 50). Ziembinski coordinated the cast as a whole, which encouraged ensemble consciousness. The star system was thus eliminated, and the prompter became a relic of the past. Ad-libbing became a vice rather than a virtue. Play selection was now based on the best of the international repertoire, and national dramaturgy of quality was encouraged. Os Comediantes raised theatrical standards and demonstrated that the public would go to see plays with literary merit and at least some social content. A new kind of theatre critic emerged, better educated in the art of theatre, more cosmopolitan and impartial.

Os Comediantes became a milestone in the history of the Brazilian stage, then, essentially for reasons of aesthetics and stagecraft.

And if some members of the company wanted to do what Teatro de Arena accomplished twenty years later—to create nationalist theatre that would bring Brazilian problems to the stage—the main thrust of their work was not ideological, at least in the political sense. They did not deal with problems peculiar to Brazil—*Bridal Gown* excepted—nor with the great questions of war and peace elicited by World War II. What Os Comediantes really accomplished was to provide Brazilian theatre with the high aesthetic standards of the European stage. Its revolutionary vision of stagecraft would be a guide for new companies demanding carefully crafted and designed stagings. It would be up to the most significant companies of later decades—especially Teatro de Arena, Teatro Oficina, and Grupo Macunaíma—to go beyond merely European artistic models and develop stagecraft and dramaturgy that would be uniquely Brazilian.

2. *Bridal Gown*

Rio theatre in the early 1940s continued to be dominated by melodramas, *revista*, and comedies of manners. However, Teatro do Estudante do Brasil, Os Comediantes, and some professional companies made significant strides in Brazilian stagecraft in the late 1930s and early 1940s, producing a number of substantial works, mostly by foreign playwrights: Spanish (e.g., Arniches), French (Verneuil, Molière), British (Shakespeare, Somerset Maugham), American (Kaufman and Hart), Italian (Goldoni), and several Portuguese authors. The few Brazilian plays—other than comedies of manners—that received stagings followed the model of thesis works like Joracy Camargo's *Deus Lhe Pague* (*May God Pay You*). If some of their social themes were progressive, their chief aesthetic feature was bombast, and they strove to imitate the "noble" Camonian model of classical Portuguese. Modernist writers like Mário de Andrade had mercilessly parodied anachronistic imitators of the *língua de Camões* (language of Camões) in the 1920s, critics like Antônio de Alcântara Machado had called for a new drama, and in 1937 Oswald de Andrade had introduced Modernist techniques with his play *The Candle King*. Not until the following decade, however, would Nelson Rodrigues (1912–1980) lead Brazilian dramaturgy out of the literary backwater.

If Oswald de Andrade was Brazil's first modern playwright, Nelson Rodrigues was the first to have a genuine influence on stagecraft and to bring new theatrical concepts to the attention of a wide public. His career as a playwright spanned five decades (1941–1980) and seventeen plays, although journalism was his profession. "Nelson Rodrigues's plays constitute the broadest theatrical picture of urban Brazilian society . . . through a language that is crisp, colloquial, concise, and vibrant. By exposing his characters' hidden selves he opened the way for all the dramatists of recent decades " (Magaldi, *Dramaturgia* 18).

Nelson Rodrigues was the only Brazilian playwright of his time to do what the European Expressionists had done decades earlier: he exploded the veil of consciousness and reason and exposed the mysteries and hidden zones of the subconscious. By examining taboos and perversions, he opened society's abscesses and attacked its violent sexual repression. His plays are filled with crimes that occur within the incestuous circle of the family, and they usually end tragically. However, "his brutal and ignominious vision of reality . . . reveals his yearning for the pure and absolute" (Magaldi, in Rodrigues, *Teatro Completo I* 34). Nevertheless, critics and audience members frequently denounced him as morbid, immoral, and perverse, because "his characters break all the conventions, to reveal themselves in their intimate nakedness, which means that the spectator becomes naked in his own eyes" (Magaldi, *Dramaturgia* 40). Many people found the themes he explored too painful or frightening to contemplate.

Nelson Rodrigues shared much with Expressionist playwrights like Strinberg. Most of his plays are extremely pessimistic, at times apocalyptic. They are filled with hyperbole, extremes of feeling, and grotesque exaggeration. The family conflicts they present are often fatal. Nelson Rodrigues's heroes follow an implacable destiny usually ending in violent death when they unleash their inner demons. Female characters are frequently victims when their subconscious desires explode against the unyielding barrier of patriarchal society.

The playwright's disaffections with middle- and upper-class society did not contain the leftist component of many Expressionists. In fact, he took a reactionary stance when he supported the 1964 military coup in his country. His motivations, though, were subjective rather than ideological. He believed above all in individualism and feared that the leftward drift of Brazilian politics could lead to its destruction. He was much maligned for his support of military dictatorship, and the irony of his position is as grotesque as the views of some of his characters. After all, how could an artist often victimized by censorship support a regime that gave carte blanche to the censors? And while leftists have regarded him with distaste for his political views, rightists have imprecated him for rattling the skeletons in the closets of "good" society. Nelson Rodrigues not only broke with tradition through content, but he did so with language as well.

The author was a consummate stylist in drama and in journalism. His newspaper column "Life as it is" was widely read by all classes of people for its stories about everyday life narrated in the spontaneous language of the street. He transposed that speech to the stage, a radical departure from the "Camonian" language of a Joracy

Camargo, verbose and full of philosophical conceits. From his first plays, Rodrigues's dialogue was clear and direct, although it became somewhat more poetic in his mythic plays. With the so-called Carioca tragedies, he made full use of the colloquial language and slang of Rio's slums. He eliminated artifice from the theatre, as the Modernists had done with poetry and narrative in the twenties and thirties. It was ironic that his lack of any connection with the Brazilian dramatic tradition, chained as it was to convention, helped him to experiment technically.

The playwright introduced specific structural innovations. He made extensive use of the flashback, breaking with linear, chronological plot organization. By utilizing techniques of psychoanalysis to search for hidden motivations in his characters' past, he defied the comedy-of-manners convention of limiting the time frame to the present. Often, in plays like *Bridal Gown* (*Vestido de Noiva*), he constructed more past than present action, as well as simultaneous actions in different time frames. Nelson Rodrigues enriched Brazilian stagecraft by removing the fourth wall and making the stage more flexible. He created a pure theatre without the spatial and temporal restrictions of realism. Under the influence of cinema, the visual image gained prominence in his work. He was willing to use any effect, borrow any technique, such as the microphones and follow spots in *Bridal Gown*. He was not concerned with verisimilitude but always appealed to spectators' imagination and fantasy.

The plays of Nelson Rodrigues have been frequently censored and have usually generated controversy. Some productions have been innovative and intelligent, while many others have failed. The attention that Os Comediantes's staging of *Bridal Gown* received would be repeated only with Antunes Filho's 1981 and 1984 productions entitled *Nelson Rodrigues o Eterno Retorno* and *Nelson 2 Rodrigues.* At the present time, more and more Brazilian companies, amateur and professional, are mounting Nelson Rodrigues's works.

Bridal Gown: Text

An examination of Os Comediantes's staging must begin with the text. The action of *Bridal Gown* takes place in the mind of Alaíde, the protagonist, as she lies dying on the operating table, after an automobile accident. There are three levels in the play: the planes of hallucination, memory, and reality. The puzzle of the young woman's life is revealed during the play's three acts: her fascination with a murdered prostitute who appears in hallucinations, the elegant Madame Clessy, and the violent and bitter love triangle involving

Alaíde, her husband Pedro, and her sister Lúcia. The play ends in the time after the protagonist's death, with images from Pedro and Lúcia's wedding. Alaíde's ghost advances toward her sister and widowed husband, reaching out with a bridal bouquet. The lights dim and a single spot representing moonlight focuses on the dead woman's tomb before the final blackout.

Alaíde is the first female protagonist in Brazilian drama to revolt against the stifling conventions of patriarchal society. Because her rebellion takes place essentially in the unconscious and in hallucination, she is in many ways an Expressionist character, her oneiric identity conforming to inner rather than external reality. Sábato Magaldi identifies *Bridal Gown*'s Expressionist heroine in this way: "Always the attraction for the unknown, the taste for adventure, the rejection of humdrum existence. Alaíde could not grow old normally, in the manner of the quiet middle class" (*Dramaturgia* 32). One sees these qualities in the theft of her sister's lovers, obsession with a prostitute, and apparent suicide. She transfers her defiance to Clessy and mimics her violent death. The protagonist searches for the madam in the diary and finds her in hallucination. In a sense, she becomes Clessy at the moment of death. To put it another way, her quest is to discover and express that part of herself the madam incarnates and which had been repressed by social and moral strictures. Clessy becomes in the final stage of Alaíde's life the voice of conscience, pushing her to reconstruct memory and therefore the truth of her life: her sordid relationships and frustrated revolt against conventions that destroy her. The madam forces her to reveal the murderous sibling rivalry with Lúcia, their regression to puerile antagonism and cruelty, and the murderous triangle with Pedro. Goaded by the phantom prostitute, Alaíde lays bare the crumbling façade of middle-class respectability, the social entrapment of marriage, and the death of desire. Clessy is a temptress beckoning her to violate taboos, while her hallucinations expose the sordid aspects of the prostitute's life. She has romanticized the madam's "ideal" union, only to find that Clessy died with her face torn off by her young lover's knife.

The playwright does not present this rather melodramatic material to reinforce social convention or to warn against revolt. While according to her class mores Alaíde's secret model is scandalous and perverse, it is the prostitute who guides her to question those very mores. She reveals a startling truth to Alaíde: society condemns the idea of women fulfilling their fantasies and hidden desires. Indeed, it is the women in *Bridal Gown* who are strong and vital and lead the revolt against sexual repression. The men are merely part of a repressive apparatus, an implacably brutal reality.

"*Bridal Gown* exemplifies clearly Nelson Rodrigues's horror in the face of reality" (ibid., 72). The play depicts the professional indifference of doctors and reporters toward Alaíde's terrible accident. Unmoved by her tragedy, they refer to her in impersonal telegraphic language as an object to be reassembled: "Facial bones crushed. Exposed fracture of the right arm. Generalized excoriation" (Rodrigues, *Vestido* 157). Brutal too is the banality of everyday life, from which Alaíde escapes into the unconscious.

The play tears away the conscious mind's veil of censorship. It draws the reader/spectator into a realm of forbidden desires and archetypal symbols. "*Bridal Gown* is supported by two pillars. It interests us for purely theatrical reasons by telling a story that holds our attention [and] it penetrates the world of unrevealed feelings that represents one of the essential aspects of the human personality" (Almeida Prado, *Progresso* 85). The play's real conflict takes place in Alaíde's unconscious mind, where memory and hallucination struggle for dominance. One critic, in fact, classified the work as a memory tragedy (Lins, "Notas" 64). On the one hand, memory represent's Alaíde's attempt to reconstitute her identity through the coherence of the past (Magaldi, *Dramaturgia* 46). On the other hand, without censorship of the conscious mind, she liberates her hidden desires. One knows her, then, through memory and through the imaginary episodes that compensate for the frustrations of her short life (Magaldi, in Rodrigues, *Teatro Completo I* 17). Through the unconscious, the dying woman reveals the forbidden zones of her *psyche,* to use the Jungian term for the mind, which she projects in the form of a phantom prostitute who dominates her life when instinct and desire come to the foreground. Those secret yearnings come to light in the play's hallucinatory scenes as Alaíde takes on the mannerisms of a prostitute or imagines murdering Pedro. To a great extent, the theme of death informs the play's structure.

As the protagonist's death approaches, the planes of memory and hallucination become increasingly confused. Her vision of the madam's demise in the past foreshadows her own. Several death symbols pertain to the wedding: the bridal gown in which Clessy is buried, the sickening smell of flowers, and the Woman with Veil, who during the second act's prewedding scene foretells Alaíde's passing. The woman thus becomes a strange prophetic figure, and like other characters in the play, she has a Jungian archetypal dimension.

Most analyses of the psychological dimensions of Nelson Rodrigues's works have focused on Freudian concepts. Director Antunes Filho, however, in his 1981 and 1984 stagings of *Nelson Rodrigues*, based much of his interpretation on the Jungian theory of archetypes—the ancient, "eternal" symbols embedded in the modern psyche and which emerge from the collective unconscious. These archetypes, according to Jungian psychology, appear in dreams, hallucinations, delirium, and artistic creation. They are especially likely to come forth in times of crisis and passage. In my view, *Bridal Gown* is well suited to Jungian archetypal analysis: its plot consists mainly of a woman's hallucinations during her time of most profound crisis and passage, her accident and approaching death.

Jungian psychology posits that the dreaming or hallucinating mind is linked to the world of myth and supernatural, and that is the case with Alaíde's hallucinations. In one scene, her mother suggests that Clessy's ghost haunts the house where she died and where Alaíde's family now lives. One might say that the protagonist is possessed by the madam's spirit, not a farfetched idea if one considers the pervasiveness in Brazil of Macumba, a neo-African religion based on ritual possession. Supernatural images pervade the play, as in the scene after Alaíde's death, with its magical atmosphere. The stage directions state: "Light on Alaíde and Clessy. Poetic ghosts" (Rodrigues, *Vestido* 167). As the protagonist's ghost climbs the stairway holding the bridal bouquet, the other characters are frozen (immobile); reality is suspended while the supernatural takes over. The final image is Alaíde's tomb in the moonlight. The lighting effect here is not merely poetic. The moon is often a death symbol in mythology and in dreams, as Jung has pointed out.

According to the Swiss psychologist, all people share a common instinctual repository, called the collective unconscious. This deepest level of the psyche sends vital messages that concern the individual's inner growth and development, and it speaks in the language of visual or pictorial images and symbols. These symbols are known as archetypes, and Jung gave them specific names and definitions: *shadow, anima, animus,* and *mandala.* They have distinct forms, represent different aspects of the personality, and perform special functions in psychological development.

Bridal Gown begins with the sounds of the accident. The first voice is Alaíde's, calling "Clessy, Clessy." She is summoning her shadow self. The accident has broken the shield of the conscious mind and plunged her into the vastness of the collective unconscious. The most shattering crisis of all, death, has placed her in direct contact with the psyche's deepest levels and produced the emergence of the ancient symbols. The shadow archetype represents the dark or hidden side of the psyche, such as repressed desires and qualities that are difficult to integrate into the personality and which the conscious mind rejects because they seem alien to one's self-image. The shadow, projected as a figure of the same sex as the hallucinator/ dreamer, is a critic of the personality, a teller of unpleasant truths. Madame Clessy is a shadow projection: she embodies the secret, dark side of Alaíde's personality, the repression of which has given rise to the tragedy. In the hallucination scenes, the shadow urges the protagonist to remember her past. And while Alaíde tries to reassemble memory, to stop the mental distintegration that comes with death, she also wants to forget painful and shameful events. In her shadow function, therefore, the madam is a catalyst for resolving the play's central conflict, in which memory struggles against unconscious desires and fantasy. She forces the dying woman to recognize her soul's hidden zones and the truth of past events. At the same time, this archetype has a prophetic dimension, when the dying woman tells Clessy she wants to live as the latter did, and the shadow figure reveals that Alaíde has unconsciously tried to imitate the prostitute's life and prophesies her death. It is the young woman's witness and collaborator; it helps her act out the fantasy of Pedro's murder.

The archetype appears as well in the memory scenes with Pedro. In her outbursts, the protagonist threatens her husband that she will become like Clessy and lies that she loves another man. According to Jung, the shadow, repressed desire, at certain times of heightened emotion may explode into external behavior. Pedro cannot believe what his wife is saying; it is as if "another" were speaking. And indeed this archetype, because it corresponds to a hidden side of the personality, is often identified with "another," the "other," or the "double." The Clessy shadow has been taking over Alaíde's life, and she is unable to reconcile it with her family relationships and with social conventions and mores.

The mysterious Woman with Veil is another figure corresponding to the protagonist's hidden side. It is she who reveals that Alaíde has stolen Lúcia's lovers and who is associated with the former's repressed desire to kill Pedro. Just as the shadow is difficult to discern clearly when it appears in dreams, the reader/spectator does not learn until Act II the identity of the Woman with Veil.

A second archetype of the collective unconscious that one would expect to be present in *Bridal Gown* is the animus. It symbolizes the masculine side of the female psyche, and its appearances are personified by various male figures. There is a man in Alaíde's first hallucination dressed as a *malandro* (rogue, hustler). The author indicates in the stage directions that the same man appears throughout the play, with different costumes and personalities. He corresponds to the animus, which lives within the woman's collective unconscious and which she projects externally on male figures throughout her life (e.g., father, lover, wise man). That the man in Alaíde's hallucinations possesses an archetypal essence is clear, since he metamorphoses, dreamlike, in different guises. His initial identity, the *malandro*, represents the underworld, the forbidden universe of the young woman's secret desires. Another man, with the same face, tells Alaíde of Clessy's sordid death. He is yet another dimension of the animus: the inner guide, whose function is to show the dreamer a more objective view. He informs the protagonist that Clessy was never loved; that is, Alaíde's inner voice suggests that she herself has never been loved. She strikes the man angrily, not wanting to listen to the vital messages that emerge from the collective unconscious.

The dying woman's hallucinations present the complexity and contradictions of dreams; the man transmogrifies into a further archetypal manifestation, the negative animus. Alaíde screams in panic that her husband wants to trap her. This dimension of the animus— an immature prolongation of the father figure—tries to entrap the woman in a dependent, infantile state. As observed previously, all the male figures in Rodrigues's play are part of a repressive apparatus. At the same time, the negative animus forces the young woman to confess that she killed her husband, a crime which corresponds not to objective reality but to repressed desire. What she has killed, or attempted to kill, has been part of the animus itself—the smothering father, which she has projected on Pedro. The "murder" represents her search for maturity and independence, for liberation from the clutches of the negative male archetype. Alaíde informs Clessy that she has "killed" her husband because he was too good and this disgusted her. His goodness, of course, was that of social convention in a patriarchal society, and it pertains to the negative animus's function of keeping the woman from self-realization. But her training in the context of the patriarchal social code does not permit her to find the path to maturity and independence. And so her efforts (e.g., the lie to Pedro about the "other man") seem perverse and ultimately are self-destructive.

Many other archetypal symbols are present in the play. Figures that keep a vigil at Clessy's coffin in the oneiric wake scene are nameless and enigmatic: Man with Beard, Romantic Boy, Woman of Old. Their antique characteristics suggest the archaic nature of the collective unconscious.

The mandala is one of the most important pictorial symbols of the collective unconscious. Unlike other archetypes, it is not a personification. Rather, it is manifested as an object or shape whose form is usually round and occasionally rectangular. It symbolizes the *self*, the center of the psyche from which all archetypes emerge, the inner fortress where the individual takes refuge from external difficulties and psychological disturbances. The appearance of the mandala represents this retreat into the inner fortress and corresponds to the attempt to establish internal balance and harmony, to order psychic disorder. Alaíde's rectangular mandala is the operating table. There she retreats to her center in search of refuge. Her mandala's form is ironic. She has taken inner flight—through the accident—from the difficulties of her life. Her tragedy is that she reaches her inner fortress and gains self-awareness only at the moment of death. She has in a sense created a mandala that serves as the altar for a ritual of self-sacrifice.

Ritual informs the entire structure of the play, which reinforces the archetypal dimensions. According to Jungian theory, archetypal patterns and images mirror ancient rituals and myths. Director Antunes Filho has also utilized a ritual interpretation in his stagings of *Nelson Rodrigues*. His principal source for the ritual aspects are Mircea Eliade's theories on the myth of the eternal return (hence the title of the director's 1981 production). Eliade posits that for archaic societies time is cyclical rather than linear; it repeats an eternal cycle, returning always to the same point. Time mirrors nature in its cycle of birth, life, death, and rebirth. Human rituals at key moments ensure that the cycle will continue; they recreate the cosmogonic paradigm, the original creation. Time is thus suspended and becomes sacred, according to Eliade. *Bridal Gown* stages the rituals of the eternal cycle—wedding, funeral—but in an ironic fashion. The play, the external projection of Alaíde's unconscious, suspends time. Ritual symbols of death and renewal—funeral, coffin, tomb and cross, wedding, gown, veil, as well as funeral and wedding marches—occur on the stage repeatedly and at times simultaneously. Death leads to renewal through ritual: during the wedding ceremony at the end of the play, Alaíde's ghost is about to hand the bridal bouquet to Lúcia. Linear time is suspended; there is only ritual, mythical time, which is also dream time. The action in the play is cyclical, the same patterns repeated. Wedding and burial scenes happen over and over. Clessy dies to haunt Alaíde, who dies to haunt Lúcia.

There is a fundamental social irony in all this. The overriding ritual symbol in the work is the bridal gown, the wedding, marriage. It is an archaic form that the play depicts not in terms of its positive function (renewal of the eternal union) but as a repressive institution that kills desire and impedes liberation. The playwright transforms a symbol of purity, innocence, and sacred ritual into a death shroud: Alaíde's post-mortem costume, a mask that hides the violence and repression of a patriarchal society.

The archetypal and ritual aspects of the work also determine its fragmented structure, as well as certain techniques that were revolutionary in Nelson Rodrigues's time. The play's most notable structural feature is simultaneous actions in different time planes and on three levels of consciousness: hallucination, memory, and reality. All of this provides great complexity, and what makes it function and gives it cohesion is the archetypal machinery of the unconscious. The ritual form allows Nelson Rodrigues to violate one of the principal conventions of realist theatre, the protagonist's actions through linear time and confrontation with an obstacle. In *Bridal Gown* there is no forward movement through time and no external obstacle to overcome or conflict to resolve. The beginning and ending point is the death of the protagonist. Dramatic time becomes ritual time. The play illuminates Alaíde's interior adventure, intermingling planes and abolishing linear time.

Plot is reduced to the simplest elements, flashbacks in fragmentary form. External action is the least important element in the play. Dialogue and situation are external projections of images by the protagonist's hallucinating mind. What turns chaos into order is the archetypal and ritual structure inherent in the dream state. Because Alaíde projects the action, she becomes the work's unconscious narrator. What she narrates on one level is the breakdown of her personality and her memory's futile effort to bring order into chaos. Although imbedded archetypal and ritual structures provide order in the dramatic sense, it is impossible for the protagonist herself to establish the logical sequence of events that conscious memory would impose: conscious and logical order and rational sequence of events. Therein lies the work's principal conflict: the collision between the conscious and the unconscious mind. Alaíde's struggle is therefore a microcosm of a universal conflict. Jung uses the term *individuation* to describe the lifelong confrontation between conscious and unconscious and the effort to achieve a balance. Such equilibrium—Alaíde never attains it—is the very essence of maturity and self-realization, according to Jungian psychology.

Internal action, then, predominates in *Bridal Gown*, but external levels are not entirely absent. The plane of reality itself, outside the protagonist's internal universe, occasionally manifests itself to situate events. Examples are sounds of the accident, doctors' voices at the operating table, and reporters discussing the tragedy. The plane of reality provides minimum necessary details to allow the spectator/reader to extrapolate chronological coordinates of linear action, to impose a structure from the outside. This external action, however, is not entirely separate from Alaíde's inner world. She herself perceives the events that go on around her—car accident, doctors' voices—and they reverberate through her mind, producing the play's cyclical patterns. Even such scenes as the reporters' comments on the accident, which she could not perceive directly, may be her own fantasies.

The play's final scenes, which take place in the plane of reality *after* Alaíde's death, have sparked a good deal of controversy. The very last "reality" scene, when the protagonist's ghost appears, creates an illusion of pure fantasy. Many critics have objected to this apparent structural contradiction. Following is Sábato Magaldi's solution to the problem, approved by Nelson Rodrigues himself: since there is a tenuous line between memory and hallucination, why cannot Alaíde anticipate what will happen in reality? She merely imagines her own death and its aftermath. Furthermore, the rapid succession of scenes after death could be projections of a mind in the final stages of decomposition (Magaldi, in Rodrigues, *Teatro Completo I* 18). Playwright Guilherme Figueiredo wrote that *Bridal Gown* is the tragedy of unconscious memory prolonged into the future, after the death of the one who remembers (Figueiredo, "Vestido," in *Dionysos* 111). One could also accept the play's implicit supernatural premise: after her death Alaíde haunts Lúcia; she lives on through her sister. According to this perspective, the final perceptions of the play are quite literally those of a ghost observing her sister marrying the man who was her husband in life.

Whichever interpretation one accepts, the after-death scene clearly provides the last twist in an ironic cycle, for it is the bitter parody of a happy ending. The work's ironic dimensions are summed up in the title. The bridal gown, *vestido de noiva*, a costume intended as a socioreligious sign of middle-class and moral propriety, is transformed by the playwright into a mask that hides ugliness, prostitution, and indifference toward the suffering of others. It comes to symbolize repression in a patriarchal society, a ritual that destroys rather than creates.

Having examined in detail the text's themes, characters, and structures, how does one classify this play? To some degree it is an Expressionist piece. Although Expressionism characterizes a specific German literary generation (1910–1925), its principles extend beyond that time and place and have become an integral part of modern literature. Walter H. Sokel cites as examples works by Eugene O'Neill, Thornton Wilder, James Joyce, Tennessee Williams, and Samuel Beckett. If he were acquainted with Brazilian drama, he surely would have included Nelson Rodrigues on his list. Among the characteristics of Expressionist drama that Sokel discusses are "bitter, intense, and often fatal family conflicts" (*Extremis* 20). *Bridal Gown*'s external conflict is the acrimonious rivalry between two sisters that leads to Alaíde's tragedy. Sokel says about Strindberg, "the physical stage . . . becomes a projection of the protagonist's inner self. . . . Scenes, therefore, change rapidly" (38–39). Alaíde's projections in the planes of hallucination and memory take the form of rapid scene changes. *Bridal Gown*, however, is far from Nelson Rodrigues's most Expressionist work. Other Expressionist elements like apocalyptic extremity, grotesque, insane, perverse, and megalomaniacal heroes, and bizarre distortion of reality characterize his mythic plays.

There is a certain futility in attempting to graft European definitions on Brazilian cultural phenomena. Nelson Rodrigues created his own unique dramatic forms. In fact, he began working completely outside the world of theatre. If German Expressionist modes reached him, it was through the cinema. A more fruitful approach is to classify his plays on their own terms. He himself used the following terms: play, drama, tragedy, tragedy of manners, Carioca tragedy, irresponsible farce, divine comedy, and obsession. Brazilian theatre scholar Sábato Magaldi places the author's works in three categories: psychological plays, mythic plays, and Carioca tragedies. Rodrigues would eventually call *Bridal Gown* his first Carioca tragedy, although he did not invent the term until long after the play's composition. According to Magaldi, the Carioca tragedy combines the archetypal dimension of the mythic plays with the local color of Rio (*Dramaturgia* 63). The element of local color, however, is almost entirely absent from *Bridal Gown*; it would become an outstanding feature of later examples of the genre.

Another question comes to mind here: What manner of tragedy is the play? Professor Magaldi has responded succinctly. It is not technically a tragedy, he writes, but it contains an essential element of that form: the futile human struggle against destiny. The inevitability of Alaíde's accident is similar to that of Greek Tragedy. After a violent argument with her sister, "Alaíde goes to the street, as if it were a place of sacrifice. There, small and wretched, she is struck down mercilessly by an automobile, an obscure and powerful force of today's world" (Magaldi, in Rodrigues, *Teatro Completo I* 20).

Perhaps the primary consideration regarding the work's possible classification is that the Brazilian dramatist was working entirely outside theatrical tradition. He was a journalist, interested in cinema, but he had no theatrical connection whatever when he began to write for the stage. Although *Bridal Gown* was only his second play, it was unique in its own time—a work of genius, a tremendous feat of the imagination. (Guilherme Figueiredo wrote that a traditional playwright would have Alaíde on the table, "babbling long-winded and annoying nonsense about the past" ["Vestido" in *Dionysos* 110]). And the theatre world had the good fortune to count on a company, Os Comediantes, that was equal to the task of mounting the play. The company and the playwright thus began a new theatrical era—the modern Brazilian stage—and relegated nineteenth-century formulas forever to the past.

Bridal Gown: Staging

Nelson Rodrigues's first play, *Mulher Sem Pecado*, was staged unsuccessfully in 1942 by a group called Comédia Brasileira (it would receive a more positive reception with its 1945 restaging by Os Comediantes). Nelson Rodrigues wanted to attack Rio audiences for their lukewarm reception, and from that impulse arose the idea for *Bridal Gown*, with its assault on middle-class institutions and mores. He was certain that the play would be a box-office failure. He asked Manuel Bandeira to read it. The renowned Modernist poet commented that "'in other surroundings *Bridal Gown* would confirm Nelson Rodrigues's talent as a dramatist. What will happen here? If it is well received . . . it will be to the public's credit'" (quoted by Magaldi, in Rodrigues, *Teatro Completo I* 15).

Ziembinski, following the advice of French director Jouvet to stage Brazilian works, presented the play to Os Comediantes. Company members were enthusiastic, and the National Theatre Service (SNT) provided funding for the staging. It was evident that the play meant a considerable technical challenge for both the director and set designer Santa Rosa; they were equal to the task. Rehearsals began in May 1943, and the company worked afternoons and evenings for seven months. Ziembinski was demanding, thorough, and precise as no director in Brazil had been before him. For example, in the final stages of the rehearsal process he wanted ten lighting rehearsals (he got only three). There were six dress rehearsals. He rarely left the theatre during that period, and he pushed the cast and technical crew to the limits of physical and emotional exhaustion.

Nelson Rodrigues feared that the production was degenerating into chaos and that audiences would boo and hiss at the play. He wrote about what he felt after seeing the final dress rehearsal: "Oh, my process of simultaneous actions in different times had no place in Brazil. Our theatre was still Leopoldo Fróes. Yes, it still wore vests, used spats, and spoke with a Lisbon accent. And no one would forgive the temerity of a tragedy without 'noble language.' When I got home, I had lost confidence in myself. I asked inconsolably, 'how could I have put slang in a tragedy?'" (Rodrigues, "ensaio" 52).

In spite of the author's misgivings, the production of *Bridal Gown* was an immediate and resounding success with its select audiences comprised of intellectuals, artists, and a young but growing public weaned on the Teatro do Estudante do Brasil and Os Comediantes's previous work. If some spectators grasped only intuitively what was going on, others saw more clearly and objectively the nature of the theatrical upheaval taking place before their eyes. The revolution was multifaceted. The play added a new dimension to Brazilian dramaturgy, the ensemble replaced the star system, the acting alternated between pure realism and Expressionist distortion, the lighting was poetic and complex, and the set design was modern, functional, and suggestive.

It is ironic that although Santa Rosa was a painter himself, he despised painted backdrops because they hindered blocking. That is, their one-dimensional character clashed with the three-dimensional movement of the actors. Sets, the designer believed, should be three-dimensional yet with simple and clean lines. "When critics write that Nelson Rodrigues's play was a milestone in dramatic literature and in the renovation of stagecraft, they often forget that it also created Brazilian set design. Santa Rosa pioneered a movement that places our contemporary designers among the best in the world" (*Dramaturgia* 95).

Santa Rosa's design followed Nelson Rodrigues's stage directions closely. Photographs show a streamlined set consisting of three levels (platforms), in descending order: reality, memory, hallucination. The plane of memory contains four arches with movable curtains and scrims, and there are two lateral staircases connecting the three levels. The downstage area is bare, and a ramp crosses centerstage. In the upstage area a low platform leads to a wall with four multifunctional arches. A curtain hanging across one arch creates Madame Clessy's boudoir. Panels painted to create the illusion of stained glass and placed in two arches, with a bare cross between them, provide the setting for the wedding scenes. The furniture is simple: a bed, a chair. Santa Rosa's suggestive and imaginative set design created varied and flexible spaces for multiple and rapid scene changes.

The set reflected psychological states. According to the stage directions, in Alaíde's first hallucination there are prostitutes, the madam, some furniture. In addition, the author mentions an invisible phonograph, upon which one of the women pantomimes placing a record. That is, the props refer to hallucination rather than to objective reality. Dreamers usually focus on some elements but not on others, and the invisible parts of the set pertain to the blank spaces in Alaíde's hallucination. Because memory is also selective, furniture in *Gown* changes within scenes or when a specific scene is repeated (e.g., an invisible mirror in the first prewedding scene materializes in the second). Actors may carry objects off the stage during a scene or use pantomime so spectators will imagine their presence. Set and props, therefore, correspond more to inner than to outer reality.

Ziembinski's lighting design reinforced Santa Rosa's imaginative set. Reports on the number of lighting changes vary. They numbered between one hundred and two hundred, a startling quantity if one recalls that lighting for comedy-of-manners plays was static, with two changes: on and off. The light changes, indicating the flux of the dying woman's unconscious mind, increased the flexibility of the scenic space. More impressive than the sheer quantity of changes were the specific lighting techniques the director employed. A spotlight was used to follow movements from one level to another, symbolizing the shifting and narrow focus within the unconscious and emphasizing its vast darkness. At one point in the production follow spots illuminated simultaneously a turn-of-the-century funeral scene on the plane of hallucination, and a prewedding scene on the level of memory. That is, fixed lights on a single area might indicate a certain stability of the psyche, whereas moving spots and simultaneous lighting on two planes suggest instability and disintegration.

The use of microphones and loudspeakers was also innovative for the period. Because Nelson Rodrigues had not worked within the Brazilian theatrical tradition, he was not concerned about the purity of the language of the stage. He borrowed freely from whatever sources he found useful to create desired effects. Microphones fit perfectly with the subject matter and structure of the play. They provided an invisible inner voice and allowed one mental plane to penetrate another (e.g., Alaíde hears Clessy's voice—hallucination—during the wedding scene—memory). The microphone permitted actors to move quickly from one plane or scene to another. For example, one might hear the protagonist's voice (hallucination) followed instantly by her appearance in a different guise within a memory scene. Loudspeakers provided music for the wedding and funeral scenes, as well as sound effects (e.g., accident and surgical tools) for exposition. The technique was, in short, cinematic. No Brazilian stage production had ever featured an elaborate sound track, but all future epochal stagings would employ sound tracks.

Ziembinski brought his greatest talents to bear on acting and blocking. He utilized an ensemble approach that broke with the star system of the professional companies. The latter relied on improvisation and slapdash methods, while the Polish director choreographed every moment with precise timing. He also employed a variety of acting styles. The hallucinatory scenes were dominated by Expressionist technique, "which deliberately violates reality in order to obtain greater plastic and dramatic effects" (Almeida Prado, *Apresentação* 15). Distortion is one aesthetic quality of Expressionism: gestures, movement, and inflection seemed filtered through a veil, a dream. The acting in *Gown's* memory scenes was more prosaic, and in the reality scenes, naturalistic. Consequently, acting styles clarified for the spectator the division of planes. Ziembinski gave "a light touch to the secondary characters, which [had] the effect of distancing and distinguishing them from the main characters" (17). The result of the director's work with the actors was, to use a current expression, a very tight production. "The acting was excellent, carefully rehearsed, strong in the smallest details. The actors' every gesture, every attitude, every feeling was studied and executed with maximum precision" (Mesquita, "Nota" 90). There were problems with diction, however, attributable to Ziembinski's foreign background and the actors' lack of professional experience (ibid.).

Nelson Rodrigues's stage directions combined with the Polish director's blocking produced actors' movements that created a visual style not only innovative but far ahead of its time. Act II contains a vision (hallucination) with two men, one young and another old, dressed in turn-of-the-century style and holding candles. They kneel slowly before an unseen corpse, their movements totally synchronized. This stylized blocking foreshadows Robert Wilson's work during the 1960s and 1970s. It is no coincidence that the American director uses synchronized movement in slow motion to communicate with the spectator's unconscious, and that Antunes Filho employs the technique in *Nelson Rodrigues*. And while oneiric movement itself is a link to the spectator's unconscious, the archetypal male figures in the above scene correspond to levels of the animus. The visual style in the production, therefore, relates in many ways to Jungian concepts and can be explained by them.

The stage directions also include several examples of nonnaturalistic, symbolic movement. At the end of a scene in Act III, Alaíde,

Lúcia, and Pedro place their heads together and lower them. As the author indicates, the movement "creates the plastic effect of a bouquet of heads" (*Vestido* 160), an ironic visual image of the incestuous triangle, Pedro's marriage to the two sisters. In addition to synchronization and slow motion, there are numerous freezes, which create the sense of time stopped and facilitate changes of level.

The play ends with its most striking visual image: Alaíde's ghost at her sister's wedding and moonlight on her grave. Without dialogue, the scene conveys the essence of *Gown*'s themes and structure. Its supernatural atmosphere, created by an interplay of ritualistic motion and special lighting effects, and its overlapping planes together communicate the finality of death and the irony of the title.

Os Comediantes's production was received enthusiastically, even ecstatically, by audiences and reviewers alike. Several critics hit the mark by declaring that Ziembinski's staging was a milestone that would bring the national theatre into the modern era. Décio de Almeida Prado would write a decade later: "The theatre, as spectacle, became universal in the manner of the other modern arts, and Nelson Rodrigues represented for the stage what Villa-Lobos brought to music, Portinari to painting, Niemeyer to architecture, and Carlos Drummond de Andrade to poetry. What is certain is that the opening of *Vestido* made Brazilian theatre lose its inferiority complex" (*Progresso* 21). It would now be up to São Paulo's Teatro Brasileiro de Comédia to take the next step in the evolution of the modern Brazilian stage.

3. São Paulo Theatre in the 1950s and 1960s: TBC, Arena, Oficina

The process of theatrical renovation in Brazil that began with Rio's Teatro do Estudante and especially Os Comediantes continued in the late 1940s with São Paulo amateur groups, was consolidated and professionalized in the 1950s with the Teatro Brasileiro de Comédia (TBC), and was nationalized and radicalized in the 1960s with Teatro de Arena and Teatro Oficina.

Antecedents to the TBC

Rio de Janeiro was the center of Brazilian theatrical activity from the nineteenth century to the late 1940s. In the São Paulo prior to 1916, when it was still a small provincial capital, the only productions staged were those brought from Rio by *mambembe* or traveling companies associated with professional groups. Although the *mambembe* theatres continued until the 1940s to tour with their comedy-of-manners farces and melodramas, from 1916 until the late 1930s amateur productions were staged sporadically in São Paulo.

Beginning in 1936, a man who would have an enormous impact on the development of theatre there, Alfredo Mesquita, wrote and produced amateur plays based on traditional São Paulo music and dance modes. In 1942 he founded, in association with The English Players—run by the British ambassador's daughter—Grupo de Teatro Experimental (GTE). Its goal was to raise the level of stagecraft in São Paulo. It remained an amateur theatre during its short existence, from 1942 to 1948. The GTE performed classics: the first Brazilian production of Aristophanes' *The Birds* (*Os Pássaros*), Shakespeare's *Merry Wives of Windsor* (*As Alegres Comadres de Windsor*), and Molière's *The Miser* (*O Avarento*). The company debuted what were for the time avant-garde plays like Tennessee Williams's *The Glass*

Menagerie (*À Margem da Vida*). It presented original Brazilian works by Mesquita and Abílio Pereira de Almeida (several of the latter's pieces would be staged by the TBC). Louis Jouvet's visit to Brazil not only influenced Os Comediantes, it had a great impact on the GTE as well: "The contrast between Jouvet's company and our wretched national theatre was devastating. . . . We had to do something to reawaken, or rather, to establish a genuine Brazilian theatre" (Mesquita, "Origens" 37).

Amateur theatre in Rio in the 1940s benefited from the presence of foreign directors and government funding. Rio companies were far in advance of their São Paulo counterparts, and their tours had a great impact on the development of the stage in São Paulo, which although outgrowing its status as a provincial capital was not yet the cultural center it would soon become. Its amateur groups had no private or official support of any kind, so they could not attract great foreign directors like Ziembinski. Even the GTE, the only forward-looking São Paulo company of its time, had minimal influence. On the other hand, events were taking place in São Paulo universities that would have a significant impact on the local theatre scene. Starting in the late 1930s, students from the upper classes, under the sway of their European professors, began to form their own groups devoted to the study of theatre and to occasional performances within the confines of the university, their perspectives based on European models and imbued with class consciousness. They were interested in producing plays for the public of their class, exclusively, albeit some of the students involved had nascent social concerns. The university connection led to the founding in 1948, by Alfredo Mesquita, of Brazil's first school of the dramatic arts, Escola de Arte Dramática (EAD). Mesquita's original purpose was to train actors, but the EAD eventually would develop talent in many other phases of the performing arts.[1] Proponents of engagé theatre in the 1960s would bitterly criticize the class origins of the São Paulo stage and destruction of native popular theatre (i.e., comedy of manners). Nevertheless, this class-university influence, once it made its presence felt, gave São Paulo a leg up on Rio: "The means by which theatre became a permanent activity in São Paulo involved a process of evolution similar to that which took place in Rio [with] Os Comediantes. Except that São Paulo did not have to overcome the burden of a pre-existing theatre with no artistic quality. . . . Theatre activity in São Paulo began with high standards and its development was aided by the participation of a school of dramatic arts that became a continuing reservoir of talent" (Doria, *Teatro* 106).

Teatro Brasileiro de Comédia

Décio de Almeida Prado, in meetings with several amateur groups during the late 1940s, planted the seed for the creation of the TBC by proposing the construction of a theatre especially for use by São Paulo amateur companies. Consequently, TBC's original membership came from the GTE, the Sociedade dos Artistas Amadores de São Paulo (Society of Amateur Artists of São Paulo), and Almeida Prado's own University Theatre Group, Grupo Universitário de Teatro (GUT).[2] Almeida Prado stated the aesthetic foundation of the proposal: "I respect and admire the older generation for having kept theatre alive in thankless times. . . . But it is with the younger generation that I align myself, with those who came after and not before Ziembinski. We can sum up the ideas we share in a single notion: all plays must be interpreted in their smallest details, whether material or spiritual, by one person" (quoted in *Nosso Século 54* 82).

Wealthy Italian-born industrialist Franco Zampari, a theatre lover who had previously tried to help the GTE, picked up Almeida Prado's idea and in 1948 founded the TBC, which he originally called the Sociedade Brasileira de Comédia. The project would combine business and art. Zampari had conducted consumer research and found São Paulo to be fertile ground for artistic activities; that is, theatre could be merchandised and sold as a refined, elegant, and quality product to appeal to a consumer class that could afford access to that product. Zampari also had a formula for stability. First, he rented a building—it had previously housed a laboratory—on Major Diogo Street in Bela Vista, an Italian district on the edge of downtown São Paulo. It would be a comfortable theatre, with an auditorium containing 365 seats, small but well-built proscenium stage, and adequate lighting and sound equipment. Zampari wanted uniform training and a stable ensemble permitting quick changes of program in case of doubtful success. To this end, he established an ongoing relationship with the EAD: the latter would be a continuous source of actors for the TBC, which in turn would provide professional experience for the EAD actors. Zampari further decided to hire directors who had proved themselves able on the European stage, and so he would bring several directors from Italy.

The TBC debuted on 11 October 1948 with *A Mulher do Próximo* (Thy Neighbor's Wife), written and directed by Abílio Pereira de Almeida, who also played the lead role.[3] Also on the opening program was Cocteau's *The Human Voice* (*La Voix Humaine*), performed in French. The theatre community was euphoric about the possibility of at last "creating a true national theatre of cultural and artistic excellence" (Mesquita, "Origens" 40). The potential appeared to be re-alized the following year with the critical and box-office hit *The Voice of the Turtle* (*Ingenuidade*), by John Van Draten. Neverthe-less, an amateur theatre like the TBC was still not solid enough as of 1949 to have a regular season, so Zampari brought in outside groups, such as the GUT and the GTE. He soon realized that it would be impossible to maintain a theatre of high quality only with amateur productions on an irregular basis, so he met with company members and proposed their professionalization under his supervision. Conse-quently, the year following its founding, the Teatro Brasileiro de Co-média became São Paulo's first professional group. To increase sta-bility and improve the level of stagecraft, Zampari hired the first of several Italian directors, Adolfo Celi, who was part of an outstand-ing group, including Vittorio Gassman, from the Rome Academy of Dramatic Arts.[4] Celi's first directorial stint was William Saroyan's *The Time of Your Life* (*Nick Bar, Álcool, Brinquedos e Ambições*), which opened in June 1949.[5] Celi provided the TBC amateurs more sense of spectacle and theatricality and gave the company an en-hanced cachet with its elite supporters, who tended to look to Eu-rope for aesthetic orientation.

In addition to its foreign directors, among the TBC's initial par-ticipants were some of the most distinguished actors in the history of the modern Brazilian stage: Cacilda Becker, Paulo Autran, Sérgio Cardoso, Tônia Carrero, Maria Della Costa, and Walmor Chagas. From early on, therefore, Zampari was the catalyst for a collection of impressive talent on all levels, and overnight São Paulo had the most aesthetically and technically sophisticated theatre the country had ever seen. The TBC responded to European-nurtured public taste, and critics especially appreciated the company's naturalistic acting style in contrast to the "violent" (i.e., Expressionistic) acting com-ing out of Rio in such plays as *Bridal Gown* and *Hamlet*.

In 1950 Celi directed Sartre's *No Exit* (*Entre Quatro Paredes*), con-demned by both the Communist party and the Catholic hierarchy, but audiences went wild over it. Ruggero Jacobbi staged John Gay's *The Beggar's Opera* (*A Ronda dos Malandros*). The adaptation in-cluded verses from nineteenth-century Brazilian poet Cruz e Souza's *The Litany of the Poor*, which were cut by censors. The play was poorly received by audiences and critics. Luciano Salce, whom Zam-pari brought that year from Italy, mounted Tennessee Williams's *Summer and Smoke* (*O Anjo de Pedra*), a resounding success both for its production values and for the masterful acting of Cacilda Becker. Ziembinski, with the demise of Os Comediantes, began a new career with the TBC, directing plays by both Brazilian and foreign playwrights (e.g., Luigi Pirandello and Tennessee Williams). The year 1950 also saw the creation of a Monday program—traditionally the "dark" night in Brazilian theatre—later to be imitated by Teatro de Arena with highly positive results.

The 1951 season was triumphant: Ziembinski directed Abílio Pereira de Almeida's *Paiol Velho* (Granary) and Mary Chase's *Harvey*; Adolfo Celi staged Pirandello's *Six Characters in Search of an Author* (*Seis Personagens em Busca de um Autor*), with Paulo Autran, Calcilda Becker, and Sérgio Cardoso; Salce directed Jean Anouilh's *Convite ao Baile* (*L'invitation au chateau*)—also with a first-rate cast including Eugênio Kusnet, Ziembinski, Nydia Lícia and Sérgio Cardoso—as well as Alexandre Dumas's *The Lady of the Camellias* (*A Dama das Camélias*); Flamínio Bollini, the last of the young Italian directors hired by Zampari, staged Gorki's *Ralé* (*Lower Depths*).

The year 1952 began with a forgettable production of a work by Brazilian playwright Edgar da Rocha Miranda, directed by Celi. However, the Italian also staged a program of both versions of *Antigone* (by Sophocles and Anouilh), which was considered at the time perhaps TBC's most significant production. But 1953, which saw productions of both Brazilian and foreign works, was one of TBC's least successful years.

The following season included plays by Sartre, Noel Coward, and Shaw, but the year's greatest achievement was nineteenth-century Brazilian Romantic poet and playwright Gonçalves Dias's *Leonor Mendonça*. Finally, Sérgio Cardoso and Nydia Lícia left to found their own theatre, a pattern that would be repeated regularly. In 1955, for example, director Celi and actors Paulo Autran and Tônia Carrero departed to form a new company. The 1955 stagings were of little note and included plays by Abílio Pereira de Almeida, Ben Johnson (*Volpone*), and Friedrich Schiller (*Mary Stuart*), translated by poet Manuel Bandeira.

The resounding success of the 1956 season was John Patrick's *House of the August Moon* (*Casa de Chá do Luar de Agosto*), staged by Belgian director Maurice Vaneau. Although it is "a mediocre play . . . justifying American imperialism in Japan . . . it develops the problem with a sympathy and verve that can win over an unsuspecting audience" (Magaldi, "Surge" 49). The year included plays by Tennessee Williams and Anouilh.

As of 1957, the only successful Brazilian plays staged by the TBC had been those by Abílio Pereira de Almeida. Maurice Vaneau attempted to rectify the situation with João Bethencourt's *Provas de Amor* (Demonstration of Love).[6] As the director wrote in the program notes: "the establishment of a genuine Brazilian theatre is unconceivable without Brazilian plays. It is therefore our duty . . . to encourage . . . young national talent. The only way an author can obtain experience is to see his plays staged before an audience. If in this way we manage to help João Bethencourt develop his play-writing techniques, one of our main objectives will be achieved" (quoted in *Dionysos 25* 107). Reviews and audience response, however, were unfavorable: "It would be difficult to talk about the third act: the staging, especially in the final scenes, compromised [the play] with an excessive addition of quaintness. In the last analysis, this is very harmful to the play, which by itself shares in the blame by refusing to carry out the action it undertakes" (Almeida Prado, *Progresso* 49). The year did see one noteworthy Gianni Ratto staging, *Life with Father* (*Nossa Vida com Papai*), by Howard Lindsay and Russell Crouse. There were also productions of plays by Abílio Pereira de Almeida and Spaniard Jacinto Benavente.

The 1958 season included works by Abílio Pereira de Almeida and Pirandello, but the most distinguished production was Arthur Miller's *View from the Bridge* (*Panorama Visto da Ponte*), directed by Argentine Alberto D'Aversa. The director also staged the year's greatest disappointment, Jorge Andrade's *Pedreira das Almas* (Quarry of Souls).[7]

The 1959 season was a year of crisis, with one failure after another, including Strindberg's *Miss Julie* (*Senhorita Júlia*) and Peter Ustinov's *Romanoff and Juliet* (*Romanoff e Julieta*). The following season, on the other hand, witnessed perhaps the TBC's greatest triumph, its first success with the staging of a drama by a contemporary Brazilian author—previous Brazilian plays successfully mounted by TBC had all been comedies and farces—Alfredo Dias Gomes's *Pagador de Promessas* (*Payment As Pledged*), which takes place in the old colonial capital of Bahia and deals with a man who makes a promise to a *macumba* (voodoo) deity and attempts to do penance in a Catholic church, which gives rise to a series of conflicts resulting in the protagonist's death. The play was later made into an award-winning film.[8]

The TBC experienced a financial crisis in 1961, resolved temporarily when the São Paulo Ministry of Culture's Theatre Commission came to the rescue with funds (the Ministry would later bankroll Grupo Macunaíma). The season witnessed another noteworthy production of a Brazilian drama, *A Semente* (The Seed), by Teatro de Arena actor and dramatist Gianfrancesco Guarnieri. Under the influence of Arena, it appeared for a while that the TBC would embark on a new path of engagé national dramaturgy. Less successful in 1961 were productions of plays by Gogol and Jorge Andrade.

The TBC scored successes the next year with Arthur Miller's *Death of a Salesman* (*A Morte de um Caixeiro Viajante*) and Federico García Lorca's *Yerma*, directed by Antunes Filho, future founder of Grupo Macunaíma. Dias Gomes's *A Revolução dos Beatos* (The Revolution of the Blessed) was a box-office failure. The 1963 season saw yet another financial crisis—the Ministry of Culture again made funds available—and a resounding success by Jorge Andrade, *Os Ossos do Barão* (The Baron's Bones). The play, a satire about the union of a nouveau-riche immigrant with a member of the decadent aristocracy, broke the TBC's box-office record; it was later adapted for a popular television series. In 1964, the author's *Vereda da Salvação* (Path of Salvation) was a flop. "One of Jorge Andrade's densest works in literary terms, the production suffered from hysterical acting that nearly sank it. And Jorge was the victim of a most unfortunate misunderstanding: the left did not support his theatre, which it considered nostalgic and rather aristocratic, and the right judged that, in the wake of the political events of 1964, it was an outrage to bring to the stage a problem relating to the poverty of the masses" (Magaldi, "Surge" 55). This failure marked the effective end of TBC as a theatre company, which from then on became—and continues to be—merely a theatre space rented out to various groups and for different productions.

There has been considerable controversy over the years regarding the legacy of the TBC. It has been accused of elitism and lack of social consciousness; some claim that it even hindered the development of Brazilian play writing, because it spent lavishly on productions to attract audiences to sophisticated foreign plays staged by foreign directors. Teatro Oficina's Fernando Peixoto has expressed the anti-TBC view in this way: "The appearance of TBC involves several problems, such as the stifling of a tradition of popular theatre . . . , the advantages or disadvantages of bringing together in a single professional company various amateur theatre movements existing in São Paulo, the imposition of imported and eclectic aesthetic values, which are profoundly commercial, ideologically tied to a social class, unrelated to the nation's cultural reality, values institutionalized over a long period of time as a sacred icon of quality" (Peixoto, "Zampari" 59). Teatro de Arena director Augusto Boal's anti-TBC argument is also based on nationalist concerns: "The financial elite, in alliance with young intellectuals and scholars, wanted to establish in Brazil a theatre that would be a carbon copy of the aesthetic standards then in vogue in the 'great capitals,' [resulting in] productions that were translations and that obeyed criteria which had roots in social milieu not our own. . . . Brazil, an underdeveloped country in search of its economic emancipation, cannot produce the same art as England, a country in economic decline. Nor can we write the torpor-inducing plays of the American imperialists, ex-masters of the world" (Boal, "Tentativa" 9). Others merely sneer at its legacy: "TBC's was a theatre of illusion, an ideological phantasmagoria, the creation of artificiality for the purpose of supplying a set of fanciful ideals for a provincial bourgeoisie in search of its roots, an ornamental formalism which, even in stagings of Gorki [or] Sartre, produced grotesque fragrances masking contradictions and highlighting melodrama" (Mostaço, *Teatro* 18).

The TBC has many defenders, however. In response to the company's detractors, one could argue that "it seems rather gratuitous to condemn . . . renovation after it has taken place" (Magaldi, "Surge" 56). Alfredo Guzik, who doubles as an academic scholar and theatre reviewer for the São Paulo newspaper *Jornal da Tarde,* places the issue in clear perspective: "The Teatro Brasileiro de Comédia occupies a position of great distinction in the panorama of modern Brazilian theatre. Its influence was fundamental in the process of modernization, and its productions were incomparable. For eighteen years, it was part of the city's soul. . . . Subsequently, as it was gradually forgotten or distorted, it became a scapegoat, blamed for all the problems of the national stage (Guzik, "Crônica" 351).

The TBC set a standard of excellence in production values, often presented serious plays (as opposed to the comedies of manners and melodramas of the old professional companies), went farther than any previous company in staging Brazilian authors, gave rise to innumerable spin-off companies, and trained a whole generation of actors, designers, and directors, allowing Brazilians to seize control of their theatrical destiny. While Os Comediantes modernized the Brazilian stage, the TBC systematized the modernization. Finally, the TBC had a faithful audience of some twenty-five thousand— mostly upper-middle and upper class, to be sure—which obviated the necessity of having to change plays and go on tour constantly; in this and many other ways it set the pattern for Arena and Oficina, even though several of their members would subsequently denounce the TBC.

Teatro de Arena

Teatro de Arena was in the beginning a modest attempt to be a "poor" version of the TBC, but it evolved into the "home of the Brazilian playwright" (Magaldi, *Palco* 8). That is, Arena moved away from the TBC model and sought ways to produce theatre with solid production values inexpensively. Later, with its 1958 production of Gianfrancesco Guarnieri's *Eles Não Usam Black-Tie* (*They Don't Wear Black-Tie*), the company began a process that would give a new legitimacy to Brazilian dramaturgy. Arena also moved into new ideological territory: leftist consciousness-raising theatre. Its impact was enormous: it encouraged the establishment of other companies with similar goals, the most important of which was Teatro Oficina. Even the TBC in its last years became the follower rather than the leader when it staged Guarnieri's *A Semente*.

Like the TBC, Teatro de Arena's foundation is associated with the Escola de Arte Dramática. On 23 January 1953, actor-director José Renato met with a group of friends—all EAD students and alumni—in his São Paulo apartment to formalize the establishment of a new professional theatre company. Due to the lack of available performing space in São Paulo and the high costs of theatrical production, the group would have to find economical and flexible ways to produce its plays. Renato, under the guidance of Décio de Almeida Prado, had tested a novel theatrical space while a student at the EAD. His 1951 production of Tennessee Williams's *The Long Goodbye* (*Demorado Adeus*), subsequently performed in the TBC, was the first staging in the round in South America. Many of the new company's founders had worked in that production, so the logical solution seemed to be theatre-in-the-round or arena, which meant that any space (e.g., museums, schools, factories) could be utilized. Thus was born the Companhia de Teatro de Arena. The group would begin working on its goal to produce plays in repertory according to the aesthetic standards set by the TBC.

Although the eventual aim of the Arena founders was to have a permanent performing space, the first year would be devoted to testing the arena form with productions in the São Paulo Museum of Modern Art. The first play would be British playwright Stafford Dickens's *Why Not Tonight?* (*Esta Noite É Nossa*). By opening with a light and unpretentious comedy, the young and inexperienced company would not be too sorely tested. The production would have a wide audience appeal, and money could be earned for subsequent productions. After two months of rehearsal Arena debuted in the museum on 11 April 1953, to an enthusiastic audience and critical praise. The arena mode intrigued both spectators and reviewers: Ruggero Jacobbi wrote that José Renato was the "apostle" of the new theatre ("Arena," *Folha*); Mattos Pacheco lamented the lack of available performing space in São Paulo and hailed the experiment as a possible solution: "Theatre-in-the-round is, in short, like a circus ring. A theatre without a stage, without sets. Light and sound 'decorate' the space" ("Arena", *Última Hora*). Former Comediantes member Miroel Silveira, however, mused over the irony of the former EAD students' play selection: "All our young actors . . . coming out of the schools of the dramatic arts, whenever they went to see professional theatre, would turn up their noses . . . at the repertoire [and say] 'mediocre plays,' 'commercial theatre.' What is amazing is that these same people, when they decide to face the footlights professionally, . . . choose precisely those mediocre plays associated with the much-maligned 'commercial theatre'" ("Noite," *Folha*).

On 1 August 1953, the group offered a program of one-acts in the museum: *The Long Goodbye, Judas em Sábado de Aleluia* (Judas on Hallelujah Saturday), a farce by Martins Pena, and José Renato's own *Visita de Pésames* (Visit for Condolences), which he himself described as a pale imitation of foreign comedies (José Renato, interview). The plays received mixed reviews, although some critics responded positively to the fact that Arena was staging a Brazilian play, still an unusual circumstance in 1953 in spite of the fact that both Os Comediantes and the TBC had included national works in their respective repertoires. Arena toured *Why Not Tonight?* and the one-acts, performing in schools, clubs, homes, and a factory, thus demonstrating the flexibility of theatre-in-the-round.

The company added only one new play to its repertoire in 1954, Marcel Achard's *Voulez-Vous Jouer Avec Moi?* (*Uma Mulher e Três Palhaços*), directed by José Renato. The circus setting of Achard's boulevard comedy lent itself to staging in the round, and while the critics had reservations about the production, audiences were overwhelmingly supportive. The play toured extensively, and the company was flown to Rio to give a command performance for President João Café Filho. The production was especially important in a formal sense: "*Uma Mulher e Três Palhaços* was, I think, a great leap forward. We managed to produce a show that was totally extroverted and aimed at the audience" (Renato, interview). There are ironies here that reach into the past and into the future: Os Comediantes had staged this work in 1940, and Arena was far from the revolutionary company it would soon become. There is a further irony in the notion that with a light comedy Renato purported to demolish the distance between audiences and actors nearly twenty years before Teatro Oficina made the same claim with such self-righteousness and deadly seriousness for its production of *Gracias Señor*.

The success of 1954 resulted in financing that allowed the group to inaugurate, on 1 February 1955, the first permanent theatre-in-the-round in South America, called, of course, Teatro de Arena, located on Theodoro Bayma Street in downtown São Paulo. A small performing area and limited seating (150 spectators) would hamper the company throughout its existence. The first production in the new space was French playwright Claude Spaak's *The Rose of the Winds* (*A Rosa dos Ventos*), which was considered both more intellectual and less spontaneous than previous Arena offerings. Nevertheless, since all its previous stagings were kept in repertory, the company was not dependent on any single production. José Renato's second play, which he also directed, opened in May. Reviewers compared the piece, entitled *Escrever Sobre Mulheres* (Writing about Women), unfavorably with Pirandello and Noel Coward.

The following July Arena opened a Pirandello festival with a production of *The Pleasure of Honesty* (*O Prazer da Honestidade*), which pleased both critics and audiences, followed by *No One Knows How* (*Não Se Sabe Como*), directed by Renato, which was criticized for its mechanical staging and unconvincing youthful cast. But the company was growing in artistic maturity and professionalism. The final production in 1955 was Tennessee Williams's *Glass Menagerie* (*À Margem da Vida*), a reasonably fortunate venture staged by television and cinema director José Marques da Costa.

The year 1955 marked the founding of the Teatro Paulista do Estudante (TPE), which included actors and future playwrights who would have a profound impact not only on Teatro de Arena but on Brazilian theatre as a whole. The TPE opened in the Arena space and later merged with the company when its members opted for professionalization, bringing to Arena a concern for social problems and initiating a sixteen-year focus on *concientização* or consciousness-raising.

The next season, José Renato began looking for a director to share the onus of staging the company's many productions. At the urging of Sábato Magaldi, his choice was Augusto Boal, who would eventually become the group's principal director and theorist. Boal debuted with John Steinbeck's *Of Mice and Men* (*Ratos e Homens*), a triumph in terms of stagecraft and box-office receipts. The production was a turning point, in that its essential characteristics would become Arena's trademark language of the stage: engagé social consciousness, "gritty" photographic realism, and Actors Studio methods, which Boal had studied at Columbia University with John Gassner. Renato directed the company's four other productions in 1956, the most fruitful of which was Molière's *School for Husbands* (*A Escola de Maridos*): "In the case of *A Escola de Maridos*, for example, we tried to do the same thing we did with *Uma Mulher e Três Palhaços*. We found a Brazilian way of presenting a French text—sophisticated up to a certain point—and added the charm of the Brazilian circus" (Renato, interview). One can see here the persistent influence of the TBC, Arena's precursor, which also fed the public a steady diet of European scripts, with a special place reserved for Molière and Pirandello. This fact makes Boal's later pronouncements regarding the TBC sound rather hollow, if not self-serving. Three other works presented in 1956 were more commercially viable French boulevard comedies (e.g., *Dias Felizes* [*Les Jours Heureux*], by Claude André Puget). A further significant event in 1956 was Arena's founding of a permanent children's theatre under the direction of Fausto Fuser, the first time a Brazilian company had ever undertaken such a venture. The stated purpose was to "develop children's artistic taste and prepare their emotions for more authentic childhood experiences" (quoted from the 1956 *Ratos e Homens* program).

In 1957 Boal staged Sean O'Casey's *Juno and the Paycock* (*Juno e o Pavão*). The play, although not a financial success, gave further impetus to Arena's new social-realist phase. Nevertheless, Boal, the future ultranationalist, continued at this juncture to stage foreign plays, which meant, as he said of the TBC, "productions that were translations and that obeyed criteria which had roots in social milieu not our own"("Tentativa," *Arte em Revista*, no. 6). He also wrote and directed *Marido Magro, Mulher Chata* (Skinny Husband, Boring Wife), a would-be Broadway comedy about the "Coca Cola" youth of Rio's Copacabana district. Once again, it is instructive to recall Boal's condemnation of the TBC: "Nor can we write the torpor-inducing plays of the American imperialists" (ibid.).

José Renato invited Alfredo Mesquita, his instructor and guide at the EAD, to direct two one-acts, Octave Mirabeau's *Old Couple* (*Casal de Velhos*) and farceur Georges Feydeau's *Madam's Late Mother* (*A Falecida Sua Senhora Mãe*). This would be the professional debut of São Paulo's amateur theatre guru: his direction at Arena was highly praised and compared favorably to that of the TBC professionals. Renato himself directed, for the first time since his group's founding, a work by an established Brazilian playwright, Silveira Sampaio's *Só o Faraó Tem Alma* (Only the Pharaoh Has a Soul).[9] Although the play is a light political satire, it by no means carries the banner of social consciousness that Arena would take up later. It does, however, foreshadow the group's subsequent Brazilian dramaturgy phase. Due to pressing financial needs—a constant in the history of the Brazilian stage—José Renato staged in 1957 another French boulevard comedy, Vernon Sylaine's *As Long as They Are Happy* (*Enquanto Eles Forem Felizes*); nonetheless, the crisis deepened to the point that the director decided in his own mind to close the theatre. Since he now had nothing to lose, he resolved to stage what seemed at the time the most unlikely vehicle for regaining financial solvency, former TPE member and current Arena actor Gianfrancesco Guarnieri's *Eles Não Usam Black-Tie*. That decision would not only initiate Teatro de Arena's most productive and original phase and establish its unique identity but would give impetus and credibility to Brazilian engagé play writing.[10]

Black-Tie opened on 22 February 1958. Amazingly, or so it seemed at the time, the production was an instant success, and it played for twelve months, an unheard-of run, even for established companies like the TBC. Although in retrospect the work may appear obvious and sentimental,[11] it had several unique features that fascinated the São Paulo theatregoing public. For the first time in a Brazilian play, an author placed his focus on the urban proletariat—in this case, workers living in a Rio de Janeiro slum. Moreover, the play deals sympathetically with the cause of unionization and class solidarity. And also for the first time on the Brazilian stage, audiences heard the colloquial language of slum dwellers in a manner other than caricature or folklore. A euphoric nationalist phase was about to begin in Brazilian theatre—Brazilian plays about Brazilian problems—and the way was paved for a whole new generation of playwrights.[12]

Flushed with the overwhelming success of *Black-Tie*, Arena initiated its renowned play-writing workshop, or *Seminário de Dramaturgia*, which would launch several new authors in the Arena space alone. The workshop was the first systematic attempt in Brazil to develop play writing. It had taken over a decade for a theatre company to put French director Louis Jouvet's suggestion into practice—that the Brazilian stage would only flourish with Brazilian plays. Arena, almost by chance, with the fortuitous success of Guarnieri's play, undertook a nationalist project that had far-reaching consequences. Although the *seminário* itself was short-lived, in the long run national playwrights came into their own in part as a result of Arena's efforts. The first play to come out of the workshop was Oduvaldo Vianna Filho's *Chapetuba, Futebol Clube* (*Chapetuba Soccer Club*), which began the 1959 season. Like *Black-Tie* a microcosmic view of the nation's labor relations, the work focuses on a uniquely Brazilian phenomenon, the fortunes of a professional soccer team from a small town in the state of São Paulo. *Chapetuba* examines the dreams, corruption, and exploitation of small-time soccer players. Finally, the work marked the beginning of an illustrious play-writing career for Oduvaldo Vianna Filho.[13] A further outgrowth of the *seminário* was Arena's inauguration—following the lead of the TBC—of a Monday-night experimental series, which presented four original plays in 1959, including Vianna Filho's *Bilbao, Via Copacabana* and Plínio Marcos's *Quando as Máquinas Param* (When the Machines Stop). The latter thus began a fruitful, if rocky, play-writing career.[14] In July Boal staged another original play, Roberto Freire's *Gente Como a Gente* (Folks like Us), which of all the *seminário* plays was the least effective. As a result, Arena restaged *Black-Tie* to win back its audiences. The final new *seminário* work of the season achieved a measure of success: a Boal production, Edy Lima's *A Farsa da Esposa Perfeita* (Farce of the Perfect Wife), set in the southern state of Rio Grande do Sul, on the Brazil-Uruguay border. Utilizing local color and a distinct regional dialect, the play weaves a paradoxical tale of a woman who saves her husband's honor by sleeping with another man. The work's "unique flavor of amorality and liberty in the face of conventional ethical commandments, places it squarely in the vein of the admirable universal tradition of the farce" (Magaldi, *Panorama* 257). Arena's other activities that year included tours to several cities, as well as the sponsorship of a performance by a new theatre group: Teatro Oficina's production of José Celso's *A Incubadeira* (The Incubator).

Arena produced only one major new play in 1960, Augusto Boal's *Revolução na América do Sul* (*Revolution in South America*), directed by José Renato, a box-office hit and favorite of the critics. The work established Boal as an important new product of the playwriting seminar, but it has not withstood the test of time. Like most of Boal's later plays and dramatic theories, his *Revolution* looks in retrospect like a pale imitation of a Brechtian piece (i.e., *Mother Courage*), with its fusion of the typical Arena photographic realism and use of epic technique: excessively episodic structure, archetypal central character—José da Silva—and didactic songs. The year saw the beginning of another Arena hallmark, the musical show, with the staging of *Um Americano em Brasília* (An American in Brasília)— equal parts satire of the Broadway musical, rebirth of the old *revista* (vaudeville), and original theatrical form. Variations of the new Brazilian musical would be staged by Arena, Oficina, and Rio's Grupo Opinião. Arena's musicals would later be termed *bossarenas*, in reference to the neosamba known as the bossa nova. All these phenomena, musical and theatrical, corresponded to the growing nationalist fervor in Brazil that would come to a head during the precoup Goulart administration (1961–1964).

In 1961 Arena continued its Brazilian dramaturgy phase, but the system was wearing thin. Audiences were beginning to tire of plays that were long on the *povo no palco* (common people onstage) formula, but short on artistic merit. Examples were Arena's two major productions that year, *Pintado de Alegre* (Painted with Joy) and *O Testamento do Cangaceiro* (The Bandit's Testament). The former play, by Arena actor Flávio Migliaccio, staged by Boal, was a comedy modeled after *Revolução na América do Sul,* and the latter, by Francisco de Assis and also directed by Boal, utilized northeastern Brazilian folkloric modes. Their failure signaled a three-year hiatus in the company's Brazilian dramaturgical phase. Two other events during the 1961 season were a tour to Porto Alegre, which led to that city's creation of its own Teatro de Arena, and Teatro Oficina's staging—albeit with mediocre results—of Boal's sequel to *Revolução na América do Sul* entitled *José, do Parto à Sepultura* (José, from Cradle to Grave). Whereas the former play was highly successful with audience and critics—even if today its Brechtian mimicry stands out—the latter play was characterized by "shoddy craftsmanship, repetition of *Revolução's* formulas, and simplistic analysis of the [capitalist] system" (Magaldi, *Panorama* 253).

Arena embarked on an entirely new trajectory in 1962, its "nationalization-of-the-classics" phase—utilization of classic works as vehicles to criticize contemporary Brazil—which would continue through 1964 and reappear in 1966 and 1967. José Renato broke with the Brazilian dramaturgy formula by staging Brecht's *Señora Carrar's Rifles* (*Os Fusis da Señora Carrar*), which received a lukewarm reception. The second production of the year was Machiavelli's *The Mandrake* (*A Mandrágora*), directed by Boal, who, in the Brechtian manner, added songs and attempted to emphasize the Florentine statesman's political theories. The audiences, however, seduced by the love story of Calimaco and Lucrecia, missed the political lessons, while many critics objected to them. Although Boal's intentions seemed to go awry, the ironic fact was that *A Mandrágora* was a very popular play: he won for his direction the São Paulo Association of Theatre Critics Award. His second production of the season was Tennessee Williams's *A Streetcar Named Desire* (*Um Bonde Chamado Desejo*) in Teatro Oficina.

The year 1962 would see many changes in personnel. José Renato turned over the artistic direction of Arena to Boal and moved to Rio de Janeiro. There has been a great deal of speculation regarding Renato's departure from the company he had founded; the most common theory/rumor is that he was forced out by Boal in a power struggle. Indeed, in his many writings in later years Boal appears to take full credit for Arena's many accomplishments. The founder himself, however, stated in our interview that he was tired of working in the confined space of the tiny theatre-in-the-round and wanted to branch out. His chance came when he was invited to direct the Teatro Nacional de Comédia in Rio. He has continued to work in that city and remains one of Brazil's most accomplished directors. Lending credence to the power-struggle theory, several other Arena members left to work in Rio, including playwright-actors Flávio Migliaccio and Oduvaldo Vianna Filho, who would later be identified with Grupo Opinião. The leaders of Teatro de Arena were now Augusto Boal, Gianfrancesco Guarnieri, Paulo José, Juca de Oliveira, and Flávio Império.[15]

In 1963 Boal directed Martins Pena's comedy of manners about bigamy, *O Noviço* (The Novice). Pena (1815–1848) is the father of the comedy-of-manners genre, which would become the worn-out formula favored by the Rio professional theatres in the first decades of this century. Boal and the Oficina director José Celso have criticized the TBC for staging sophisticated foreign plays and consequently putting an end to the formula, which they claimed was an authentic Brazilian popular mode, ignoring the fact that the modern comedy of manners was an anachronistic corruption of what once had been fresh and mordant social satire. Arena touted *O Noviço* as a period piece and held in conjunction with the play an exposition of colonial furniture and music recitals. Although the production received considerable audience support, some reviewers complained that the staging was mere entertainment and that the political and historical significance of Martins Pena's work was lost.

Boal continued the nationalization-of-the-classics phase that season with an adaptation—by Boal, Guarnieri, and Paulo José—of Lope de Vega's *O Melhor Juiz o Rei* (*El Mejor Alcalde, el Rey*). All the company's classic productions were marked by an attempt to establish correspondence with Brazilian reality, but this was especially true of Lope de Vega's play. In Arena's version, the aristocrat's punishment is administered not by the king himself but by a peasant dressed in royal garments. The change, obviously, added to the production a "power-to-the-people" cachet. *Juiz* was especially popular with student groups and toured extensively.

The following season opened with a brief return to Brazilian dramaturgy, Guarnieri's *O Filho do Cão* (Son of the Hound), one of the author's least credible works, a cliché-ridden portrayal of the arid Brazilian Northeast. Directed by Paulo José, its most distinguishing feature was Flávio Império's set design. The second staging of 1964, Molière's *Tartuffe* (*O Tartufo*), would be Arena's final classic until 1967. Once again Boal emphasized the social significance of the work, relating its theme of religious hypocrisy to political repression.

Boal initiated an important new direction in 1964, staging in Rio *Opinião*, a musical show co-written by Oduvaldo Vianna Filho and others, with music by veteran *sambistas* from that city's slums. The production, which led to the formation of Grupo Opinião in Rio, solidified the musical show, begun in 1960 with *Um Americano em Brasília,* as a serious art form and vehicle for social protest. The fundamental idea of *Opinião* was to use Brazilian popular music to express the concerns of the working class and to demonstrate that this class was the true source of national music. The production consisted basically of songs—samba and bossa nova—with the three performer-singers speaking briefly about such themes as rural and urban poverty, exploitation and protest, and the history of the Afro-Brazilian samba form. The show was an overwhelming success and went through several revivals with such future megastars as Nara Leão and Maria Bethânia. And therein lies another irony of Brazilian 1960s social protest theatre: the bossa nova—not to mention the singers—became the great favorite of the middle class, particularly students and intellectuals, and lost its connection with urban working-class roots. The irony goes deeper: the eventual fate of the bossa nova was its transformation into muzak played in American elevators and supermarkets.

The year 1965 would be all music for Arena. Besides the *bossa-renas,* Boal wrote and directed *Arena Canta Bahia* (Arena Sings Bahia), often listed in programs and reviews of the time as *Arena Conta Bahia* (Arena Narrates Bahia), with Gilberto Gil and Caetano Velloso. Although the Arena shows belonged to the nationalist protest school of Brazilian popular music, those two singer-composers would subsequently embark on a collision course with the school when they joined the vanguard of the *Tropicália* movement. Another Boal protest musical production in 1965 was *Tempo de Guerra* (Time of War), with Maria Bethânia, based on songs and poems by Brecht and Brazilian poet Sá de Miranda. The show played in Teatro Oficina and had a great deal of trouble with the censors. Boal also staged *A Criação do Mundo Segundo Ary Toledo* (The Creation of the World According to Ary Toledo), with the singer-composer of the title. But all of this was only preparation for the phase that gave Teatro de Arena its greatest notoriety: the *Arena Conta,* or "Arena Narrates," formula.

The first, and most memorable, of that series was the 1965 *Arena Conta Zumbi,* written by Guarnieri and Boal, directed by the latter, with music by Edu Lobo, about a colony of escaped slaves—the Palmares *quilombo,* 1630–1694—led by the legendary Zumbi.[16] The authors intended that the historical circumstance of the *quilombo* serve as a metaphor of the struggle against the military dictatorship in postcoup Brazil. The destruction of Zumbi's Palmares *quilombo* and the slaughter of its inhabitants by federal troops is one of the most shameful moments in Brazil's history, making the parallel to the present that much more poignant. The implicit criticism of the military regime installed in 1964 was the strongest condemnation of the dictatorship any artistic medium had until that time presented in Brazil. The play is based on narration in word and music by an ensemble of actors who exchange roles in the Brechtian manner, and it has a thin episodic structure, providing the minimum necessary details to move the story along. *Zumbi* is not, however, a sixties version of the "docudrama"; uninterested in characters and psychology, the staging presented historical fact as a protest against injustice and tyranny. The episodic structure also arose from the fact that *Zumbi* was a nationalist Brazilian protest musical, not a sugarcoated Broadway song-and-dance. Some of the songs, however, such as "Upa, neguinho," recorded by Elis Regina, are now pop standards. "*Zumbi* confirmed Arena's leadership in theatrical experimentation and in the struggle against the despotism in control of the nation" (Magaldi, *Palco* 71). *Arena Conta Zumbi* would become the company's greatest theatrical achievement and box-office success: it went through a succession of revivals and toured to both Europe and the United States.

From the success of *Arena Conta Zumbi* emerged a new system known as *coringa*—literally, the Joker in a deck of cards—which sheds light on the relationship and response of the modern Brazilian stage to foreign models. Augusto Boal devised the *coringa* to be a unique Brazilian codification of certain principles of Bertolt Brecht's Epic Theatre. Distilled from several features of *Zumbi*, the Joker was first applied to the 1967 *Arena Conta Tiradentes*, co-authored by Guarnieri and Boal and directed by the latter, which narrates the story of the *Inconfidência Mineira*, the late eighteenth-century failed plot led by Tiradentes, the father of the Brazilian independence movement and official national hero. History is idealized in the play, which presents Tiradentes as the champion of the masses. Following the Brechtian notion of *Lehrstücke*—instructing ideologically while entertaining through the use of popular music—the primary function of Boal's system is a didactic treatment of the myth of Tiradentes and its historical and contemporary implications. Using popular music as an integral part of the dramatic structure, the *coringa* attempts to combine Brechtian alienation (or estrangement) and empathy (or audience identification with the central character). The members of the ensemble exchange roles, while a single actor plays Tiradentes to maintain empathy. The *coringa*, played at times by a single actor and at others by the chorus, serves the general function of setting the scene, interrupting and explaining the narrative, and making comments and speeches to the audience. Alienation, which in Brecht has a Marxist economic meaning—the people do not control the means of production—in *Tiradentes* has a political focus: the independence movement, or *inconfidência*, failed in part because the people were not involved. As in Brecht, the collective principle is held above the individual: the ensemble is more important than the individual actor, the chorus is central to the dramatic structure, and Tiradentes is presented as a collective hero, whose famous utterance is sung repeatedly by the chorus: "If I had ten lives, ten lives I would give" (*Dez vidas eu tivesse, dez vidas eu daria*). Boal took from Brecht thematic episodes and semidocumentary style: *Arena Conta Tiradentes* includes self-contained episodes relating to the *inconfidência*, in addition to such documents as transcripts of Tiradentes's trial. The final Brechtian dimension is the use of irregular verse forms interspersed with prose dialogue. The *coringa* techniques did not have the desired effect but made the production unwieldy, overly cerebral, and schematic; it fell far short of *Zumbi*'s success, and a 1968 revival in Rio, directed by Teatro Oficina's Fernando Peixoto, achieved mediocre results.[17] A whole series of *Arena Conta/coringa* projects were planned, but only one reached the stage, the 1971 *Arena Conta Bolívar*, written and directed by Boal.

The years from 1966 to its demise in 1971 represented, for the most part, a period of decline for Arena. There were productions in the nationalization-of-the-classics mold (e.g., Gogol's *The Inspector General*, Molière's *L'École des Femmes*), works by Brecht (e.g., *The Resistible Rise of Arturo Ui*), Brazilian dramaturgy plays, several musical shows, and contemporary plays such as *Macbird*.[18] Those productions failed to rise above a general panorama of mediocrity, with one fruitful exception, the 1968 *Primeira Feira da Opinião Paulista* (First São Paulo Opinion Fair). Organized by Boal, the fair was based on the idea of soliciting opinions, especially political ones, in the form of sketches, skits, vignettes, and playlets. The *Feira* included contributions from several playwrights: Guarnieri, Jorge Andrade, Plínio Marcos, and Boal himself. Among the pieces were a parody of the military mentality and censorship, an examination of the pre- and postcoup conditions for workers' organizations, problems of rural poverty, and a paean to Che Guevara. Interspersed among the episodes were songs by some of Brazil's leading pop composers, such as Sérgio Ricardo, Gilberto Gil, and Caetano Velloso, who would become the enfant terrible of Tropicalism the same year. Several well-known actors performed in the *Feira*. The fair was equal parts wildly comic absurdism, melodrama, and didacticism;

staged in the large space of the Teatro Ruth Escobar, it gained enthusiastic audience support. Concurrently playing in another of Ruth Escobar's three performing spaces was Chico Buarque's *Roda Viva*, which was the object of a violent assault by a right-wing paramilitary squad. At the same time, the *Feira* participants received threatening letters; fortunately, the expected attack never materialized. However, the production was closed by the censors following the military government's declaration of state of seige in December 1968. Other opinion fairs were planned for Brazil and for Latin America—rather grandiosely, an international fair was discussed—but they never took place. This fruitful idea, like so many others, fell victim to military repression. A book entitled *Feira Brasileira da Opinião*, with selections by critic Décio de Almeida Prado, and distinguished playwrights including Dias Gomes, Guarnieri, and Leilah Assunção, was published in 1978 but never staged.

The final promising Arena experiment was conducted by Augusto Boal in 1971, and he would subsequently reap enormous personal prestige from it. He staged, with mixed results, a Brazilian adaptation of the American depression-era Living Newspaper entitled *Teatro Jornal, Primeira Edição*. Like the *coringa*, both a didactic theory of performing and a stage production, the *Teatro Jornal* utilized amateur actors in a series of readings, skits, and episodes based on current news, with musical accompaniment (e.g., samba, tango). Frivolous and tragic news items were juxtaposed for ironic contrast.

In great part due to increasing pressure from the police-state apparatus, company members went on a number of tours in Arena's final years. In 1969 the New York–based Theatre of Latin America, Inc. (TOLA) invited Arena to perform *Zumbi* in St. Clement's Theatre for a one-week run, which was extended to a month due to the play's success. TOLA director Joanne Pottlitzer invited Arena back in 1970 for a tour of several universities, culminating in an appearance at the Public Theatre, where the company debuted its *Arena Conta Bolívar*, which was never presented in Brazil. The tour was subsequently extended, and the two *Arena Conta* pieces played in Mexico, Peru, and Argentina, where the group participated in the First Latin American Theatre Festival of Buenos Aires. There was a final tour to Europe in 1971, and *Arena Conta Zumbi* and *Teatro Jornal* were performed at the Nancy International Theatre Festival, and subsequently in other French cities.

Upon his return to Brazil, Boal was arrested and tortured, and he went into exile. He subsequently achieved international recognition with his experiments in Latin America and Europe, where he elaborated his *coringa* and *Teatro Jornal* didactic theories with stagings, variously named Popular Theatre, Theatre of the Oppressed, Invisible Theatre, and Forum Theatre. He also published a number of theoretical works.[19] While he continues to use Paris as his base of operations, Boal occasionally returns to Brazil to direct, conduct workshops, and lecture.

Teatro de Arena's long history came to a close with its final production, *Doce América Latina* (Sweet Latin America), an unsubstantial collective creation, under the coordination of Luis Carlos Arutim, in the manner of the Living Theatre and Teatro Oficina's later work. Teatro de Arena closed its doors in August 1971, although Arutim continued to administer and rent out the theatre until 1977. That year, the Serviço Nacional de Teatro took over the Arena space and renamed it Teatro Experimental Eugênio Kusnet, which continues to this day to house productions by assorted student and other noncommercial groups.

Teatro de Arena's legacy is vast. It spearheaded a movement that gave impetus to Brazilian play writing. When the company began its existence, most playscripts produced were foreign and few were Brazilian; now that formula has been inverted. From its beginnings as a bargain-basement TBC, it evolved into the latter's mentor. Arena's experiments encouraged the theatrical treatment of national problems, characters, and speech, combined with engagé social consciousness. It helped break the national dependence on the Italian-style proscenium stage and paved the way for a myriad of other groups that could now mount inexpensive productions in unconventional spaces. The *bossarenas* established their own tradition: plays with and even about popular music remain a staple of the Brazilian stage.

Augusto Boal's stagings and writings have justifiably brought him international renown but have served as well to cloud the picture regarding Teatro de Arena and indeed the modern Brazilian stage in general. That is, Europeans and Americans have come to identify contemporary Brazilian theatre almost exclusively with Boal, and the result has been that other theorists and practitioners of theatre, whose contributions are equal to Boal's, are virtually ignored. Moreover, some of his theories have been widely circulated, propagated, and studied (e.g., *coringa*), while in practice they produced meagre results. *Arena Conta Zumbi*, a collaboration by some of the most luminous figures in Brazilian theatre and music, was a genuine breakthrough, but it predates Boal's theoretical formulations. In spite of all that has been written about the post-*Zumbi coringa* system, where did that experiment lead? Guarnieri stated in our interview that the *Arena Conta* plays he co-authored were useful because of their collective dimension and the economic advantage of a few actors playing many roles. He did not, however, agree with Boal's quasi-Brechtian *coringa* theory surrounding the *Arena Conta* efforts, because in the end it "impoverishes the stage" by leaving the audience "trying to guess who is who." The main problem with the *coringa*, according to Guarnieri, is that it attempts to "express the essence of the mask without the mask." The reference here is to the social "mask" the *coringa* utilizes in place of the physical masks of Greek theatre, which represented the characters. That is, Boal sets out for the *coringa* a judicial analogy: the audience is like a jury that must see several witnesses to judge objectively. According to the theory, then, several actors sharing a role allow the audience to judge the character objectively; whatever remains constant about the character—the social mask—corresponds to the objective truth. All other characteristics— emotions and psychological motivation— vary from actor to actor and have no "social" significance. The *coringa* social mask did catch on in Brazil with many amateur groups, and indeed it persists to the present time. The idea is that anyone using the social—or Living Newspaper—techniques can perform theatre. Stagecraft—acting, directing, play writing, design—is deemphasized. The result is an amateur theatrical milieu in which social intention is the only important factor; rigorous study of acting technique and focus on aesthetic values are "fascist." The upshot is that new amateur groups usually spend most of their time arguing over social and ideological questions, and rarely do they manage to bring anything to the stage. Those that do tend to produce plays that are weak, if not slapdash, in stagecraft. Amateur troupes that venture into the territory of aesthetic concern are stamped as "alienated" by the heirs of *coringa*.

The above reservations aside, Arena's contributions were undeniably vital, and its stance in the face of repression was heroic. In aesthetic terms, while the company specialized in a kind of gritty realism, it would be up to Teatro Oficina to carry on the Os Comediantes and TBC tradition of refining the elements of stagecraft.

Teatro Oficina

Teatro Oficina was founded in 1958, the year of Arena's *Eles Não Usam Black-Tie*. Although Arena's pioneering efforts toward the development of a national dramaturgy and the direct contributions of Arena playwright and director Augusto Boal gave Oficina a strong push in its early years, the latter is more clearly a descendant of the Teatro Brasileiro de Comédia. While Arena's great contributions to

Brazilian theatre pertain to play writing and engagé social consciousness, those of Oficina lie more in the realm of stagecraft. Another important facet of Oficina's legacy was to rescue from oblivion Modernist Oswald de Andrade's drama and to bring to the stage for the first time his aesthetic-ideological concept of Anthropophagy. Oficina's outstanding figure was José Celso Martínez Correa (José or Zé Celso, as he is usually referred to), in my view one of the three leading directors—along with Ziembinski and Antunes Filho—in the history of the modern Brazilian stage.

Oficina's earliest beginnings focus on a group of young artists in the provincial São Paulo town of Araraquara. The group belonged to an organization called the Centro Cultural Alberto Torres. Since Alberto Torres was one of the principal theorists of the Integralist or Brazilian fascist movement, the group's political background provides a stunning contrast with its subsequent leftist and eventual anarcho-utopian tendencies. The center, which included José Celso and Inácio Loyola Brandão,[20] organized annual samba and poetry festivals. In 1956, several members of the center entered the University of São Paulo Law School, where they continued their cultural activities. In spite of the Integralist, provincial, and upper-class origins of the group, in 1958 the members had no specific political agenda, beyond the euphoric nationalist sentiments shared by many Brazilians during the Kubitschek administration. Teatro Oficina was born modestly during an informal meeting in the courtyard of the law school that included the young men from Araraquara and other students. One of the latter, Carlos Queiroz Telles, suggested the name *oficina* (workshop) for the new amateur company. Since few of the students had any theatre background, they decided to assign specific roles according to their limited experience. The first playwrights would be Queiroz Telles, a poet, and José Celso, neither of whom had ever written a play. Nevertheless, Arena's success with *Black-Tie* had engendered the hope that aspiring Brazilian theatre artists could produce their own works. Amir Haddad, who had staged a play in secondary school, would be the director, and he went on to direct the group's first three productions. The remaining members were to be actors in the new company.

Two plays were composed: *A Ponte* (The Bridge), by Queiroz Telles, and *Vento Forte Para Papagaio Subir* (Strong Wind for a Kite to Fly) by Celso. The group sought sponsorship from the law school's academic center, but the plan was rejected because another theatre company was already being funded. This marginalization established a pattern that would characterize much of Oficina's work throughout its existence. Although Oficina's members were discouraged, they decided to produce the two plays independently with their own meagre finances. Rehearsals were conducted in private residences until a performing space was secured in a building on Jaceguai Street where séances had previously been held, a fact which some claimed, not always with tongue in cheek, would influence Teatro Oficina's ofttimes bizarre destiny. The place on Rua Jaceguai would eventually become the company's permanent home, and to this day the space is controlled by José Celso Martínez Correa, who, some would say, inhabits the space like a ghost of Oficina's bygone days. But that is getting ahead of our story.

Oficina 58, as the group first called itself, performed its productions on two successive evenings in late October. In spite of a bus strike, they played to sold-out audiences, comprised of "representatives of the São Paulo bourgeoisie, each one with his own car" (Carlos Queiroz Telles, interview). In spite of Teatro de Arena's influence, the two plays expressed only the most superficial social concerns. The author himself calls *A Ponte* "an awful psychological-religious melodrama" (interview). The play deals with the coupling of a young man and woman; when she becomes pregnant, the conflict centers around her decision whether to abort the child. She comes under the influence of a "progressive" priest and decides to keep the child in the face of social disapprobation. *Vento Forte Para Papagaio Subir* is an autobiographical play about the trials of a young man in a small São Paulo town and his flight from the stultifying provincial environment, the kite carried off by a heavy wind.

Décio de Almeida Prado, with a touch of irony, deemed Oficina's opening promising: "Everything will depend on the future." *A Ponte*, he wrote, has an insipid, cut-and-dried plot without literary or theatrical merit. On the other hand, the critic found *Vento Forte* excessively symbolic, and the production itself was marred by pointless movement and the omnipresent heavy hand of the director ("Dois Grupos"). Nevertheless, José Celso's play was subsequently entered in an amateur theatre contest sponsored by a São Paulo television network, where it received awards for best author, director, and actor. Encouraged by this success, Oficina 58 planned its next program.

Oficina originally announced it would stage Clifford Odets' *Waiting for Lefty* but subsequently decided to perform José Celso's *A Incubadeira* (The Incubator). In July 1959, the company presented the play in the port city of Santos, at the Second National Student Theatre Festival, organized by Carlos Paschoal Magno. *The Incubator* was awarded prizes for best director (Amir Haddad), best actress (Etty Frascr), and best actor (Renato Borghi). The latter two would remain with Oficina for the following decade and would become two of the most illustrious names on the São Paulo stage. When the company returned to São Paulo, it sought a theatre to perform its award-winning play. The only space available was Teatro de Arena, which would be dark for several months following the failure of *Gente Como A Gente*. Oficina members met with Boal and Guarnieri to discuss the terms of rent. The first contact between Arena and Oficina, therefore, had nothing to do with nationalist ideology, Brazilian dramaturgy, or consciousness-raising. The two groups began their association as landlord and tenant, and in fact the relationship was exploitive because according to the rental contract Arena would receive 80 percent of the box-office receipts. Fortunately for both companies, *A Incubadeira* was favorably received by audiences and critics and played to full houses for nearly four months, a long run for an amateur production.

The play continued the themes explored in *Vento Forte:* the stifling atmosphere of provincial life, the symbol of which is the incubator of the title, from which the young protagonist attempts to break out and strive toward maturity. Once again, central to the conflict are oppressive family ties. The latter theme would reappear often in Oficina productions. José Celso's piece also contains the seeds of social consciousness (*conscientização*) and nationalism, which would increasingly motivate the group's work. According to the program notes for *A Incubadeira*, Oficina was concerned with "the future of Brazilian theatre and dramaturgy." Celso wrote his third and last play, *Cadeiras na Calçada* (Chairs on the Sidewalk), but it was never staged.

To finance its operations, the group began performing light pieces in the private homes of the wealthy—a program called *teatro a domicílio*—and even in a night club. The young company's association with the wealthy, as well as the upper-class background of its members, created an image of "rich brats" trying to be artistes, a far cry from the future fire-breathing *épater les bourgeois* Teatro Oficina.

In December 1959, the company staged Sartre's *The Flies* (*As Moscas*) as part of a Franco-Brazilian Festival sponsored by the Alliance Française. The production was directed by Frenchman Jean-Luc Descaves, who had been in São Paulo for only a few years staging amateur theatricals in French. Although the play deals in many ways with themes that had characterized previous Oficina works (e.g., individual liberty), the staging of Sartre's work received little audience support. The critics, however, considered it praiseworthy as an amateur effort in the right direction. José Celso, Renato Borghi, and Etty Fraser did not participate in *The Flies*, reflecting a widening schism among Oficina members. Several of them, led by Celso, wanted to turn professional, while others wanted to maintain their amateur status. The latter group, including Amir Haddad and Carlos Queiroz Telles, would soon leave the company.

In 1960 the paths of Arena and Oficina began to merge. The first play of that year, *Fogo Frio* (Cold Fire) by Bendito Ruy Barbosa, dealing with the problems of a rural family in the southern state of Paraná whose crops have been destroyed by frost, fit the national dramaturgy mold of Teatro de Arena. The production was directed by Augusto Boal in the Arena space, with actors from Teatro Oficina. Some observers maintain that *Fogo Frio* and subsequent co-productions went beyond mere cooperation, that Boal was attempting to absorb Oficina into his company, while according to another viewpoint the Oficina group was seeking to annex itself to the more established theatre. Important for the young performers was the fact that they received their first formal acting classes from Boal. The Arena director also staged the year's second production, *A Engrenagem*, which he and José Celso adapted from a film script, entitled *L'Engrenage*, by Sartre. That was Oficina's initial foray into engagé territory, since the work deals explicitly with revolutionary movements in the Third World. Sartre himself, during a 1960 visit to Brazil, stated that "*L'Engrenage* takes place in an imaginary country that could actually be Brazil" (Magaldi and Vargas, "Cem anos"). Sections of the script were cut by the local censors. In response the company members staged a public protest, wearing gags, in front of the independence monument in downtown São Paulo.

In 1961 the group opted for professional status, which along with its newfound engagé stance sent those opposed packing, while continuing its semiautonomous association with Arena and the acting classes with Boal. In spite of the latter's influence, José Celso had clearly emerged as Oficina's leader. The company also obtained its own performing space that year, the building on Jaceguai Street, where it had its debut and which would become its permanent home. The group launched an intensive fund-raising campaign to rehabilitate the theatre. Under the direction of an architect, the seating was increased while the stage was transformed from a small proscenium to a semithrust, the audience seated above the performing space, a novel concept for Brazil. The thrust stage allowed closer contact with the public yet avoided the blocking headaches of a theatre-in-the-round like Arena. While the space was being renovated, the company spent six months rehearsing Clifford Odets' *Awake and Sing* (*A Vida Impressa em Dólar*)[21] and conducting intensive workshops based on method acting. Although Ziembinski and Boal had already pioneered the Stanislavski system, Oficina went further than anyone else in Brazil in utilizing interior psychological acting. The group was aided in this direction by American actor James Colby, who had trained in the Actors Studio under the tutelage of Lee Strassberg, and by Russian emigré Eugênio Kusnet, Brazil's leading expert on Stanislavski. As in the case of Ziembinski and Os Comediantes and the Italians and TBC, foreign cultural influence—the Method, in this case—would be crucial for the group's development. *Awake and Sing,* directed by José Celso, was extremely well received by audiences, and students in particular identified strongly with the play's social concerns. According to the program notes, "critical analysis of American society is a means to examine the social and existential problems that affect us." Support for the production was aided by the local censors' heavy-handed attempts to cut scenes and language "contrary to public morals" and, incredibly, to change the title, because its negative use of the word *dollar* might offend the United States. Although it is by no means the only company in Brazil to have suffered at the hands of the censors, Oficina would be haunted throughout its existence by repressive measures, by "one drama on the stage and another bureaucratic drama in the wings" (Sérgio da Silva, *Te-Ato* 28). But at least the publicity generated by *Dollar's* censorship problems enhanced audience support for the production. The play was also significant because it confirmed the directorial talent of José Celso, who, in the context of the company's subsequent radical direction, would denigrate the staging as a pale imitation of American theatre, and worse yet, "liberal."

The second production of 1961 was *José, do Parto à Sepultura* (José, from Cradle to Grave), written by Augusto Boal and directed by Antônio Abujamra.[22] *José,* which opened in late December, flopped due to the text's heavy-handed use of Brechtian techniques and to what critics called the cold, geometric blocking. According to Décio de Almeida Prado's review, the play followed Arena's usual formula: "more or less equal doses of leftist political preaching and farce, [but] instead of harsh criticism of capitalist society, what we are left with upon leaving the theatre is the impression of a gigantic, two-and-a-half-hour sketch. José's path from cradle to grave seems at times to go on and on" (Almeida Prado, *Progresso* 225).

In 1962, Boal would direct for the last time at Oficina. His *A Streetcar Named Desire* (*Um Bonde Chamado Desejo*) was the first in a succession of Oficina stagings characterized by highly sophisticated production values, in the tradition of the TBC. The play was distinguished by the participation of a renowned actress, Maria Fernanda, in the role of Blanche Dubois. Many of Oficina's subsequent productions would include top professional actors. *Streetcar* was also notable for Flávio Império's set design. The production marked a definitive break with the Arena formula, in spite of Boal's direction. Oficina's North American cycle came to an end with its second 1962 production, Ketti Fring's theatrical adaptation of Thomas Wolfe's novel *Look Homeward Angel (Todo Anjo É Terrível)*, directed by José Celso. The production was elaborate and expensive; it pleased the critics but received weak audience support. The company had to face up to the realities of the professional stage; it needed new sources of inspiration and a commercial success to make up for its losses. The answer was supplied by Eugênio Kusnet, who introduced the group to Russian theatre with his translation of a little-known Russian comedy by Valentin Kataev, *Square the Circle (Quatro num Quarto)*. The play, dealing with the misadventures of two couples—one from the old aristocratic class and the other from the newly ascendant working class—forced to share a single-room honeymoon "suite" in postrevolutionary Moscow, represented the requisite change of focus. After presenting exclusively realist drama, utilizing interiorized Method acting, Teatro Oficina staged a light and graceful comedy. The actors thus expanded their style and repertoire, and the company earned a significant sum of money, all of which permitted the consolidation of a stable ensemble. *Quatro num Quarto* would undergo several revivals over the years, which along with other occasional forays into the commercial arena, put finances on a less precarious footing and allowed further aesthetic experimentation. The play represented a transition to another phase, which would lead the company to the vanguard of the Brazilian stage, alongside Teatro de Arena.

The new phase began with the 1963 production of Maxim Gorki's *Petty Bourgeois (Pequenos Burgueses)*, which takes place in the period immediately preceding the Russian revolution. The play was translated by José Celso and Fernando Peixoto.[23] Celso was also the director. The experiments, workshops, and stagings based on the Stanislavski system were brought to fruition in the play, and the presence of Eugênio Kusnet in the role of Bessemonov aided the production immeasurably. In addition to the brilliance of its formal aspects, Celso communicated successfully his intentional linking of Gorki's work to the Brazilian sociopolitical situation, with its atmosphere of prerevolutionary aspirations and questioning of class relationships. The public supported *Pequenos Burgueses* overwhelmingly, and the consensus of the critics was that it represented "the most perfect Brazilian performance within the realist mold" (Magaldi and Vargas, "Cem anos"). Its success was comparable to that of Teatro de Arena's *Eles Não Usam Black-Tie*. It ran until the military coup of 31 March 1964, when it closed in the cloud of uncertainty that had descended over the entire nation. The production reopened a few weeks later, and revivals would continue for decades.[24] Besides its year-long run in São Paulo, *Pequenos Burgueses* toured to several other Brazilian cities and won the grand prize in the Latin American Theatre Festival in Uruguay.

The company intended to follow with John Ford's *Too Bad She's a Whore* (*Pena Que Ela Seja uma P . . .*) but suspended rehearsals on the day of the coup and turned to the politically safer *Toda Donzela Tem um Pai Que É uma Fera* (Every Maiden Has a Ferocious Father), a light comedy written by Gláucio Gil and directed by Benedito Corsi.

The final staging of 1964 would add to Oficina's growing reputation as a creator of beautiful and daring productions. The play was Max Frisch's *Andorra*, directed by José Celso, who, as a result of his brilliant staging of *Pequenos Burgueses*, was now widely considered the nation's finest director. The production of *Andorra* was notable for its stunning visual effects, including a highly acclaimed set design by Flávio Império, and for its use of Brechtian estrangement—a step in a new direction for Oficina—which offset many of the work's realist facets and underscored its application to Brazilian political reality. Although the plot concerns Nazi persecution of the Jews, the production was taken by many to be the first theatrical response, albeit somewhat allegorical, to the military dictatorship and its anti-Communist witch hunt. Arena's 1965 *Zumbi* was of course an even stronger condemnation of the coup. In December 1964, Teatro Oficina presented *Pequenos Burgueses* and *Andorra* at yet another Latin American Theatre Festival in Uruguay and came away with the bulk of the prizes. Fernando Peixoto also directed Gianfrancesco Guarnieri's *O Cimento* (Cement) for Uruguayan television.

In 1965 José Celso traveled to Europe to study theatre techniques with the Berliner Ensemble, while the remaining members carried on the company's work. Eugênio Kusnet directed Alexei Arbusov's *It Happened in Irkutsk* (*Aconteceu em Irkutsk*), Fernando Peixoto directed a musical show with samba artist Nara Leão, and *Toda Donzela Tem um Pai Que É uma Fera* was adapted for television. Other group members toured throughout Brazil with productions of *Quatro num Quartro*, *Pequenos Burgueses*, and *Andorra*.

In 1966, Teatro Oficina opened a new play on the stage of the Teatro Brasileiro de Comédia, Gorki's *The Enemies* (*Os Inimigos*), directed by José Celso, who applied the lessons he had learned by observing the Berliner Ensemble. The director came to believe that psychological realism fused with techniques of Brecht's Epic Theatre represented an excellent solution for the Brazilian stage because it would lead the audience to the reason, and not merely to the emotion, of a text. Celso worked closely on this project with Fernando Peixoto, who was quickly establishing himself as Oficina's second-in-command and who would later become Brazil's leading expert on Bertolt Brecht. *The Enemies* received strong public support but mixed reviews from critics skeptical of the attempt to fuse psychological realism and Brechtian distancing techniques. Flávio Império's bold set design, however, was unanimously praised.

In May 1966, the company's building on Jaceguai Street was gutted by fire, an event that would become charged with symbolism. Oficina received immediate support from other theatres, the municipal government, and the press. During the process of rebuilding, the group presented a retrospective of its most important works on the stage of the Teatro Cacilda Becker: *A Vida Impressa em Dólar, Quatro num Quarto*—the latter production also toured extensively around São Paulo's outlying districts—and *Pequenos Burgueses*. In early 1967 the company took the latter two productions, as well as *Andorra*, to Rio. The support received after the fire and the success of the retrospectives gave the group a chance to rethink its mission. The fire would signify a symbolic burning of the theatrical past and would lead to a production that would become Teatro Oficina's great legacy to the Brazilian stage.

On 29 September 1967, the rebuilt theatre was inaugurated with Oswald de Andrade's *O Rei da Vela* (*The Candle King*), directed by José Celso, again with significant contributions from Fernando Peixoto. The staging was a milestone for debuting Andrade's 1937 play, thus demonstrating the importance of a little-known facet of the Modernist writer's oeuvres. It synthesized and parodied most avant-garde theatrical styles of the 1950s and 1960s, as well as several specifically Brazilian genres like comedy of manners, *revista*, circus, and São Paulo opera. The result was the first application on the stage of Oswald de Andrade's concept of Anthropophagy, subsequently transformed into the *Tropicália* movement. The staging scandalized some—company members received death threats, and the production was later banned outright—and was hailed by others as a new and original performance mode. In 1968 *The Candle King* toured Europe and participated in two international festivals: the IV Ressegna Internazionale dei Teatri Stabili (Florence) and the Festival Mondial des Jeunes Compagnies (Nancy). The production was received more enthusiastically in France than in Italy. Owing to its success in Nancy, the company was invited to Paris, where its presentation of *O Rei da Vela* coincided with the 1968 student protests. The European tour had no official support and incurred debts from which Oficina never fully recovered.

José Celso directed another controversial play in 1967: popular singer-composer Chico Buarque de Hollanda's *Roda Viva* (Spinning Wheel).[25] Although the production had no official link to Teatro Oficina, it meant a continuation of the performing aesthetic introduced by *O Rei da Vela:* theatre of aggression and Tropicalist elements. *Roda Viva* had both supporters and detractors. Among the latter was a right-wing paramilitary organization, known as the Communist Hunting Command (Comando de Caça aos Comunistas, or CCC), responsible for a number of terrorist acts prior to the 1968 declaration of state of siege. During a performance at São Paulo's Teatro Rute Escobar, the CCC attacked and beat actors and musicians, destroyed sets and props, and ransacked the theatre because of its objection to the play's "immorality" (profane language and simulated lovemaking) and "subversion" (scenes of student protest). When *Roda Viva* subsequently toured to Porto Alegre, the performers were again terrorized by the "command": the leading actress and actor were kidnapped and threatened with execution (they were released after a short time). The censors eventually banned both Chico Buarque's play and *O Rei da Vela*.

Fernando Peixoto returned to popular music in 1968, directing the Arena-like *Show Musical Oficina*, with singers Nara Leão and Maria Bethânia, composer Chico Buarque, and Tropicalists Caetano Veloso, Gilberto Gil, and Jorge Ben. Peixoto also staged his first drama, Leroi Jones's *The Dutchman* (*Poder Negro*),[26] but only after overcoming strong resistance from censorship. The director intended that the production represent the struggle for liberation of oppressed peoples in Latin America, but the reviews of the play were very negative. The consensus was that Peixoto, in his directorial debut, had failed to match the blocking with the dialogue and to communicate the violence contained in Jones's story of a white prostitute and the black subway passenger whom she humiliates and then murders.

In December 1968, Oficina presented another of its milestones, Brecht's *Galileu Galilei* (*The Life of Galileo*), translated by Roberto Schwartz and directed by José Celso. The inquisition of Galileo symbolized for the company tyranny at the hands of the dictatorship, and the Renaissance the birth of a new era to be brought about by forces resisting political and cultural oppression. Ironically, the opening date coincided with the imposition of the Institutional Act Number Five, which gave the military government state of siege powers.[27] A split among group members came to a head during the production, which would lead to a new phase for the company. On the one hand were the professional actors who considered theatre's function to be the transmission of ideas, a source of reflection, and on the other were the young amateurs from the *Roda Viva* ensemble who, under the influence of Tropicalism and 1960s counterculture, viewed theatre as ritual and magic. The latter faction participated in a now legendary carnival scene which changed improvisationally with every performance and brought audience members on stage with the actors. The carnival scene expanded over the course of *Galileo*'s run and indicated Teatro Oficina's future direction. In spite of the Tropicalist inclusion of carnival and rock music, José Celso captured the work's Brechtian spirit: "a prodigiously rational performance, which constitutes a clear demonstration of the value of reason" (Peixoto, "Oficina," *Ciclo*). The play sold out during its run in São Paulo and subsequent tour to other Brazilian cities, during a period in which most productions played to near-empty houses. The critics were divided: the traditionally minded reviewers turned up their noses at what they saw as antitheatre and anticulture, but the more adventurous (e.g., Sábato Magaldi) considered it a masterful staging.

Celso staged another Brechtian piece in 1969, *In the Jungle of the Cities* (*Na Selva das Cidades*).[28] For this production, the company came under a new influence—as usual, Oficina was the first to detect the latest theatrical trends—that of Jerzy Grotowski's Polish Laboratory Theatre. Following Grotowski's concept of an actor-centered theatre, the ensemble underwent intensive and painful vocal and physical training, practicing disciplines like karate and conducting lengthy rehearsals. This new method drove some of the veteran actors out, but most went through the process. The training allowed the company to stage the early work by Brecht, perhaps his most anarchic piece. The play was, of course, very physical, with actors literally throwing themselves about the stage, and Oficina's longest (about three and a half hours). Most critics agreed that, while not his greatest aesthetic experiment, it was one of Celso's most fascinating productions. Symbolic of the internal crisis into which Oficina had plunged, the set—a boxing ring—was destroyed during each performance.

In 1970, Fernando Peixoto directed Molière's *Don Juan*, which he saw as a play about protest and youthful passion (he was under the sway of the youth culture expressed in the music of the Rolling Stones and the film *Easy Rider*). Arena's Gianfrancesco Guarnieri played the title role.[29] The ambivalence regarding the rational and the irrational—the latter referring to the chorus, like the Carnival revelers in *Galileo*—continued in this production. Inspired by the music and singing of Mick Jagger, the director added rock music, and the action took place among the spectators, seated on the floor. Oficina also produced a film in 1970, *Prata Palomares*, directed by André Faria, which was banned by the censors and not exhibited until the 1977 Cannes Festival. It debuted in Brazil in 1979, at the annual Festival do Gramado. The film constituted a massive drain on the already financially strapped comedy, leading to another of its fund-raising retrospectives, which featured *Galileo* and *Don Juan*. Finally, the year would provide a fascinating and promising—although some would say ultimately disastrous—association with the Living Theatre, a story that sheds light on the vital questions of imposed cultural models and Anthropophagical devouring.

The Living Theatre was founded in the late 1940s by Judith Malina and the late Julian Beck.[30] It was initially an off-off-Broadway avant-garde troupe whose early influences were Erwin Piscator, with whom Malina had worked, and Bertolt Brecht. Among its productions from 1950 to 1964 were William Carlos Williams's *Many Loves*, Pirandello's *Tonight We Improvise*, Brecht's *In the Jungle of the Cities* and *Man Is Man*, and *The Brig*. In 1964, due to income-tax problems, the group departed for Europe. During their four-year sojourn abroad, company members immersed themselves in Antonin Artaud's Theatre of Cruelty and began to experiment with prelogical and ritual forms of communication. They reduced the position of the word, created works collectively, focused on physical techniques, and invited spontaneous involvement by the audience. Ideologically, they saw themselves as anarchists and mystics combating the evils of modern society: bureaucracy, massification, instinctual repression, and materialism. They espoused an international order in which humankind would live communally and harmoniously with nature in order to achieve physical and spiritual plenitude. They were opposed to violent revolution, believing that it only changed conditions; rather, they sought a revolution of consciousness that, as Julian Beck was fond of saying, would change man. In an article on the Living Theatre, Brazilian critic Anatol Rosenfeld refers to Peter Brook's criticism of the group's ideology: it seeks sainthood without tradition and sacred sources, leading it to the creation of a "bizarre spiritual cocktail" (Rosenfeld, "Living Theatre"). Brazilian actors in direct association with the American company would have their own complaints.

After Malina and Beck's performing commune returned from Europe, it staged a body of work in the Brooklyn Academy of Music and Yale University that would have an international impact, its revolutionary—and controversial—productions of *Mysteries and Smaller Pieces, Antigone, Frankenstein,* and *Paradise Now.*

In 1969 the troupe once again traveled to Europe, where José Celso and Renato Borghi met Beck and Malina through Cinema Novo director Glauber Rocha and invited them to work in Brazil with Oficina. A faction of the Living Theatre, under the guidance of its founders, arrived in São Paulo in 1970. The responses to the Living Theatre's sojourn in Brazil were mixed. On the negative side, the group was criticized for its countercultural mysticism and alleged colonialist mind-set. Following are views on the subject expressed by Oficina members.

According to Fernando Peixoto, an attempt was made to create a joint theatrical piece with Oficina, Living Theatre, and Grupo Lobos.[31] The Latin Americans, however, objected to "a certain spirit of colonization, whether conscious or unconscious." To complicate matters, the Living Theatre was "searching for new paths," which the Brazilians could not provide. In the end, no agreement with the Living Theatre could be worked out (Peixoto, "Oficina," *Ciclo*).

Designer Flávio Império, the only South American participant in the collaborative experiment who had actually seen Beck and Malina's performances, recalled in our interview that one difficulty was the Living Theatre's profound communal experience, cohesive organization, highly developed theatrical methods, and working discipline, which their would-be partners could not match. According to Império, there was a single joint workshop. But the physical training of the Americans was so awesome that the Brazilians dropped out after five minutes and merely observed the rest. Many of the younger Brazilians "were terrified, panicked by the Living folks, as if they were beings from another planet." There were other conflicts, especially ideological. The Americans claimed to believe in equality and to be opposed to any form of leadership, but according to Império they imposed their values and ways on the Latin Americans and refused to relinquish or even discuss their leadership role. As a result, there was no shared process or growth. The Living Theatre, moreover, made specific demands in terms of the necessities of survival. For example, they wanted a house isolated from others. They were told that such a luxury was impossible, that Latin American artists got by as best they could, sharing housing, food, clothing—some even living with their parents. It was suggested to the Americans that they do a retrospective of their works, which was the Oficina modus operandi for raising funds during lean times. The Living Theatre members refused, maintaining that those works belonged to a now dead past. Império viewed their response as the utopian attitude of a developed society and the inability to comprehend and face the realities of an underdeveloped country. During their six-month stay, they did not even learn rudimentary Portuguese. The only possible way of relating to the Living Theatre, therefore, was to become an integral part of its community, to embrace its values—which some Brazilians did—handed down by Julian Beck and Judith Malina. Império saw the commune as more a cult surrounding two people than a theatre group. Finally, Império accompanied the Living Theatre to Rio de Janeiro, where it performed a Christmas procession in the streets of a slum. Although the procession was meant to be serious, even tragic, the local residents found it merely amusing. Império did see one positive outgrowth of the Living Theatre's stay in Brazil: Oficina's subsequent production entitled *Gracias, Señor* (sometimes written as *Gracias, Senhor*).

The third view is that of José Celso, who became the classic person caught in the middle. He recalled in an interview with Hamilton Almeida ("Don José") that the Living Theatre accepted Oficina's invitation because the two groups were in similar states of crisis. Once discussions began in São Paulo, Celso perceived the foreigners as having "a strong imperial consciousness, as if they were to be the saviors of South America." The Latin Americans wanted to examine the question of their cultural relationship and the "colonial disease," but Celso felt that because the Living Theatre was a closed group with a long history, it was not open to new information that might jeopardize its ideological underpinnings. Moreover, outsiders were looked upon as subjects for indoctrination. So the only possible view was that the Brazilians follow the guidance of the Americans and enter into their scheme. The result was a collision of opposing forces: "On the one hand there we were, faced with this puritanical chief, Julian Beck, and on the other hand, ourselves, that chaos, that contradiction." Celso saw the Living Theatre as "that perfectly formed, monolithic being, that computer, that creature from the Salvation Army." The nature of the confrontation made no sense to the Americans, who never understood the character of nationalist struggle, according to Celso, since they were themselves utopian internationalists. Although Beck and Malina expressed solidarity with the Third World—as Jews, they considered themselves equally oppressed—the Brazilian director viewed the very term *Third World* as a colonialist designation coined by people from industrialized nations who "were into consuming the cycle of the Southern Hemisphere." The abrasive relationship also had specific causes. While Celso was spending his own time and money to aid the foreigners, they saw him as a mere "impresario," while he viewed them as "merchants, forever Americans," in spite of their antimaterialist protestations. Yet a decade later Celso would tell me the two companies had made a great deal of effort to reach an understanding, and furthermore there had been mutual benefit, especially for Oficina, which "devoured their stuff Anthropophagically" (José Celso, interview). The result was *Gracias, Señor.*

In December 1970, after the departure of the Americans,[32] in order to pay off the debts incurred by the filming of *Prata Palomares,* the troupe decided to go on tour with a retrospective of *O Rei da Vela, Pequenos Burgueses,* and *Galileu Galilei,* and to establish a community of actors to be called Oficina Brasil. With few professional actors remaining from the pre–Living Theatre days but with an eagerness to experiment, the new company, also led by José Celso, played to packed houses in Rio until March 1971 and then embarked on a seven-month sojourn through the Brazilian heartland. The group defined the tour by the catchphrase—the first of what would become an avalanche of slogans—"journey through utropia"; that is, through the "utopia of the tropics." The trip became a metaphor of itself, a way to move forward, to break old bonds and search for a "new star" (Almeida, "Don José"). Oficina was attempting to break with cultural dependency: "I always feel that in art there is a close link to colonialism, something submissive and servile. You almost never see anything free in Brazilian art." Oficina's path had always been to "break, leave, travel, unleash" (ibid.). During the voyage, the company chose a communal life-style and supported itself by presenting the retrospective in several cities. By staging plays in unconventional areas like town squares and engaging in open debate—this at the height of state-of-siege repression—the group created a stir wherever it went. Performances sold out everywhere, and intellectuals, artists, and students gave Oficina Brasil strong support; but local officials were less than enthusiastic. Free presentations were banned—the authorities judged the common people insufficiently cultured to appreciate theatre—and the company was kicked out of some cities for holding postplay public discussions.

During its pilgrimage through the Brazilian interior, the company improvised on the themes of the old plays from the retrospective and tested new ideas in workshops, which led to a piece entitled *Trabalho Novo* (New Labor), "a kind of re-creation that encompassed a thousand and one utopias, carried out during a utopian journey" (José Celso, interview). *Trabalho Novo* was first presented at the University of Brasília, where the entire campus was used as the performing area. With some two thousand students in attendance, the actors began in a circle, experiencing a trancelike state—"something African"—and then applied clay from the ground for makeup, "as if they themselves had come from the earth."[33] In the first part of the improvisation, the actors silently confronted the audience, an "assembly of the dead," in reference to Oficina's "dead past" and to a "dead institution," the university. The group next executed a "lobotomy," in which slogans were shouted, such as "intelligence is stupidity" and "creating is obeying," an Orwellian parody of what the group saw as a repressive and moribund society. Once the "atrophied brains were destroyed, symbolizing the end of the old order," the audience aided the actors in a scene of "resurrection." Finally, the collective assembly passed around a *bastão*, or staff, to point the way to an ending; the performance came to a close with the *te-ato*—another of the catchwords José Celso was becoming increasingly fond of, a pun on the word *teatro* meaning "thee I bind"—in which all barriers between performers and public were broken and a chant was created spontaneously and seeds were planted in the ground. The structure of that performance would become the nucleus of *Gracias, Señor,* and *te-ato* its guiding principle.

After Brasília, the improvisations continued in small towns in the Northeast and North of Brazil, where the actors worked with local residents. The most significant of those "happenings" took place in the village of Mandassaia, located in the *sertão*, or arid plateau region, in the state of Bahia. Without prior notice, the Oficina group entered Mandassaia as a silent band on a pilgrimage. Carrying a staff in the tradition of the local mystics, they walked silently through the village marking seven spots where the seven parts of the spectacle would take place. In the central plaza they formed a processional with the populace and went to the first point, a cemetery, where they performed a symbolic resurrection with the "sacred" staff. The actors pantomimed blindness, a common malady in the region, and upon returning to the village square touched the staff to create vision, in the physical and spiritual senses of the word. Subsequently, the actors helped the townspeople to build a bridge over the river dividing Mandassaia and neighboring villages. Finally, the procession crossed the bridge and the actors sang a song promising to return for a pilgrimage to Joazeiro, the holy city of the *sertão.*

José Celso viewed the communal bridge construction as a ritual of decolonization. The townspeople were accustomed to waiting passively for outside forces to organize and lead them. He felt that the ritual demonstrated they could accomplish things for themselves, collectively. There is an apparent contradiction in Celso's interpretation of the event, since Teatro Oficina, an outside force, organized the villagers to perform the task. According to Fernando Peixoto ("Oficina," *Ciclo*), the bridge caused the river to rise and nearly flooded Mandassaia. At the same time, Oficina did not fulfill its promise to return for a pilgrimage to Joazeiro. In spite of these objections, it is clear the company members attempted something rare for engagé theatres in Brazil: they explored firsthand one of the poorer regions of their country and sought involvement with its diverse inhabitants.

After traveling to other towns and cities in northern Brazil, presenting Oficina retrospectives and developing variations on the *Trabalho Novo* and the *te-ato* theme, the group returned to São Paulo in early 1972 and began the collective writing of *Gracias, Señor*. The new play, or happening, was defined by yet another catchphrase, *revolição* (revolition), a revolution or return of the will. That is, Oficina had lost its will, conditions were adverse—financially, politically, artistically. However, the "utropian" voyage had revitalized and transformed the *company*—a term associated with business and capitalism—into a collective theatre community. At least in theory. *Gracias, Señor* contained most of the *Trabalho Novo* improvisational structure, with one significant difference: it was performed in traditional theatre spaces. The play opened in Rio's Teatro Teresa Raquel on 1 February 1972. Its key feature was audience participation, based on "'techniques removing the spectator from his passive state of contemplator of information; he will then become the very medium of communication'" (Celso, quoted in Macksen Luiz, "Espetáculo"). Audience response to participation and physical contact with the actors was divided. Some critics found it diverting, others groundbreaking, and yet others artless. In response to a negative review from Sábato Magaldi, who heretofore had been one of Oficina's staunchest defenders, the group circulated a letter, which the following paragraph sums up: "Sábato Magaldi is a *critic*, perhaps the most respected, because he is the most reactionary: his function is to stabilize, to keep theatre just as it is, like a vampire sucking a little new blood here and there for his own survival. His ideological position is blind due to his inability to distinguish what he sees as long as its stagecraft is high-level and lends seriousness to the pap consumed by the dead clientele of the Theatres. Every year he tries to 'save' the season by praising its diversity; he is a perky model selling a nice, clean product." Young counterculture-oriented spectators were enthusiastic participants, while the traditional theatregoing public was intimidated, offended, or bored. Fernando Peixoto, representing the leftist viewpoint, would sum up the experience five years later: "This opens the way to a type of fascist theatre: the celebrants of this improvised ritual are the enlightened bearers of truth, while those who attend are a formless mass—passive, dead, useless, and colonized" ("Oficina," *Ciclo*). Similarly mixed reactions had been expressed some years earlier on the occasion of the Living Theatre's performances at the Brooklyn Academy of Music and Yale University. After a subsequent and equally controversial run in São Paulo at the Teatro Rute Escobar, *Gracias, Señor* was closed by the censors.

In spite of all the complaints of the Living Theatre's "colonialist" venture in Brazil, it is ironic that Oficina's collective period was so clearly modeled on the American group: improvisation around a structure; deemphasis of the verbal; didacticism to change consciousness; audience participation and direct physical contact; emphasis on counterculture values, mysticism, and ritual; theatre in the streets; voyages of discovery; and the apparent contradiction of a collective organization under the firm control of a charismatic leader. Seen in retrospect, *Gracias, Señor* was a desperate attempt to respond to the disintegration of engagé theatre's desire to effect political change. The military coup of 1964, the 1968 AI5, and the dark forces of censorship and torture closed off most avenues of protest. The American and European counterculture and collective theatre were seductive to many Brazilian artists, because they offered a means to disassociate from a repressive society. But the countercultural experiment in theatre that was *Gracias, Señor* alienated Oficina's supporters and was cut off by the censors, signaling the death knell for Teatro Oficina.

Once back in São Paulo, Oficina would turn the building on Jaceguai Street into a center of counterculture experiments and would call the space *Casa das Transas*—loosely translated into the jargon of the period, House of Groovin'—featuring avant-garde and rock music and Super-8 film festivals. (More catchphrases and buzz words here, such as *revoli-som*, "revoli-sound," and *off-cine*.) In late 1972, in an attempt to recoup financial losses, José Celso elected to stage Chekhov's *Three Sisters* (*As Três Irmãs*). The visual style was stunning in the manner of José Celso's earlier phase, but his brilliant direction was undermined by the inexperienced actors' inability to cope with Chekhov's text. For the first time ever in Oficina's history, audiences and critics were unanimously cool toward the production, which had very short runs in São Paulo and Rio. Thus, a dismal failure would mark the end of Teatro Oficina, which had been established fourteen years earlier. Renato Borghi, who quit after the opening of *Three Sisters*, would have this to say about the company's death throes: "'What was really going on during this last phase before I left was a group of 40 people—the vast majority of them professionally inept—revolving around 3 or 4 people who made all the rules. I found this deeply disturbing. After working so long with so many people I cared about—and professionals to boot—I was suddenly surrounded by people who were incapable of delivering a single line on stage'" (quoted in Peixoto, "fascinante" 99).

José Celso has kept the name Oficina to this day. In 1974 he was arrested and tortured by the São Paulo police, and after his release from jail he went into exile, first in Portugal, where he started the Teatro Oficina–Samba. In 1975 he went to Mozambique, where he filmed a documentary on the independence movement entitled *25*, which was shown at the Cannes Festival in 1977. Celso returned to São Paulo in 1979, under the terms of an amnesty decreed by President João Figueiredo. He resumed control of the old performing space, as well as the former company name, with new variations and catchwords (e.g., *Oficina/Uzyna*, or "Oficina/Faktory"). During the intervening years, he has intermittently staged plays in the space but has never regained the prestige he had in the 1960s. Teatro Oficina, which began in a state of marginalization in the São Paulo Law School in 1958, remains marginalized more than three decades later. José Celso is a phantom of the 1960s.

Oficina left an important legacy for the Brazilian stage. In the tradition of Os Comediantes and the Teatro Brasileiro de Comédia, it raised Brazilian stagecraft to the level of a high art form, while fusing the demands of aesthetic principles and social consciousness. And if it found inspiration in foreign models—Stanislavsky, Brecht, Berliner Ensemble, Living Theatre—during its most productive period, it transcended its role as a receiver of imported culture as no other company had previously. With its greatest production, *O Rei da Vela*, for the first time a theatre became the initiator and catalyst of an entire cultural movement: Tropicalism. Finally, writing about Arena, Sábato Magaldi could be talking about Oficina as well: "If the expansion of the group corresponded to the developmentalist spirit that so excited Brazil in the 1950s, Arena's decline and disappearance are intimately associated to the repression unleashed by Institutional Act Number Five on 13 December 1958" (*Palco* 9). Eight years after the effective demise of Teatro de Arena and seven after that of Oficina, Antunes Filho would take up the banner of national stagecraft and form yet another great company: Grupo Macunaíma.

4. *The Candle King*

There were three stagings in the 1950s and 1960s that had great impact on the evolution of the Brazilian stage: Teatro de Arena's 1958 *Eles Não Usam Black-Tie*, its 1965 *Zumbi*, and Teatro Oficina's 1967 *O Rei da Vela*. With its production of Gianfrancesco Guarnieri's *Black-Tie*, Arena initiated its most productive and original phase, established its unique identity, and contributed to a process that would culminate in the establishment of engagé Brazilian dramaturgy. It created the opportunity for Arena to carry on its *Seminário de Dramaturgia*, the first systematic attempt in Brazil to develop play writing. Guarnieri's text has, for its time, several unique features: it focuses on the urban proletariat, deals sympathetically with the cause of unionization and class solidarity, and presents the colloquial language of slum dwellers. *Black-Tie* paved the way for a whole new generation of playwrights, including Oduvaldo Vianna Filho and Plínio Marcos. The 1965 *Arena Conta Zumbi*, written by Guarnieri and Boal, kicked off the *Arena Conta* series. It constituted a new genre, an authentic Brazilian protest musical, and its use of history to criticize the 1964 coup was the earliest artistic condemnation in Brazil of the dictatorship. Oficina's 1967 *O Rei de Vela*, however, contributed most clearly to the development of original forms of Brazilian stagecraft. It represented "for our contemporary theatre an event comparable to what the 1943 opening of *Bridal Gown* meant for its own time." The production "brought to fruition a genuine aesthetic and cultural project, which would initiate a new phase in Brazilian theatre and serve as inspiration for numerous offshoots and imitators" (Michalski, *Teatro* 28). The legacy of Oficina was to rescue from oblivion Modernist Oswald de Andrade's drama and to bring to the stage for the first time his aesthetic-ideological concept of Anthropophagy, subsequently transformed into the cultural movement that came to be known as *Tropicália*, or Tropicalism.

Oswald de Andrade's *The Candle King* was written in 1933, five years after the appearance of his *Manifesto Antropófago*, and was published in 1937. It represented, to some extent, a dramatic application of the nationalist aesthetic formulated in the manifesto. The first Modernist generation, famous for the 1922 Modern Art Week, held in São Paulo, revolutionized literary language by emphasizing unique aspects of Brazilian Portuguese. The arts focused increasingly on national themes: Modernism attempted to "Brazilianize" literature, music, and painting. Oswald de Andrade's main contributions to the first phase of Modernism were his manifesto and poems entitled *Pau-Brasil*. Subsequent works, such as *Manifesto Antropófago* and Mário de Andrade's narrative *Macunaíma*, were more socially conscious. The 1930s heirs of *Modernismo* produced neo-realist engagé works: the novels of northeastern writers Jorge Amado, Rachel de Queiroz, José Lins do Rego, and Graciliano Ramos.

The Modernist aesthetic failed to revolutionize the stage. According to Sábato Magaldi, the reason for the late development of the theatre in Brazil is that it is a synthesis of the other arts, and they must develop first ("Marco Zero" 7). Modernist Mário de Andrade wrote his operetta, *O Café*, in 1934, but it was never staged. The stage adaptation of his narrative work *Macunaíma* would have to wait until 1979. "The theatrical projects undertaken in the spirit of the 1922 movement appeared some years later, and the only texts that could be considered to belong entirely to the movement were written by Oswald de Andrade, particularly *O Rei da Vela*, which clamors against Brazil's subordination to foreign interference (now including the U.S.)" (Heliodora, "Influências" 46). Oswald de Andrade, poet, prose stylist, essayist, has to his credit a large number of plays, mostly unstaged. The most memorable, those written in the Modernist mode in the 1930s, were *O Rei da Vela*, *O Homem e o Cavalo* (The Man and the Horse), and *A Morta* (The Dead Woman). Thirty years would pass before any would be produced.

One important question remains: why were none of the plays in Oswald's trilogy staged before 1967? Sábato Magaldi believes that if "*O Rei da Vela* had been produced in 1937 by a foreign director, it would unquestionably have become a milestone in the renovation of modern Brazilian theatre" ("Marco Zero" 4). There were problems of censorship under Getúlio Vargas's dictatorship. The play's criticisms of Brazilian socioeconomic conditions were too harsh to be acceptable to an authoritarian government. Brazilian theatre critics and historians have put forth various hypotheses: "*O Rei da Vela* was so far ahead of its time, it foresaw with such clarity a more Brazilian Brazil, that we are forced to admit that, within the panorama of Brazilian theatrical history, *O Rei da Vela*—as theatre, not as a text—is not relevant in its own time. Only in the latter part of the 1960s would there exist a sufficiently supportive attitude among the nation's general public to enshrine the work on the stage" (Heliodora, "Influências" 46). Or in the words of Yan Michalski,[1] the play "had never before been staged, nor could it have been: its corrosive spirit, its *deboché* language, the stage directions openly suggesting a chaotic and aggressive performance—all that was light years away from the previous decades' canons of theatrical behavior. On the other hand, its spirit seemed made to order to channel the rebellious non-conformity of the young people of 1967" (Michalski, *Teatro* 28).

Another school of thought has maintained that the author's dramatic texts lacked literary and theatrical merit: "Our most enlightened men of the theatre considered on several occasions the possibility of staging an Oswald de Andrade play, but they always backed off due to the fragility of his texts, picturesque oddities, elaborated in the manner of the *revista* scripts of the period in which they were written, but they hardly were sufficient to be turned into a full-fledged production, without a monumental contribution from a director" (Doria, *Teatro* 172). In a sense, Doria was right; it took a major undertaking on the part of director José Celso and his Oficina colleagues to resurrect the play.

The Tupy Potpourri

Teatro Oficina's 1967 production of *O Rei da Vela* illustrated for the first time the applicability of Anthropophagy to stagecraft, formulated by Oswald de Andrade in his 1928 *Manifesto Antropófago.* Anthropophagy means literally, of course, cannibalism. The basic premise of the manifesto is the existence of an Indian or Tupy golden age in which instincts were not repressed, goods were shared communally, and humankind lived in harmony. Furthermore, the Tupy mode of being is the foundation of Brazilian ontology, and the culture that has flowed from Europe—and later the United States—has masked that truth. As Andrade frequently stated the principle: "Tupy or not Tupy, that is the question." Although Anthropophagy is not a carefully worked-out cultural theory, it does have several useful applications. Primarily, it refers to a metaphor for a nationalist aesthetic, a literary code that would "devour" rather than imitate foreign literary models, while incorporating uniquely Brazilian popular, primitivist, and folkloric modes. Armed with parody and sarcasm, the new cannibals would grind up rigid social, moral, and aesthetic codes and roast the colonial legacy of imitation and subservience. But still, why Cannibalism? Because at one fragile point in the nation's history the native population had an effective means of dealing with the onslaught of colonialism. The Indians' first response was swift and direct: they ate the colonizers, shipwrecked explorers, and missionaries, and they even devoured an occasional bishop. Indeed, Oswald de Andrade dated his *Manifesto Antropófago* "Year 374 since the swallowing of Bishop Sardinha." The natives' tasteful notions of how to deal with would-be colonizers stimulated Andrade's palate, who turned Cannibalism into a nutritious way of dealing with cultural modes imposed from the outside and slavishly imitated by Brazilians. And so Anthropophagy translates artistically into a devouring of imported culture to neutralize its dominance of national culture and to gain its strength (i.e., to employ freely useful aspects of imported models). Anthropophagy does not respect the authority of foreign modes; rather, it blends them into a native cultural stew. To put it another way, imported spices enhance the flavor of native dishes but do not overwhelm them. But still, what is Anthropophagy: an aesthetic theory, an anti-imperialist ideology, a nationalist cultural platform, a colossal joke, an avant-garde casserole, artistic thievery? A bit of each, actually. Maria Eugênia Boaventura (*Vanguarda*) defines as its main technical feature the intertextual collage. Benedito Nunes hits the tooth on the head by calling it a word-guide (Nunes, in Oswald de Andrade, *Obras*), a metaphor utilized in many ways by several generations of artists, including the Tropicalists of the 1960s. Most users of the word-guide have privileged the verb *to devour*. That is, the colonial paradigm has meant that Brazilians have always been devoured (exploited economically and culturally) by foreigners. Brazilians must now devour them. Anthropophagy, in this sense, translates into what I will call the Tupy potpourri: unfettered utilization of a myriad of sources, whatever their origin, without respect for the integrity of those sources.

The Candle King: Text

The "Tupy-or-not-Tupy" guide in *O Rei da Vela* pointed its teeth in many directions, first of all toward France. The French avant-garde was the main outside influence on Brazilian Modernism, and Oswald de Andrade particularly was steeped in French culture. In fact, he wrote his first, and forgettable, plays in French. Anthropophagy led the author to go beyond imitation of French avant-garde and to transform it into a unique Brazilian cuisine. What Andrade clearly did in the case of *The Candle King* was to cannibalize Alfred Jarry's *Ubu Roi* and strain its themes, characters, and symbols through a native crafted sieve, placing them in the service of Brazilian reality. At the same time, the basic structures of Jarry's play—its corrosive satire, and what Mikhail Bakhtin calls grotesque realism—were utilized by Andrade as burlesque and piquant counterpoint to the wilted Brazilian theatre of the 1930s. "When *Ubu* was written the dramatists who seemed most forward-looking were pursuing with determination the ideal of an increased physical or moral 'realism'. In *Ubu* . . . Jarry embodied a theatrical aesthetic exactly the opposite of those preoccupying the most 'progressive' dramatists of his day" (Benedikt, *Modern French Theatre* ix–x).

As for Brazil, the outmoded comedy of manners could be characterized by physical realism, and the bombastic thesis plays of Camargo and Vianna by moral realism, while *Rei* was unabashedly avant-garde. What is more important is that Andrade's play was an out-and-out parody of the comedy of manners and of all the other popular theatrical forms of the 1930s: *revista*, melodrama, operetta. As for *Ubu Roi*, there are several minor parallels (for example, Andrade borrowed from Jarry the device of a disembodied voice of doom). On a larger scale, the author stirred in a Tupy potpourri of ingredients from the French playwright's text.

Andrade sliced his main character Abelardo from the flesh of Ubu and cut into serving pieces the latter's naked ambition and greed and open admission of them, as well as his cowardice and amorality. Both characters are *arrivistes* seeking social ascension by whatever means. Ubu's denigration of the nobles is analogous to Abelardo's humiliation of the coffee aristocrats. Ubu butchers his enemies as Abelardo carves up the debtors. There is a constant obsession with finances in both works.

O Rei da Vela is set in Rio de Janeiro and São Paulo in the 1930s, a period of severe economic crisis. From the opening scene *The Candle King* focuses on the coffee market crisis, the Great Depression, and the consequent financial ruin. The cruel usurer Abelardo I is a junior partner in Mr. Jones's business of exploitation, American capitalism, which, according to Andrade's play, takes advantage of Brazil's economic crisis and historical vulnerability and saddles it with an onerous foreign debt. Clearly, the author's nationalist economic vision applies to the present as well. At the time of this writing, the entire nation is reeling under the burden of a foreign debt of well over $100 billion, usury on a truly grand scale. In Abelardo's own words, "inferior countries have to work for superior countries just as the poor have to work for the rich" (Andrade, *Rei* 94). In Anthropophagic terms, Brazil is being devoured by outsiders.

The Candle King and *King Ubu* present their social criticism without high-minded seriousness but with derision, vulgarity, and bad taste. Both works sink their incisors into classic literature: *Ubu Roi*, Shakespeare (*Hamlet* and *Macbeth*) and Calderón de la Barca (*La Vida Es Sueño*); *O Rei da Vela*, the story of Abelard and Heloise. The plot of Andrade's play is rather simple, at least on the surface: the *arriviste* Abelardo I intends to marry Heloísa, from an old and now destitute São Paulo coffee family. The marriage for him signifies climbing the social ladder, and for her entrée to his bank account. Her true sexual proclivity is summed up in her full name, Heloísa de Lesbos. Her parents are the patriarch Colonel Belarmino, a ruined coffee baron, or as director José Celso liked to call him, the "tragic redneck," and Dona Cesarina, a simmering sexpot masquerading as a grande dame. Hungering after Abelardo's money, they both support the marriage. But another upstart, Abelardo II, the first Abelardo's assistant, overthrows his superior and supplants him as candle king and Heloísa's mate. Heloísa betrays Abelardo, just as Mother Ubu betrays her husband. On a symbolic level, the rise of one candle king, his fall, and the rise of another suggest that Brazil's socioeconomic structure is cyclical and unchanging, that events are shaped by outside forces. To put it Anthropophagically, while Brazilians devour each other, they are devoured by foreigners. Abelardo II, in a parody of the ancient love story, states during his wedding: "Heloísa will always belong to Abelardo. It's classic" (*Rei* 158). The "classical" reference is to Brazil's eternal ritual of subjugation to imperialism. It is then fitting that Mr. Jones, the stereotypical American capitalist, intones the last line in the play: "Oh! Good business!" (158). Mr. Jones is the phantom protagonist of *The Candle King*, the puppeteer. The marriage of Abelardo II and Heloísa is held to make her available to the American. That is, in the post-Tupy world Brazilian social institutions always garnish outside interests. "Oswald's anarchic text, written between 1933 and 1937, submitted the corrupt structure of the workings of our *tupiniquim* capitalism to a critical analysis with an unprecedented virulence" (Michalski, *Teatro* 28).[2] While the author's radical view of Brazil's *tupiniquim* economic system borrowed from Marxism, it also reflected widely shared nationalist feelings not only of his era but of more recent times as well.

Brazilian history may be seen in terms of cycles of boom and bust, the rise and fall of an export commodity and the region or regions tied to that product. Examples are sugarcane (the Brazilian Northeast), gold (the second colonial capital of Vila Rica or Ouro Preto), rubber (Manaus), and coffee. The latter commodity lay at the financial heart of the Old Republic or *República Velha* (1889–1930), and its production center was the state of São Paulo. While the coffee growers of the region exercised considerable control over the government, the importance of the export commodity for international trade and foreign exchange meant that international capital also had a powerful influence. Foreign investors, especially British, gained control of Brazilian coffee marketing and export operations. Dependence on a single commodity and the vagaries of the international market, as well as overplanting and subsequent surpluses, gave rise to a series of coffee crises. The great disaster of 1929 brought on a new bust cycle, and the coffee economy was shattered. The coffee aristocracy that had dominated São Paulo society entered a period of decadence. Finally, the coffee bust spelled doom for the Old Republic, and a military revolt swept Getúlio Vargas into power in 1930.

Vargas, a political *cacique* from the southern state of Rio Grande do Sul, quickly assumed dictatorial powers in the wake of his overthrow of the old regime. There was widespread censorship and suppression of political dissent. The dictator modeled his government after Mussolini's and called it the Estado Novo, or New State. His economic policies to some degree reflected nationalist sentiments. He initiated a drive toward industrialization and established the first state-owned industries. Nevertheless, poverty remained epidemic and foreign economic influence—now American more than British—actually increased.

Andrade spooned these socioeconomic trends on his play. And because the trends begun during Vargas's Estado Novo also characterize later periods in Brazilian history, the play speaks beyond its own time. When it was finally staged in 1967, it served as a viable protest vehicle against the military dictatorship that had ensconced itself firmly in power with its 1964 coup.

If *O Rei da Vela* were merely a treatise on economic nationalism and a compendium of Marxist clichés, it would elicit little interest on the part of readers/performers. It is the means of conveying those ideas, Andrade's chafing burlesque, the Tupy potpourri, that draw attention to the work. Its finely chopped aesthetic tidbits were drained from the São Paulo avant-garde literary experiments of the 1920s, and parallel artistic currents in Europe before and contemporaneous to the time of the play's writing. That is, through his application of Anthropophagy and attempt to define national identity, the author has created a total theatrical language.

The titles of Jarry's and Andrade's plays contain the word *king*, and the Brazilian play has skimmed off for its title Father Ubu's oft-repeated oath "by my candle" or "by my green candle" (*"De par ma chandelle verte"*). A constant in the set, candles, and the "king" of the title, have shifting symbolic values as the plot unfolds. In Oswald de Andrade's play, *vela* is primarily a symbol of the economic crisis, which has caused an interruption of electric power and brought the candle back into use. The usurer Abelardo I has cornered the market, making him the candle king, the lord of underdevelopment. But Abelardo is destroyed by the same code of greed by which he lives, and that transforms *vela* into a death symbol, *velório* (wake). The death symbolism of the candle is cyclical: when one candle king falls another replaces him, Abelardo I is overthrown by Abelardo II. All this suggests the concept of the unchanging cycle of a Latin American country, where events are repeated endlessly under the domination of outside forces.

The domestic agents of this domination are Oswald de Andrade's grotesque characters, reminiscent of the bizarre *guignol*-based characters in *Ubu Roi*. In the case of the Brazilian work, they were taken not from puppet shows but were based on the stock characters of comedies of manners and *revista* (director José Celso devoured others from carnival and comic books). The characters are Brazil's elite classes, whose humiliating servility to foreign domination the playwright mocked. He put their relationships in the Anthropophagic cooking pot and barbecued classical love motifs, as Jarry parodied traditional themes of honor. Among the stock characters from the comedy of manners are the gallant and wealthy romantic hero and his plucky love interest, the ingenue from the other side of the tracks. Andrade kept the relative economic positions intact, but he pushed the ingenue up the social spit (Heloísa, impoverished coffee aristocrat) and the romantic hero down (Abelardo, the petty bourgeois speculator). The gallant, rather than the ingenue, is now the social climber. Gone also is the romance, replaced by his cruel usury and "imperialist" sycophancy and her financial "prostitution" and lesbianism (*O Rei da Vela* was written long before the era of gay rights). The relationship of Heloísa and Abelardo revolves around finances and sexual aberration, as do most of the other relationships in the play. Andrade quartered another stock comedy-of-manners character, the devoted mother, in this case Dona Cesarina, whom he turned into a sex-hungry matron. Oswald de Andrade boiled the characters' sexuality in the second act kettle, entitled "Frente Unica Sexual" (United Sexual Front).[3] Another way to view the question is this: if sexuality in the Tupy golden age was pure and unfettered, in the context of an unjust social structure and imperialism sexual relations are reduced to commercial transactions and repression of instincts, the obverse of the Tupy golden age.

The family crises and quarrels typical of the comedy-of-manners genre are now lethal financial rivalries and ideological struggles. *The Candle King* skewers the acting methods of the comedy of manners. Comic stars like Procópio Ferreira indulged in constant ad-libbed asides to the audience. Andrade parodied this practice by writing such asides into the script. Abelardo II, for example, tells the audience that he is the first socialist in Brazilian theatre. Critics have admired these asides and defined them in terms of proto-Brechtian anti-illusionist techniques, which is certainly a valid perspective. But the essential reason for their presence in the play is to smoke comedy-of-manners fluff until it ignites into ideological warfare.

There is a Tupy potpourri of parodic references to other genres and works in the play. The characters are constantly comparing themselves to those of European authors, such as Flaubert and Oscar Wilde. Abelardo I sees himself as a character from Freud, whom he calls the "last great novelist of the bourgeoisie" (*Rei* 107). Oswald de Andrade used his play as a kettle for the Tupy potpourri: he rendered what was useful from *Ubu Roi* and other texts, discarded the rest, and spicing them with Anthropophagy he poured them on a plate of Brazilian reality.

Finally, much of what has been written about *Ubu* applies to *Rei:* "King Ubu is, in Jarry's own words, 'un être ignoble', and in the untraditional indifference to nobility of this irrational king we see marked foreshadowings of the spectacular irrationality of approach which would be so important a part of the avant-garde theatre to come. With Ubu's rise to power, effected through the openhanded employment of a kind of childishly ingenuous deceit, a dreamlike atmosphere is evoked—not by any means the gloomy atmosphere of nightmares—full of the strange, the unlikely, and the scurrilously humorous" (Benedikt, *Modern French Theatre* xiv). As for *O Rei da Vela*, it is the acerbic, playful, and subversive character of Andrade's language that saves it from becoming a mere didactic exercise. That language is not only verbal, it is visual. It required a director, José Celso, and designer, Hélio Eichbauer, both of considerable stature, to reveal the richness of Oswald de Andrade's stagecraft to the Brazilian public.

The Candle King: Staging[4]

There is some debate over the circumstances that led Teatro Oficina to select *The Candle King* to inaugurate its rebuilt theatre. Some facts are clear: after the 1966 fire rendered the group's theatrical space inoperable, it organized a fund-raising retrospective festival in Rio de Janeiro. Company members engaged in improvisations and wide-ranging discussions about their past activities and about the course of national events. José Celso and his group were tired of Stanislavskian interiorization and were becoming increasingly interested in the visual and gestural aspects of stagecraft. At just the right time, apparently, Oswald's script made its appearance. According to some reports, it was critic Sábato Magaldi who suggested a reading of the play. Fernando Peixoto ("fascinante") wrote that the reading was suggested by director Luiz Carlos Maciel, who was working with the company in Rio. José Celso claimed he had previously felt the text "reeked of stale Modernism and Futurism" (Celso, "Manifesto" 45), a position shared by Décio de Almeida Prado. Fernando Peixoto's view is more balanced: "We were already familiar with the text, we thought it was intelligent and amusing, but historically out of date, a manifestation of twenties literary avant-garde" ("fascinante" 71). But all reports indicate that a group reading in a single night made everyone an enthusiastic adherent to Oswald de Andrade's vision, both theatrical and political. The play written more than thirty years before appeared to strike at the heart of recent political events and passive response to military takeover. In three decades, from dictatorship to dictatorship, in spite of outward signs of progress, *The Candle King* made it appear that Brazil had been frozen in time.

The Second World War changed Brazil's economic circumstances by producing a significant increase in foreign exchange reserves and industrial expansion and diversification, leading to the belief that the country could develop import-substitution manufacturing and export industrial goods on a large scale. That belief gave rise to the doctrine of developmentalism, or developmental nationalism (*desenvolvimentismo*), which characterized government policy until the 1964 military coup. The developmentalist doctrine "called for government control of natural resources, limitations on foreign capital, continuing industrialization, and greater commerce with all nations" (Burns, *History* 320). The heyday of developmentalism occurred in the euphoric climate of the Kubitschek administration (1956–1961). Brazil experienced spectacular industrial and economic growth in those five years. Nevertheless, runaway inflation, expensive government programs, budget deficits on all levels of government, and increasing foreign involvement—especially on the part of multinational corporations—brought about a shift in thinking from the capitalist developmentalist model to a socialist and anti-imperialist model. This change in thinking, which especially influenced the Goulart presidency (1961–1964), was one of the motivating factors behind the right-wing military coup and its U.S. support. When the military took over on 1 April 1964, one of its first stated goals was to control runaway inflation, which it succeeded in doing with an austerity program whose main feature was wage control. The three decades of nationalist economic reforms were abandoned; multinational capital was favored over national, to the point that many previously nationalized enterprises were denationalized. (Nevertheless, some state-run corporations became bloated, and corrupt bureaucracies drained the country's resources during the military dictatorship.) Repression steadily increased, but so did opposition from the left, although some middle-class sectors supported the dictatorship for its control of inflation and successful efforts to increase the gross national product (the economic successes were known as the Brazilian "miracle"). By the late 1970s, when the economic policies of the military government had failed miserably, the opposition had become open and widespread among all sectors of Brazilian society, and in 1985 there was a return to civilian government (see Furtado, *Brasil*, and Skidmore, *Military*). At the time of this writing, Brazil finds itself in an economic crisis of unheard-of proportions.

The initial mass movement opposed to military rule came to a head in 1967; it was met with ever more brutal responses from the armed forces, police, and a loose alliance of right-wing paramilitary organizations, such as the Comando de Caça aos Comunistas, or CCC. When the military decided it would tolerate no more opposition, it declared a state of siege—the infamous Institutional Act Number Five, or AI5—in December 1968. "We all felt we were suffocating under the daily grind of the consequences of '64, we could barely control our impatience, we were overwhelmed by angry rebelliousness, brought about by the loss of illusions and skepticism toward reformist and pseudorevolutionary projects" (Peixoto, "fascinante" 72).

O Rei da Vela would constitute a Cannibalist rending and tearing at the flesh of Brazil's nationalist mythology. Teatro Oficina members felt that the Cannibalist hot sauce should be poured on the cultural, political, and economic ingredients of 1967, because they believed that the sociopolitical soup of the 1930s, described in

Andrade's play, had been reheated in the 1960s. With this notion, the company's intention was to ridicule Brazil's political leaders, who in the 1960s had brought back the repression of Getúlio Vargas's Estado Novo. The players extended this theatrical derision to the urban middle class and its belief in Brazil's progress. In fact, they all felt it was time to wield in the 1960s the same meat cleaver that Oswald had earlier taken to 1930s Brazil-is-the-country-of-the-future chauvinism. Like Oswald de Andrade before them, José Celso and his actors were convinced that some classes of Brazilians benefitted from stagnation, poverty, and obsequiousness to foreign power and influence. "It is significant that what José Celso was searching for in Oswald de Andrade was a text affirming the essence of Brazil in an essentially imitative environment" (Heliodora, "Influências" 51). Consequently, *The Candle King* was to be Teatro de Oficina's manifesto, a rebirth of the *Manifesto Antropófago*.

Inspired by Glauber Rocha's film *Terra em Transe,* Oficina director Celso decided to go on an Anthopophagic diet: he wanted no more and no less to create a new theatrical language that would express the deepest roots of Brazilian culture, to find a path back to the Tupy golden age. José Celso read in Oswald de Andrade's word-guide the message that to return to the Tupy as a theatrical creator, he must devour or be devoured by colonizers and their doctrines, by artistic modes imposed from the outside and imitated by Brazilians, by tourists and their exotic Tropicalist vision of Brazil consumed by Brazilians themselves. Celso wanted to develop a new Brazilian form of stagecraft by serving up a rich sauce of folklore and primitive motifs and stirring in key ingredients of the international theatrical avant-garde. The Tupy potpourri turns its users into thieves in the night, and in this case the Oficina members selected what they wanted from a myriad of sources and discarded the rest. A popular guessing game spectators attending performances of *O Rei da Vela* played was to speculate about the origin of aspects of the set, props, and costumes.

The new Oficina manifesto was intended to be an act of "decolonization," a raising of consciousness through provocation, outrage, ridicule, and bad taste. But Teatro Oficina was not out to criticize only the easy targets, meaning the Americans, generals, and the usual bourgeois straw man. "*O Rei da Vela* was an unrestrained critical discovery of Brazil. An implacable and merciless revision of values . . . during a period in which we underwent a dizzying process of liberation from preconceived ideas and colonized cultural training. And in the end we turned all this against the public, including the so-called intellectual and political elite. Because what we had done was to develop a critical focus based on scorn and irreverence. Nothing was spared, neither myths nor stereotypes, and we pulled no punches when we went after sacrosanct codes of behavior" (Peixoto, "fascinante" 72). The means to accomplish this end was to apply Anthropophagy as a kind of aesthetic terrorism against official culture and stick a knife into past and present nationalist ideologies. "*The Candle King* was a means to take what amounted to an x-ray of the country, revealing its rottenness, its internal cancerous yet still resistant tissue, resistant because it fed on our passivity and on our naive conformity. The play thus became a radical banner, an explosive and creative political-cultural manifesto. All of our uncontainable and immeasurable vomit gained an organic structure that was worked out in its smallest details. . . . Mixing circus and vaudeville, opera and critical theatre, carefully worked out yet sloppy gestural languages, ritual and pornography, protest and celebration. An act of breaking with the past" (72).

The production extended its Anthropophagic process by incorporating certain popular forms that had been marginalized by international aesthetic standards of good taste, forms such as circus, Carnival, and *revista*. In other words, the production raised to the level of an art form Brazilian kitsch, which was the main influence in the subsequent *Tropicália* movement, a Brazilian pop art. The important thing was that Teatro Oficina's recipe for a theatrical cornucopia included a myriad of forms, modes, and ideologies to the end of creating a new and original way of doing theatre. It was the quintessential Tupy potpourri: in the words of Oficina actor Fernando Peixoto, "we used influences shamelessly" (Peixoto, "Oficina," *Ciclo*); or as José Celso repeated constantly, the production "used everything, devoured everything."

The theater had been rebuilt after the fire: "We went back to the Italian style proscenium. But with one innovation—a revolving stage [that] came out of our idea of one day putting on Brecht's *Arturo Ui*" ("fascinante" 73). The electronically controlled platform, inspired by the Berliner Ensemble's revolving stage used in its production of Brecht's *Arturo Ui*, was put on the *The Candle King* rotisserie. In spite of this and other additions, most of the set design described in Oswald de Andrade's text was included in the performance. Modifications of the playwright's original conception were intended to bridge the three-decade gap, from 1937 to 1967.

The playtext stipulates that each act have its own theme, a concept followed to the letter by José Celso and Hélio Eichbauer. Following Oswald de Andrade's stage directions, they set the first act in a moneylender's office—a sign over the window read Abelardo and

Abelardo's Office of Usury—and a waiting room in the form of a cage for debtors. The overall conception for the Act I mise-en-scène was the circus. That is, the production was flavored with motifs from the circus, a truly popular performance mode expressing the irrepressible Tupy spirit. Because the Anthropophagic word-guide points in different and often contradictory directions, the circus ambience also symbolized the "buffoonery of the nation's capitalist system" (Sérgio da Silva, *Te-ato* 145). Circus elements included the debtors' cage, a lion-tamer's outfit for the character Abelardo II, and clown skits. José Celso also cannibalized for the first act something he called the "industrial show," a reference to Modernist Andrade's early Futurist phase (the Futurists were obsessed with machines and industrialization). Director Celso used the term ironically, because the play depicts what he saw as Brazil's "feudalism."

Eichbauer stuffed the set design with both early and contemporary avant-garde styles. The revolving stage was covered with a canvas tarp painted in yellow and red to resemble melted candles (and candles of all sizes and shapes were scattered about the space). Its revolutions at times allowed the audience a full view of the set, and at others a partially obscured view through a large Futurist window. The idea was to suggest the cyclical and ephemeral nature of power in Abelardo's corrupt world of exploitation. That is, in the same way the stage/world turns, so does power slip from one's grasp. The furniture for the first act, the setting of which was the moneylender's office, was placed on this revolving platform: a Futurist window with "chrome" frame, which measured about six feet by six feet and opened out like French windows; a divan, also in Futurist chrome, rounded on one end and squared on the other; a Louis XV table; in the Bauhaus style, a large boxy functional chair—one can see the origin of the glass-box skyscrapers so beloved of the U.S. architects spawned by the Bauhaus—and buffet table. Eichbauer added to his skillet the architectural design of Warchavchik—he championed the Internationlist style of the late period of São Paulo Futurist architecture—and painted furniture silver to resemble Futurist use of chrome. (The divan was a leftover from Oficina's production of *Pequenos Burgueses*.) The buffet table and chair were based on designs by Bauhaus architect Mies Van der Rohe (1886–1969), a leading exponent of the Internationalist style, later a seminal figure in Chicago architecture who stripped the skyscraper of its masonry and championed the glass-walled design. Eichbauer also borrowed from the Expressionists, for example, a grotesque, outsized filing cabinet where the debtors were classified in separate drawers: "punctual, unpunctual, con men, sure things, loin cloths [i.e., not a shirt on their backs], pawned, suicides." Following Oswald de Andrade's stage directions, there was a large iron gate on rollers that could be open and shut to reveal the bars of a cage, where debtors were kept. Located upstage was a brass candelabra with a large candle, flanked on one side by a portrait of Getúlio Vargas—the "father of the poor"—and on the other by a statue of the São Paulo patron saint Our Lady of Aparecida. The original script calls for a portrait of the Gioconda, who gave us, in Oswald de Andrade's words, "the first bourgeois smile" (*Rei* 82). José Celso and Eichbauer, however, felt that the Vargas and Aparecida images were more appropriate, as they were to be found in most Brazilian homes, particularly in those of the poorer classes: the visual image thus conveyed Abelardo's mocking of others' misfortunes. The first-act set, in addition to its grotesque description of Abelardo's universe and Brazil's economic crises, corresponded to the author's own life experiences. Always in debt, his life was in a sense an endless sojourn from one loan shark to another. Finally, the set design clarified one important aspect of the Tupy potpourri: a menu of diverse dishes, foreign and national, cleverly assembled to create an original and uniquely Brazilian cuisine, and at the same time to mock the colonial mind-set behind susceptibility to outside influence.

Costume design and makeup revealed the Tupy potpourri at its most carnivorous. While reacting against Oficina's previous alliance on Stanislavskian techniques, a new influence would now be privileged. Brecht would replace the Russian master, the exterior would be favored over the interior, the blatant over the subtle; that is, the design was aimed at exposing the characters from the outside in. In some scenes, characters' faces were divided in two, representing social dualities and deceitfulness. In the case of the two Abelardos, for example, the right eyebrow arched diabolically upward. The idea for this duality was stripped from the Berliner Ensemble's *Arturo Ui*.

The actors, in collaboration with Eichbauer, designed their own dress styles according to their perceptions of the *dramatis personae* they were playing. Fernando Peixoto, in the role of Abelardo, fused Oswald de Andrade's idea of a lion-tamer's outfit with the clothing (e.g., *bombachas*, or wide breeches) of traditional Rio Grande do Sul politicians like Getúlio Vargas and João Goulart, thus linking two populist figures from different eras. He manipulated the butt of a lion-tamer's whip onstage to emphasize its phallic symbolism (phallic paraphernalia abounded in the play). The attire also evoked the image of a *pelego*, a union infiltrator, an Estado Novo scab. The costume of Abelardo II suggested Arsène Lupin—cape, top hat, and spats—the ingenious thief of Maurice Leblanc's stories, with a cigar in allusion to the clever buffoonery of Groucho Marx. Following Oswald de Andrade's stage directions, Heloísa in the first act was dressed in a white linen suit, vest, tie, and hat, and she carried a cigarette holder, the outfit of a 1930s businessman, which corresponded simultaneously to three levels of meaning: the emancipation of women, Heloísa's lesbianism, and the "business" of her marriage of convenience to Abelardo. Heloísa's makeup divided her face into blue on one side and white on the other. Blue indicated both the color of the tropical sky and the colloquial meaning of "happy" or "up" (blue in English conveys the opposite, "down"). Blue thus projected her public guise. The ghostly white bespoke the decadence of her social class, the São Paulo coffee oligarchy. Heloísa's family was decked out in coffee sprigs as reminders of past greatness, which were tied with black, white, and red ribbons, the colors of the São Paulo flag. Representing the family coat of arms, the ribbons were inscribed with its motto, *non ducor, duco* (Latin for "I am not led, I lead"). Dona Cesarina, Abelardo's mother-in-law, dressed from the waist up in the traditional attire of a São Paulo grande dame (her social class) but wore from the waist down the skimpy costume and net stockings of a *revista* chorus girl (her repressed sexuality). Dona Poloca, Cesarina's sister, dressed like a pious old maid. Her costume was inspired by old photo albums: hair in a bun, shawl, rosary, down on her upper lip. She carried a small whip in reference to sadomasochistic tendencies; that is, her aristocratic family's past practice of whipping slaves and her own devotional self-flagellation. Heloísa's sister Joana, or João dos Divãs, the spoiled daughter of the upper class, dressed like Shirley Temple, the child movie star of the 1930s: pink organdy dress, a wide taffeta sash around her waist. Integralist or fascist family member Perdigoto was dressed in his party's green uniform, to which was pinned a parodic version of the family moto, *non ducor, Duce.* Mr. Jones wore the safari getup of the explorer (*explorador* in Portuguese means both "explorer" and "exploiter"). He also represented the stereotypical American tourist, wearing sunglasses and carrying a camera, with red, white, and blue socks (the authorities forbade a display of the American flag). Eichbauer and Celso turned again to Expressionism for the costume of the debtor Pitanga, who wore beneath his ragged suit a leotard painted to resemble lacerated flesh. Characters not in the original playtext heightened the kitsch effects associated with *Tropicália:* the hackneyed *baiana,* or street vendor from the city of Bahia, whose dress is worn in the annual Rio carnival parades; actors in the costumes of American comic-book figures like Batman and Superman, allusions to foreign mass cultural influence. "The costumes, also by Hélio Eichbauer, are, if possible, even more intelligent and expressive than the set. Extremely bold in the carnivalesque tone and in their awesome bad taste, they explain the characters in an exemplary fashion" (Michalski, "Considerações").

The omnipresent phallic elements in the staging provoked considerable controversy among audiences, authorities, and some critics. Dona Poloca licked an all-day sucker shaped like male genitalia. All of the male attire, as well as Heloísa's pants in Act II, included a codpiece worn on the outside, a tidbit garnered from Oswald de Andrade's prose work *Serafim Ponte Grande*. The most controversial phallic prop was a gigantic papier-mâché puppet, Abelardo's double. Located downstage right, it loomed over the audience and was the first thing spectators saw as they arrived in the theatre. The fifteen-foot-tall puppet wore a pin-striped suit, like Abelardo in the first act, and a tin Father Ubu crown on its head. Its right arm was cocked in an obscene gesture, and it had a "cannon"—as it was referred to—that flipped up between its legs and lit up whenever an execution took place. The statue was inspired by a small doll sold by Brazilian folk artisans, which depicts a monk. When a string beneath the cassock is pulled, a red phallus pops up. The "cannon" was at one point seized by censors. "One day the police pulled up and four plainclothes detectives came into Oficina and actually 'arrested' an immense plywood cylinder . . . the penis of a giant puppet. . . . The next day, José Celso, Renato, and I went to the federal police headquarters, made a short statement, and after signing an agreement according to which the 'penis' wouldn't be used onstage again, we carried that great and dangerous wood cylinder through the streets of São Paulo and back to the theatre. The 'penis' regained its freedom when *O Rei da Vela* was presented in Florence at the start of our European tour" (Peixoto, "fascinante" 75).

Armando Sérgio da Silva explains that one of the elements the director utilized to unify the three acts was a kind of sexual obsession: sex in the first act was an instrument of power and domination wielded by the Brazilian macho; in the second act it gave the lie to class and political relationships; in the third it functioned in dramatic counterpoint to the first act. "Abelardo I went from the vertical position to the horizontal, ending up precisely in the classic position, on all fours, Abelardo II, his successor, stood erect with candle in hand, the same one that he would plunge into the anus of Abelardo I. . . . A new king was arising. The macho exhibited his power. The nonmacho was penetrated, sexually, by power" (*Contrainte* 202).

Candle symbolism extended beyond the phallic. Candles were central to the lighting design, providing a Tupy potpourri of references. To use as footlights Eichbauer placed ten can lights downstage bearing the Shell Oil logo. The can lights also resembled candle holders, reminiscent of theatre lighting during the pre-electricity days when candles were in use. Furthermore, Shell Oil cans were commonly used as candle holders by the rural poor and in urban slums; thus, the influence of U.S. capital was associated with poverty.

"The sound track completed the 'salad'; from Villa-Lobos to Carlos Gomes, sampling on the way tunes from carnivals past, the Fascist 'Giovinezza', and the Communist 'Internationale'" (Peixoto, "fascinante" 73). Although José Celso wanted to have a score composed for the play, that proved to be financially unfeasible, and so he and Renato Borghi chose a salad of recorded musical pieces, which served as a constant and critical counterpoint to the action. Heloísa's first entrance was accompanied by a Dave Brubeck blues piece, an auditory reference to Brazil's melancholy state of affairs. The first act also included songs about rural São Paulo, ironic allusions to the coffee crisis, such as "São Paulo da Garoa" ("Drizzly São Paulo"), a paean to the region's bountiful harvest and natural beauty. A children's song, "Casinha Pequena" ("Little House"), was heard throughout the play, Abelardo's theme song, an innocent counterpoint to his avarice. The latter, in a mock romantic scene, also sang with Heloísa a duet, "Giovinezza," from the Mussolini period. The first-act musical salad was complemented by morsels from Puccini, Vivaldi, Gounod ("Ave Maria"), John Philip Sousa, and Brazilian Modernist composer Villa-Lobos.

Acting styles obeyed the Tupy/Brechtian thrust of costumes and makeup: "Creative freedom, which burst beyond our limits on a daily basis and revealed to us an unsuspected potential, was not lost in chaotic improvisation; instead, we managed to harness it in a rational and disciplined manner. . . . The cast threw itself heart and soul into the elaboration of the new conception of acting. The actors drew on their own provincialism, to which they added the lessons they learned from Brecht, as well as the most spontaneous and dynamic manifestations of Brazilian popular theatre" ("fascinante" 72). Abelardo, for example, exhibited the gross gestures of Brazilian-macho (e.g., scratching genitals). Renato Borghi, who played Abelardo, explained that "'this is the easiest role of my career. That's because it's easier to play a funny, grotesque Brazilian bourgeois . . . than to create a character like the one I played in *Andorra*, a persecuted Jew who is condemned to death.' To construct Abelardo I, Renato spent weeks watching TV programs, *revistas*, Brazilian slapstick comedies. . . . 'I had to lose my fear of showing the ridiculousness of

Abelardo I. I reached the conclusion that to play him correctly I must have no respect for his character. My criticism would be implicit if I could accomplish that'" (Rodrigues, "incêndio").

As in the case of the costumes, exterior Brechtian distance was privileged over interior Stanislavskian psychological realism. Arena, Oficina, and other groups during the 1960s came to believe that the Stanislavski approach, and its U.S. progeny, the Actors Studio Method, were bourgeois. The Tupy result, in the view of Yan Michalski, was "a modern Brazilian style of acting: a fusion of Brazilian anti-illusionist techniques with our national characteristics of rude and sarcastic mischievousness, a fusion achieved by taking generous portions—naturally and properly stylized and criticized—from our great cultural tradition, slapstick comedy" ("Considerações"). José Celso explained the development of Oficina's new acting style this way: "Initially I followed the Stanislavski method of interpretation, then it was Brecht that fascinated me with his epic theatre (the actor, onstage, interprets the character and at the same time criticizes him). Now what concerns me most is Chacrinha's mass communication. He represents national reality: our opportunism and *ufanismo*." *Ufanismo* is Brazilian jingoism, less bellicose and more sentimental than that of other nations. Oswald de Andrade and, later, José Celso scorned *ufanismo* because its nationalism was based on gloating over Brazil's natural wonders. They saw it as the ideological descendant of the sixteenth-century "texts of information," letters sent to the king by the early Portuguese explorers, filled with propaganda about the exploitable wealth in the newly discovered lands.

Act II, which takes place on a tropical isle in Guanabara Bay near Rio de Janeiro, parodied Brazilian stagnation by absorbing flavors from yet another performance mode, in this case *revista*, with its elements of political satire, sketches, dance, jokes, and music. The temples of *revista* in the 1930s had been Tiradentes Square in downtown Rio and the Urca Casino, located at the foot of Sugar Loaf Mountain, always featured in Rio postcards and therefore the ideal location for Brazilian kitsch. The second-act set souffléed the postcards—consumed by millions of tourists—into tacky painted backdrops depicting the visual clichés of Sugar Loaf (its cable car makes it the city's primary tourist destination), Corcovado (where the gigantic Christ statue looms over the city), and the apartment buildings lining the shore along Flamengo and Botafogo beaches. The backdrops featured tropical plants and birds, with a few clouds and a 1930s blimp floating above, and in contrast two warships anchored in Guanabara Bay, a reminder of the U.S. naval vessels cruising off the coast of Brazil at the time of the 1964 coup. The backdrop depicting the Bay of Guanabara was at times backlit, conveying the truly spectacular vista of Rio at night as seen from Sugar Loaf or Corcovado. To a stage-right mast was secured a sail-shaped flag, which originally was to be the U.S. flag, an idea banned by the censors so as not to offend Brazil's friends. All that remained were the colors red, white, and blue (Eichbauer used the same cloth for Mr. Jones's socks). The censors also banned the Brazilian flag, but the designer included its yellow and green colors everywhere in the set, which made the parody of *ufanismo* even stronger than a display of the flag itself would have. The tarp covering the revolving stage, in addition to melted candles, was painted to resemble a large tropical sun; on it were placed a beach umbrella and chaise longue. The Rio beach setting parodied the stereotype of Brazilian indolence. A small table held a 1930s-style radio. Painted scenery in the form of banana and palm trees was lowered and raised. Painted cloth backdrops were the norm for the 1930s comedy-of-manners Rio theatre—itself a nineteenth-century relic—prior to the revolution spearheaded by Os Comediantes. *The Candle King* set based on *revista*, therefore, was a scathing commentary on the idea that in Brazil *plus ça change, plus c'est le même chose,* or as José Celso stated the matter in the 1967 program, "*O Rei da Vela* . . . depicts life as a burlesque show. . . . There is no History, only the performance of History."

If for no other reason, the second-act set would be noteworthy as the most self-consciously kitsch scene in the history of the Brazilian stage. The only thing as kitsch was the television variety show hosted by Chacrinha, the principal contemporary survivor of the *revista* form, on the air for over two decades, until the 1980s. Chacrinha's show, however, did not have the acerbic intent of *The Candle King.* It was kitsch for kitsch's sake, the very thing that caused many Brazilian participants in the *Tropicália* movement to look uncritically at and even to lionize the program. It took a director of José Celso's acumen to discover the full significance of the kitsch elements explicit and implicit in Oswald de Andrade's play and to rub the audience's face in them, just as Antunes Filho would later reveal those same dimensions in the work of Nelson Rodrigues. One of the inspirations behind Oficina's kitsch potpourri was a Carmen Miranda movie, designed by Busby Berkeley, to parody Brazilian exoticism for export. The idea is that foreigners consume images of Brazil—Rio and *Carnaval* and Sugar Loaf, Pelé and soccer, Carmen Miranda and her fruit-laden hats—and distort them into grotesque stereotypes that replace notions of Brazil's complex sociocultural reality. Brazilians then reimport and in some cases participate in the production of those distorted images of themselves, particularly in the form of movies and music.

A recent example of the latter phenomenon is the lambada, which has shaped a new generation's image of Brazil. Although the lambada, one of a myriad of folkloric-popular dance forms practiced in Brazil, originated in the northern state of Pará and was popularized in Bahia during the 1980s, it was devoured by French impresarios who promoted it aggressively as a Brazilian "dirty dancing" and turned it into a fad that swept first Europe and then the United States. Following is a Brazilian view of the lambada craze: "World, get your tambourines ready and light your dance halls: The Brazilians, those indolent and sensual people who do not pay their foreign debt and who are burning their rain forests, are back. This time, they are doing the lambada." Referring to two America-made lambada films showing in São Paulo, the author opines: "Anyone who thought that Carmen Miranda movies portrayed a distorted image of Brazil should now rush out and buy a big fruit-salad hat. Carmen Miranda was much more real than the caricature of Brazil in these two movies." The article cites a number of distortions. The two movies depict lambada as an "'authentic ritual dance' of the Indians of the Amazon jungles." (No, one might add parenthetically, the filmmakers are not referring to Oswald de Andrade's Tupy golden age.) Those same Brazilian Indians in the film speak Mexican Spanish. And the lambada, it seems, "has been banned in Brazil for the past 50 years because it is considered 'obscene.'" Furthermore, as one would expect, the lambada danced in the films "is a pale imitation" of the genuine version. The article concludes: "It is high time for Brazil to send someone overseas who can represent quality amid all of this stupidity. Until that happens, though, get ready for more tambourines, palm trees and sensual dancing. It seems that people— whether they remember Brazil for Carmen Miranda or for the lambada—will continue to believe that our capital is Buenos Aires" (*Veja*, "Lambada"). The lambada, stripped of its folkloric-popular roots and reimported into Brazil, is consumed in its altered form by the middle classes in São Paulo and Rio. Were José Celso to restage *O Rei da Vela*, he would surely include the lambada in Act II.

In the second act Abelardo I wore a nouveau-riche sports ensemble: yellow satin jacket and velvet pants. Heloísa's brother Totó, his costume based on the traditional Rio homosexual carnival ball, sashayed about the stage in a burgundy velour bolero jacket bordered with rhinestones and coffee sprigs, wine-colored shorts, chiffon pants, hat covered with chiffon and feathers, fur-lined cape, gold-colored sandals, and anklets: a truly carnivalesque potpourri.

The sound track featured the song "Cidade Maravilhosa," about the "marvelous city" of Rio de Janeiro, from the 1935 carnival, reminding spectators that Brazil was still the "country of carnival." Another popular song from the past was "Yes, nós temos bananas," which in the 1920s was popularized in the United States with the title "Yes, We Have No Bananas," a good example of Tropicalist kitsch for export if ever there was one. Rimsky-Korsakov's "Scheherazade" was played for Totó Fruta do Conde's first entrance (his costume also evoked that of a belly dancer). Other finely chopped edibles added to the second-act musical *feijoada* included a piece by Villa-Lobos, a rock tune, and to represent the African roots of Brazilian culture, the sound of a *berimbau*, a one-stringed instrument played to accompany *capoeira*, an Afro-Brazilian martial art set to music.

There was much gnashing of teeth over *The Candle King*'s second-act celebration of sexuality, indolence, and kitsch. Some critics accused Oficina of purveying pornography and others of perpetrating the same stereotypes as Chacrinha. Those stereotypes, however, were not simply invented by foreigners; Brazilians do celebrate carnival and its carnal excesses, and *revista* and its variations have long been popular. That is, festive Tropicalism is part and parcel of Brazilian reality. José Celso and company devoured kitsch to criticize what they saw as a colonial mind-set. Not only was the nation wallowing in festive Tropicalism, they believed, but foreigners were using it to create distorted images of Brazil, which Brazilians themselves were consuming, a notion borne out by the recent lambada craze. The critics, nevertheless, had a point. The second-act set and costumes displayed the ambivalence at the heart of the Tropicalist movement. Inspired by the radiant canvases of Modernist painter Tarsila Amaral, Celso and Eichbauer indulged in an explosion of light, color, and exuberant tropical fauna and flora.[5] All of this echoed Oswald de Andrade's Anthropophagical concept according to which, before it was ravaged by successive waves of colonizers, the Tupy Brazil was a garden of earthly delights. The ambivalence would be carried over to the Tropicalist movement of the late 1960s and early 1970s.

In Act III José Celso applied the Tupy potpourri to opera. It is logical that José Celso would smack his lips over a form of popular entertainment that was a favorite of the coffee barons, many of them of Italian extraction. The director delighted particularly in opera's own kitsch motifs. Opera, at least the São Paulo variety, was ripe for Teatro Oficina's table. Coffee money sponsored both touring European companies and native operas, such as those composed by Carlos

Gomes. But São Paulo opera was a poor imitation of European grand opera, and so the third act revealed its poverty: the stage was bare but for a dilapidated wheelchair, like something out of a junkyard, where Abelardo I sat after his fall from power. There was a patchwork red curtain made of canvas rather than velvet. The lighting in the third-act opera design was dim, reinforcing the atmosphere of dissolution. Act III was framed by what one might call an antiset representing the falsehood of imitative culture. Abelardo I wore the costume usually associated with Father Ubu, a long bathrobe with a gold-colored cord dragging on the stage. The crown on his head, made from a Shell Oil can, as were the footlights used in the production, symbolized his subservience to U.S. capital. Abelardo II was dressed in the suit Abelardo I wore during the first act, and for the final scene he wore black. Heloísa featured a Tupy potpourri of costumes in the third act: she wore a long white medieval gown with a red sash suggesting a chastity belt, the bartered woman-object; her gown was also a devouring of Tennessee Williams's romantic and futile Blanche Dubois, from *A Streetcar Named Desire.* Her last costume, a black tulle gown worn during the final wedding-cum-funeral scene, came from two sources: Oswald de Andrade's own play *A Morta* and Shakespeare's (Lady) *Macbeth.* Several characters in the closing operatic scene had on silver-painted monkey masks, a dual reference to Tropicalism and the national penchant for imitation. Totó was dressed in a bat costume, which fused the image of American comic-book horror with operatic tragedy. A painted flat replaced the traditional theatre comedy/tragedy masks with glow-in-the-dark skulls. A funeral dirge was heard simultaneously with the wedding march (a musical fusion which also appeared in Nelson Rodrigues's *Bridal Gown*). Mr. Jones, in a Lone Ranger mask, opened his arms like the Christ statue on Corcovado, and the audience heard the song "Aquarela do Brasil" (Brazilian Watercolor), a paean to "Brazilianness" (something akin to "America the Beautiful"). At this point in the performance, a screen was lowered and on it was projected a sympathy card with the King's epitaph in black lettering, a passage from Oswald de Andrade's *A Morta* in which he called his nation's theatre a "gangrenous corpse." The final blackout for *The Candle King* was accompanied by a drum roll inspired by Buñuel's film *L'Age d'Or.*

The cannibals' banquet that was the staging of *The Candle King* had as its immediate objective to revive the gangrenous corpse, "to put the same old audiences on the spot, because they seemed to us to be anesthetized, asleep. That way, we could put theatre itself on the spot" (Peixoto, "fascinante" 72). The irony was that the opening-night crowd included a group of unsuspecting sponsors: "As part of Oficina's grand reopening, *O Rei da Vela* debuted for an audience filled with avid and startled guests, including—like something out of a 'happening'—our sponsors from the Paraná state government, as well as the wife of São Paulo's Governor, First-Lady Maria do Carmo Abreu Sodré, our patroness" (73).

From the opening night on, Oficina's theatre of aggression gave rise to heated charges of pornography and to threatening letters and phone calls. "The São Paulo run would be tumultuous. Critics shocked, the public either fascinated or hate-filled. During some performances people would stand up and attack the actors (verbally) or Oswald himself (one spectator issued a loud challenge that he give himself up to the police). There were nearly daily threats" (74). There was a lighter side to all of this: "The [case] most commented upon was that of a couple that disturbed the actors and the audience during the second act. He was furious about the staging of such 'audacity' and 'pornography', while his wife defended the 'greatest national playwright'" (Rodrigues, "incêndio").

Censorship was amazingly inactive, at least in the beginning. "The censors put up with us in unexpected and surprising silence. Sometimes they phoned to let us know that the denunciations, including those from the military, were on the rise. And that pressure from Brasília was increasing. But all they did was recommend a certain degree of moderation so that everything could go on its merry way. We lucked out: state censors went so far as to resist, in defense of their autonomy, the clearly repressive suggestions coming from the federal censors" ("fascinante" 74–75).

The authorities did, in fact, insist on cuts in the text, but the director considered them so minor that at one point he actually praised the censors, as related in a newspaper article: "Groups of people have gone to the police and to the Division of Public Entertainment (censorship) to ask that the play be banned, alleging that it is immoral. Director José Celso, however, maintains that the censors have understood the artistic value of the work—'a gesture that will go down in the annals of the history of the theatre'—they have not banned it, and in spite of a few cuts they have not altered its content, they are providing an umbrella for its performance. He thanked Mr. Geraldino Russomano, director of the Division, by saying: 'fortunately we have a censorship that comprehends the artistic nature of the play and is ensuring that it will be staged, in spite of protests by out of touch people who consider it offensive, subversive, and obscene" (*Folha*, "reações"). Things would, however, get worse, the text and performance would both be subject to progressive mutilation by the censors, and José Celso would change his tune: the censors "'claim they've been receiving outside pressure and they've had to make concessions to that pressure. . . . Their cutting makes no sense. If anything, their changes have made the scenes even more pornographic'" (*Última Hora*, "Rei").[6]

Reactions on the part of Celso's "out of touch" detractors became increasingly belligerent, prompting this comment by the director: "'The play has been considered pornographic and subversive. Nevertheless, the telephone calls I receive daily from spectators are more obscene than the pornography of the text and more contentious than the subversion alleged by the censors'" (*Última Hora*, "Rei"). Threats became so bellicose that security measures were taken at the theatre. One paranoid evening, Fernando Peixoto, as part of his lion-tamer costume, wore loaded pistols while performing. Friends of the company often waited in the wings acting as armed guards. Audience members were searched on their way into the theatre. There was even an emergency escape plan. "Each day we faced new risks, which convinced us that what we were doing was working" (Peixoto, "fascinante"). All negative reaction, however, cannot be attributed to the aggressive sexuality in the production. Teatro Oficina's assault on symbols of Brazilian nationalism struck a raw nerve among defenders of the status quo and particularly the super-patriots who were willing to go to any lengths to stop "defilers of the flag."

The response of many who saw the play, however, was over-whelmingly favorable, so much so that it became one of the biggest box-office hits in Brazilian theatrical history. Several critics saw the play as a revolution in stagecraft. Yan Michalski wrote that the production design was "baroque, grotesque, excessive, vulgar, and grandiose, all at the same time, conveying the impression of a false vitality masking a hopeless decadence—it is a perfect example of creative collaboration between a director and a designer" ("Considerações"). According to Van Jafa, the director "constructed an intense and energetic production worthy of Oswald de Andrade, while leaving room for the playwright to be seen and heard" (Jafa, "Rei").

Following is a potpourri of Brazilian reviews quoted in the 1969 program: "We must and we can create an authentic Brazilian theatre. A giant step has been made by José Celso in *O Rei da Vela*" (Carlos Van Schmidt, São Paulo, *Artes*); "The most superficial spectators will judge to be pornographic that which we consider 'erotic sublimation' of the text . . . , a production destined to make history" (João Apolinário, São Paulo, *Última Hora*); "Oficina took precisely the right step toward the dramaturgy we needed to add an aesthetic dimension to the kind of didactic theatre that is so typical of this period of war and transition" (Luiza Barreto Leite, Rio, *Jornal do Comércio*); "It will be difficult for any play, no matter how good, to take the place of *O Rei da Vela*" (Marisa Alves de Lima, Rio, *O Cruzeiro*); "One can point a finger at the production's faults, but . . . no one can ignore the fact that it is one of the most significant works of art created for Brazilian theatre, as well as one of the most innovative, in spite of the fact that it was written in 1937" (Luiz Alberto Sanz, Rio, *Última Hora*).

While the vast majority of reviews were single-minded in their praise of Oficina's production, some highly regarded Brazilian critics were ambivalent. Paulo Mendonça, while praising José Celso's stagecraft, affirmed that "the play itself, in terms of the themes that it concretely proposes and develops, is hopelessly dated. Those things it says that were shocking for the standards of 1937, are today clichés or simplifications [and their] power to stimulate the imagination and to awaken the conscience or to provoke indignation is now extremely limited" ("Rei"). Décio de Almeida Prado, the dean of Brazilian theatre critics, wrote: "The result is surprising in some scenes, especially in the second act. . . . The directing is singularly penetrating, inventive, imaginative, picaresque in terms of details and powerfully aided by Hélio Eichbauer's set and costumes. . . . Not everything is good in *O Rei da Vela*, but what is good is very good" ("encenação").

Almeida Prado had grave doubts about Andrade's text, as did other critics. He explained his skepticism to me in our interview:

The twenties had been a happy, festive decade. Coffee was fetching high prices [and] São Paulo was progressing rapidly. There was a certain economic euphoria and a certain joy in literature. This comes out in Oswald's own work and in the playful atmosphere of the Modern Art Week [of 1922]. But with the 1929 crisis, the global crisis, there was a very clear change in Brazil's artistic climate. Playfulness came to be viewed in a very negative light. It was the beginning of a period of seriousness, of politically engagé literature and concern with the problems of the common people. That's when the first novels of Jorge Amado, José Lins do Rego, and Graciliano Ramos came out. And the common people made their appearance; they had been almost entirely absent from [Oswald's] work. There was a new literary style. The twenties style was very experimental. It was the era of all the -isms: Dadaism, Surrealism. These -isms disappeared from the world literary scene in the thirties. The main concern was now political. Oswald himself considered that phase over when he wrote in the introduction to *Serafim Ponte Grande* that *O Rei da Vela* was, in his words, "the epitaph of what I used to be." Most people considered *O Rei da Vela* outmoded, something belonging to the twenties.

He also explained why he changed his mind: "The sixties saw the return of experimentalism for various political and aesthetic reasons. Antonin Artaud, a once forgotten name, was being read again and having quite an impact. Surrealism, too. And it was then that *O Rei da Vela*, particularly because of Zé Celso's staging, was suddenly very modern. Now, when I saw the production, I had a certain reaction. But at the same time I was influenced by *O Rei da Vela* as a critic. I see it as a turning point in the evolution of Brazilian theatre."

Not all critics were so generous nor willing to change their minds. Regina Helena ("rei") wrote that "the play is tedious. It explains too much, it is too much of a 'manifesto', its endless speech-making is far too exhausting for it to be a good play." Gustavo Doria, in his 1975 retrospective consideration of the production, had this to say: "Although the production was replete with interesting ideas, the main reason for its success was its shock value, [its] success by scandal, which actually allowed the cast to travel to Europe in search of acclamation it failed to receive" (*Teatro* 172).

Most critics in retrospect have reaffirmed the production's preeminent place in the history of the stage. Michalski would comment nearly twenty years later on the significance of its response to the historical moment: "The year 1966 would mark the appearance of a tendency toward anarchic reaction to the pressures the nation is constantly subjected to, but this tendency would leave its definitive stamp in 1967" (*Teatro* 28). The critic refers, of course, to *O Rei da Vela*. "The production exploded like a bomb, eliciting applause from most critics, but leaving the traditional bourgeois São Paulo public perplexed and shaken, and because of its provocative tone, awakening suspicion among the authorities" (31).

Whenever *The Candle King* went on tour, it received both violent reaction and lavish praise. The authorities repudiated the play, although ironically Oficina had received official funding for rebuilding the theatre after the 1966 fire and for the initial staging of Andrade's play. Federal censors excised many passages from the text, and local censors made almost daily cuts in the performance. Eventually, the climate in Brazil became quite dangerous for artists who did not toe the line, culminating in the violent assault of Comando de Caça aos

Comunistas on the cast members of *Roda Viva*. The temporary solution was a tour to Europe.

Teatro Oficina's performances of *O Rei da Vela* in Florence, Nancy,
and Paris brought the company considerable notoriety. Not until
Grupo Macunaíma's tours that began a decade later would a Brazilian theatre troupe receive such wide attention abroad. The European critics (quoted in the 1969 program) had this to say about
Oficina's production: "*O Rei da Vela* is a spectacle that cannot be
judged, artistically or ideologically, by the yardstick of European
criticism. . . . Corrêa and his companions chose the path of provocation and irreverent satire to destroy the old and construct the new on
the stage: a theatre that oscillates between intellectual scrutiny and
pop phenomena" (Carlo Degl 'Innocenti, Florence, *L'Unità*); "The
Nancy Festival has fulfilled its mission by introducing us to the
Bread and Puppet theatre and to Teatro Oficina" (Emile Copfer-
mann, Paris, *Les Lettres Françaises*); "History will be made only
through revolution: this is the implicit lesson in *O Rei da Vela*"
"Françoise Kourilsky, Paris, *Le Nouvel Observateur*); "At last, with
Oswald de Andrade's *O Rei da Vela*, São Paulo's Teatro Oficina
staged a spectacle that was genuinely rude, vulgar, in bad taste. Vulgarity used with a clear purpose by the Brazilians and by director
José Celso Corrêa, who presented one of the most important productions in the Festival" (Nicole Zand, Paris, *Le Monde*); Sorbonne professor and renowned theatre critic Bernard Dort wrote notes bearing
the title "Uma comédia em transe" for the Paris program of *O Rei
da Vela*, widely circulated in Brazil through reprints in newspapers,
magazines, and in all subsequent programs for *The Candle King*:

> We unquestionably lack references: it is to a Brazilian public that
> the spectacle is aimed. Where we only suspect that José Celso
> Martínez Corrêa and his actors wallow and lose themselves in
> bad taste, the spectator from São Paulo or Rio has no doubt: it is
> his own bad taste, that of his own preferred forms of entertain-
> ment, which is being put on stage here. But that is of no impor-
> tance whatsoever. The essential remains in this grotesque and
> bold mask, which rather than distancing us from historical real-
> ity, forces us to bear this reality in mind through the medium of
> theatre itself. It is impossible to avoid thinking about the *Three
> Penny Opera*. Brecht also tried to reflect back to the 1928 public
> the image it created for itself in its "culinary" entertainment.
> But perhaps Brecht and Weill were somewhat timid, to some de-
> gree prisoners of our good taste and our Western theatrical tradi-

tion. Teatro Oficina has taken a further step, toward the use of obscene language and gesture. This comedy-farce of a Brazil *em transe* is also a means to put an end to the sterile imitation of Western theatre, to wipe the slate clean. We are witnessing not a tranquil attempt to found a national folkloric theatre (like the Brazilian play presented in Nancy and Paris two years ago: *Morte e Vida Severina*) but an angry and desperate appeal for another kind of theatre: a theatre of insurrection.

Subsequent to the European sojourn, there were several revivals of the play until it was finally banned entirely by the censors in 1971. José Celso filmed *O Rei da Vela*, but it, too, fell victim to censorship. Although the film is useful from a research point of view— it includes many scenes from actual stage performances—it is limited and unfocused in terms of cinematic values. José Celso stated in our 1984 interview that the film has failed to receive support because he is trying "to gain control of the means of cinematic production, and the film departs from the cinema's structures, formulas, and taste. There is no room for innovation." Although José Celso reedited the film several times, he was never able to find a distributor.

Teatro Oficina's staging of *The Candle King* left a profound and in some ways curious legacy. The company enriched Brazilian stagecraft immeasurably by liberating the Brazilian imagination and overturning Western notions of propriety and good taste. It gave directors and companies a new sense of artistic freedom. Although the dictatorship created terrible obstacles, the influence of Oficina's production has endured. *O Rei da Vela* took over the *Bridal Gown*'s two-decade position as yardstick for measuring innovative stagings, and José Celso became the "new Ziembinski." When Antunes Filho began his successful experiments ten years later, he became the "new Zé Celso." It is curious that Oficina's *The Candle King* did not lead to new innovative productions of Oswald de Andrade's dramatic opus. In fact, other than a few timid amateur productions, theatre artists have continued to avoid his plays, just as they did before Oficina's resurrection. The reason may be that José Celso's interpretation was so definitive that its now legendary status frightens away directors. It may be that the works themselves continue to present too great a challenge, with their bizarre mix of historical figures (Beatrice, Horace, Saint Peter, Job, Cleopatra, "Lord" Capone) and extravagant settings (the red planet, heaven, an aerodrome that doubles as a morgue). Or perhaps their unabashed avant-gardism has little appeal in an age (the 1970s and 1980s) in which the avant-garde has lost the cutting edge or at least the appeal that it had in the

1960s. Finally, the problem may be the one addressed by Décio de Almeida Prado and Paulo Mendonça: Oswald de Andrade's theatrical language is "hopelessly dated." In spite of the dearth of Oswald de Andrade productions, Oficina's breakthroughs did have an immediate and powerful impact, not only on stagecraft but on popular culture, particularly the brief and shining moment of *Tropicália*, before that movement faded into mass commercialism and pale imitation.

Anthropophagy, Tropicalism, and Art for Export

Anthropophagy was initially an outgrowth of the broad movement known as *Modernismo*. It had its own *Manifesto Antropófago* and journal (*Revista Antropofágica*). It was Modernism's first attempt to confront contemporary social problems and to place them in historical and ideological contexts. It called for a permanent rebellion based on the paradigms of an imagined Indian golden age fused with technological progress. In its struggle against colonialism, it sneered at national imitators of foreign culture. Yet Anthropophagy also derided *ufanismo* and all other forms of sentimental and xenophobic nationalism, insisting that Brazilian culture could be nourished by devouring imported culture. While nearly dormant for three decades, but for some occasional literary snacking, it was not until the 1960s that Cannibalism became a feast and the word-guide was revived to influence a whole generation of artists. This cultural Cannibalism has bloomed, and a thousand teeth have taken root.

The staging of *The Candle King* utilized Anthropophagy to focus the problem of cultural dependency, to attempt to demonstrate that most national theatrical modes have imitated European and American models, and that Brazilians have consumed foreign-made stereotypes of their cultural traditions. Using irreverence and parody, José Celso and his company intended to subvert those models and stereotypes, to lampoon submission to them, and at the same time to criticize the other end of the spectrum, xenophobic nationalism. Their end was to clarify a national cultural essence, which Modernist Mário de Andrade defined as a mosaic; that is, Brazilian art and folklore have drunk deeply from a great many wellsprings, both native and foreign. National originality relates to the way those sources are organized. The mode of organization characteristic of Anthropophagy and its latter-day offshoot, Tropicalism, was to use freely and defiantly any and all cultural models, whatever their origin. While drawing a bead on the future, the word-guide points toward the living past, toward the roots of Brazilian culture still present in carnival, folk music and dance, African-based religious practices, and myriad forms of kitsch. All this would ideally lead to a definition of national identity through art, an exportable rather than imported identity.

Tropicália exploded in 1967 with the release of Glauber Rocha's film *Terra em Transe*—a tragic-comic "opera" of underdevelopment reflecting the disillusion of the Left and the failure of populism—and the staging of *O Rei da Vela.* The latter performance especially lit the spark for the rekindling of Anthropophagy. According to Caetano Velloso, "I changed my style of composition after seeing *O Rei da Vela.* That play is the most important thing I've ever seen. I find Oswald's work enormously significant. . . . I love the idea that contained in Oswald's work is a movement which expresses the violence I'd like to turn against stagnation and pretense. It should be easy for you to understand why Oswald de Andrade is so important to me, because I've gone through the same process, felt the burning desire to mock bossa nova ever since it started taking itself so seriously. . . . Tropicalism is a neo-Anthropophagism" (quoted in Campos, *Balanço* 183). *Terra* and *Rei* were followed by Tropicalist manifestations in all art forms: several more Teatro Oficina productions, particularly *Galileu Galilei*, Hélio Oticica's and Antônio Dias's paintings of tropical fruits, the poetry of Torquato Neto, and the music of Caetano Velloso and Gilberto Gil. The latter two composed the songs that became the anthems of the new movement, "Geléia Geral" and "Tropicália," which present several stylistic parallels with Oswald de Andrade's *Manifesto Antropófago:* the verbal collage; poetic enumeration of the fragments of the Brazilian cultural mosaic; juxtaposition of the folkloric and the erudite and of the archaic and the modern; portrayal of the "primitive" tropical universe; emphasis on parody and irreverence; and particularly the devouring of foreign modes. Tropicalist music attempted to Brazilianize imported pop culture—rock, electric guitars—and to fuse it with uniquely Brazilian musical forms, such as samba and frevo, and neo-African instruments, such as the one-string *berimbau.* A line in the song "Geléia Geral" synthesizes the process of fusion: "bumba-iê-iê-boi". *Bumba-meu-boi* is a northeastern ritual folk dance which blends African, Indian, and European motifs in the manner of the Brazilian cultural mosaic. *Iê-iê* is, of course, Portuguese for "rock and roll." The *iê-iê* is sandwiched between the two slices of the Brazilian folk dance: it is devoured. Celso Favaretto, discussing Velloso's song "Alegria, Alegria," states that it is "the product of the urban experience of young people immersed in the fragmentary world of news, shows, television, and advertising." Its language, therefore, is "kaleidoscopic" (*Tropicália* 8). According to Augusto de Campos, the Tropicalists have created a "musical metalanguage . . .

through which they are reviewing everything that has been produced musically in Brazil and in the world, to the end of consciously
creating something new, something firsthand. That is why their
records constitute an *antianthology* of the unexpected, where everything can happen and the listener goes from shock to shock, re-
discovering everything, relearning to 'listen with open ears,' just as
Oswald de Andrade used to proclaim in his manifestos, 'see with
open eyes'" (Campos, *Balanço* 262–263).

Musical Tropicalism was in part a response to the stagnation of
bossa nova and to the nationalist-protest school of music represented by such composers as Chico Buarque, Sérgio Ricardo, and
Edu Lobo, and by the *bossarenas* and the engagé musicals of Teatro
de Arena, including *Zumbi*. The protest-musical genre was characterized by direct and open criticism of social problems, such as poverty in the rural Northeast and the urban South, and by what some
have called "ingenuous" nationalism. The genre attempted to be
folkloric, to be more "purely" Brazilian, and it was aesthetically
conservative (e.g., the production of *Morte e Vida Severina* Bernard
Dort turned up his nose at). Chico Buarque composed the musical
score for the latter piece, and the author was poet João Cabral de
Mello Neto. Tropicalism's adherents identified with the work of
Teatro Oficina: they considered themselves avant-garde, participants in an aesthetic revolution, open to all kinds of music. They
were fiercely opposed to untainted nationalism; on the contrary,
Tropicalists parodied *ufanismo*. They railed against the aesthetic
conservatism of the protest school. Tropicalism, in short, initiated a
"process of deconstruction [of] the musical tradition, the ideology of
development, and populist nationalism" (Favaretto, *Tropicália* 8).
The polemic put Arena at odds with Oficina, a tension that in part
arose from the ideological dispute but also reflected more mundane
concerns: rivalry between two theatre companies vying for the same
audience and between the egos of two directors, Augusto Boal and
José Celso. The division between the two schools was in reality not
total. In the play *Roda Viva*, written by Chico Buarque and directed
by José Celso, protest music and Tropicalism crossed paths.

Tropicália's key moment was an international popular music festival held in São Paulo in 1968. Students representing the nationalist-
protest musical faction, offended by colorful plastic clothing and
electric guitars, attempted to boo Caetano Velloso off the stage. The
defenders of Tropicalism used this incident to claim that the movement was the most radical in the Brazilian arts, that it threatened
those "out of touch" with new forms and cultural revolution.

The *nouvelle cuisine antropofagique* that was *Tropicália* was in many ways a militant attempt to place Brazilian art in an international context, but whether that meant just another form of imitation is open to debate and in fact has generated a great deal of controversy. In spite of its revolutionary pretensions, the Tropicalist movement was short lived. It lacked any real ideological cohesion, and its aggression went hand in hand with self-destruction. Oficina's frustration over theatre's inability to change society through formal innovation led to increasing aggression, culminating in *Gracias Señor*, which alienated audiences. While Tropicalist exuberance in theatre led to futility, in music it meant absorption by the mass media and reduction to the status of fashion. When the kitsch element came to be appreciated for its own sake rather than for its parody, it was quickly commercialized by mass consumer culture. From parody of the language of advertising, the movement became part of that language. Tropicalists, not afraid of mass communications, wanted to function in the context of the industrial system, but ironically their creations were devoured by that very system in a process of inverted Anthropophagy.

Some critics have attempted to separate *Terra em Transe* and *O Rei da Vela* from what followed. Yan Michalski calls post-*Rei* Tropicalist manifestations "servile and stupid imitations" ("A Vela Volta"). José Celso "publicly declared his admiration for Chacrinha. But let us not confuse the two: Oficina's Tropicalism . . . is bitterly self-critical; Chacrinha's Tropicalism, by joyfully consuming ignorance and poverty for its own benefit, glorifies ignorance and poverty and zealously perpetuates them" ("Rei da Raiva").

In spite of its inevitable links with mass consumer culture, Tropicalism, like other innovative movements, suffered at the hands of police-state repression. Both Caetano Velloso and Gilberto Gil were arrested, and the former went into temporary exile in London. *Tropicália* lasted until 1972, when its principal members declared it officially defunct.

Tropicália did leave a musical legacy. Both Velloso and Gil went on to fruitful careers characterized by continuing experimentation. In the 1980s and 1990s, São Paulo groups (e.g., Premeditando Breque) and singer-composers (e.g., Arrigo Barnabé) took up Tropicalism's irreverence and Tupy potpourri openness. Their movement was known as *Paulistália*.

Whatever the intrinsic aesthetic merits of Tropicalism, it helped to revive the concept of Anthropophagy, which continues to aid Brazilian artists in their quest to define their own identity, and it has led to the widely held view that if national identity is obscured by the proliferation of imposed models and cultural dependency, then export of Brazilian artistic production should be a way to invert the colonial formula. It is not enough merely to establish autochthonous modes; it is necessary to export them and place them in an international context. And in fact that has been an increasing tendency in Brazil, particularly in popular music, lambada aside: first bossa nova and then the Tropicalist and post-Tropicalist music of Caetano Velloso and Milton Nascimento. Brazilian film has had considerable international exposure, beginning with the *cinema novo* of Glauber Rocha and Nelson Pereira dos Santos[7] and more recently the films of Carlos Diegues and Bruno Barreto. Several theatre groups have toured abroad: Arena, Oficina, Pessoal do Víctor, and most notably, Grupo Macunaíma.

5. Theatre in the 1970s and 1980s: Grupo Macunaíma

Censorship

Modest censorship, particularly on the local level, has always been a fact of life for Brazilian theatre, even during periods of democratically elected government. Examples are cuts the censors made in the TBC's 1950 production of John Gay's *The Beggars Opera* and in Teatro Oficina's 1960 staging of *L'Engrenage*, by Jean-Paul Sarte, and its 1961 *Awake and Sing*, by Clifford Odets. During the first few years of the dictatorship installed in 1964, censorship was not rigorous. When the so-called Division of Public Entertainment in São Paulo resisted pressures to ban the performance of *The Candle King*, José Celso praised the action of local censors. Beginning in 1968, however, the generals declared war on theatre companies, and with the December 1968 state of siege, or Institutional Act Number Five (AI5), the boot of military repression would attempt to grind theatrical activity into the boards. In February 1968, the theatre community in São Paulo reacted to the growing pressure of censorship by declaring a general strike. Nevertheless, the government continued to ban certain plays—deemed "immoral," a production of *A Streetcar Named Desire* was closed down in Brasília—right-wing paramilitary organizations like the Comando de Caça aos Comunistas carried out physical attacks and made death threats, theatres were targets of bombings, actors were arrested and their heads shaved, others were fired from television jobs when networks were pressured by government security agencies. Whatever misery befell the Brazilian stage before the state of siege was nothing compared to what would follow. One of the initial consequences of AI5 was to throw the theatre community into a panic. Moreover, the noisy government campaign against the "subversion" and "perversity" supposedly taking place on the stage scared off the theatregoing public. All of this served to reduce drastically the number of productions.

By 1971 the situation had become intolerable. The police began to arrest and torture some of the stage's most important figures, such as Flávio Império, José Celso, and Augusto Boal, anything and everything was subject to censorship, and theatre companies began to break up. The actions of the dictatorship had a chilling effect not only on innovative groups, but on the rather sedate commercial heirs of the Teatro Brasileiro de Comédia as well. The consequence was the emergence of a new system of theatrical production, similar to the Broadway stage, controlled by impresarios. But even for the independent commercial producers, the censors had surprises up their sleeves. In 1973, the musical *Calabar*, by singer-composer Chico Buarque and film director Ruy Guerra,[1] was one of the most expensive theatrical productions Brazil had seen. A few days before opening, the federal censors banned it, which meant a financial loss that took years for the participants in the project to recover from. Although censorship began to loosen its grip in 1974, the Brazilian stage still reeled from the shock of repression.

Rio and São Paulo in the 1970s and 1980s: Steps toward Recovery

One of the few exceptions to the dearth of stable theatre companies in the wake of the AI5 was Rio's Teatro Ipanema, which debuted in 1968 with Chekhov's *The Cherry Orchard* (*O Jardim das Cerejeiras*). Other noteworthy productions were its 1969 *A Noite dos Assassinos* (*Night of the Assassins*), by Cuban playwright José Triana; Arrabal's *The Architect and the Emperor of Assyria* (*O Arquiteto e o Imperador da Assíria*), in 1970. The company's definitive staging was the 1971 *Hoje É Dia de Rock* (Today Is the Day of Rock), by Brazilian playwright José Vicente, an homage to the peace-and-love message of the counterculture. There was audience participation, but totally unlike that of *Gracias, Señor*; the actors gave spectators flowers and broke bread with them; the production was a true Brazilian love-in. *Rock* ran for over a year. Many theatregoers went back to see it several times; some spectators felt the play's communion between actors and audience changed their lives. Teatro Ipanema's performing style was based on the celebration of "apparently primitive dramatic rituals which were in fact highly sophisticated in their elaboration of a visual and irresistibly poetic language of the stage; the actors in these rituals behaved like priests in a mystic cult" (Michalski, *Teatro* 44). With the nation suffering at the hands of the dictatorship, some thought the group's mystical and art-for-art's-sake vision escapist, "but the group's work had a nihilistic connotation, like Oficina's aggressive anger, which constituted a coherent response to the challenge imposed by the system" (45). The group's activities would be limited and short lived. In 1972 it staged *A China É Azul* (China Is Blue), by Brazilian actor José Wilker: "the company appeared to have undertaken an extremely subjective *trip*, which would lead it down the road of a beautiful but unfortunate subjectivism" (53). There would be only two more productions, one in 1974 and a final staging in 1977.

The early 1970s saw the establishment of another Rio company that showed great promise. Founded in 1974 by a group of young theatre artists, it would adopt the humorous and enigmatic name Asdrúbal Trouxe Seu Trombone, or Asdrubal Brought His Trombone. The company opened with a modest production of Nicolai Gogol's *The Inspector General* (*O Inspector Geral*), which had been staged by a group from the previous generation, Teatro de Arena, in the 1960s. In 1975 Asdrúbal staged Alfred Jarry's *Ubu Roi* (*Ubu Rei* [Ubu the King]). The group's approach in those two productions was based on an irreverent dismantling of the classics—without Teatro de Arena's engagé nationalism—and its distinctive performing style was very physical, collective, mixing music, dance, and circus technique. Its next two productions were collective creations: the 1977 *Trate-me Leão*, an unusual title loosely translated "Just Call Me Lion," and *Aquela Coisa Toda* (The Whole Bit) in 1980. The company toured Brazil and performed in New York with the latter two productions, which it kept in repertory until 1982. At that time, the company put up a circus tent on Rio's Ipanema Beach, where it presented a variety of musical and circus acts. The company members subsequently dispersed, and a few of them became well-known TV and movie actors.

The first promising theatrical troupe to appear in São Paulo after the demise of Arena and Oficina was the O Pessoal do Víctor, formed in 1975 with a group of recent graduates from the Escola de Arte Dramática, under the tutelage of veteran director Celso Nunes. The company would later steer an independent course and work with a number of different directors. Víctor has staged both foreign—Arrabal, Kafka—and Brazilian authors. Its most notable production has been *Feliz Ano Velho* (*Happy Old Year*), which ran for five years in Brazil and abroad. It played at the Joseph Papp Festival Latino in New York (1985) and at the Havana International Theatre Festival (1987). *Feliz Ano Velho* is the adaptation of the best-selling autobiography by Marcelo Paiva, originally published in 1982, a work that has been translated into English, Italian, Spanish, German, and Danish, and which was made into an award-winning film in 1988. The book recounts a middle-class family's tragedies: the author's childhood, when his Socialist politician father was "disappeared" by the generals, and his young adulthood when he became a paraplegic in a diving accident. Paiva's story has great appeal because it deals with Brazil's worst period of repression from the candid perspective of a child, tells the story of the generation that grew up under the dictatorship, and deals with the little-discussed—in Brazil—problems of the disabled.

In spite of the positive and encouraging efforts of groups like Teatro Ipanema, Asdrúbal, and O Pessoal do Víctor, it would not be until the emergence of Grupo Macunaíma that Brazil would again lay claim to a theatre company capable of investing itself with the mantle of Os Comediantes, TBC, Arena, and Oficina.

Grupo Macunaíma

The Grupo de Teatro Macunaíma, as it is officially called, has been the most successful company in the history of the modern Brazilian stage, renowned both nationally and internationally. Always innovative, always restless, it has toured all the regions of Brazil and continents of the globe. If one sought proof of the old adage according to which the most profoundly national of artistic works become the most universal—for example, *Don Quixote*—Grupo Macunaíma would supply solid evidence. While basing its productions on the roots and diversity of Brazilian culture, the company has succeeded in stirring audiences from Japan to Israel, from Rome to Los Angeles. It has received awards in such cities as Montreal and Caracas.

The company has been led for its entire existence by Antunes Filho, né José Alves Antunes Filho. While Teatro de Arena and Teatro Oficina grew up with their leaders, as it were, Antunes Filho was an accomplished professional when he founded his company. His career began with the Teatro Brasileiro de Comédia, where he studied under its Italian directors. He staged his first production in 1954, Noel Coward's *Weekend,* with the Companhia Nicete Bruno, a TBC spin-off. For the next two decades he would direct a wide variety of foreign plays by authors as diverse as García Lorca, Coward, Ibsen, Shakespeare, Beckett, Albee, and others. He directed several Brazilian works by Jorge Andrade, Oduvaldo Vianna Filho, and most importantly Nelson Rodrigues. Antunes Filho won numerous awards for his stagings. Finally, he directed for the cinema and for television.

His work, while lauded as innovative, remained essentially within the parameters of commercial theatre, and he eventually suffered "director's block [which] forced him to depart from the stage"

(Magaldi, "Consagração"). He decided to enter an experimental phase, beginning in 1977 with an acting course that he taught under the auspices of the São Paulo Ministry of Culture's Theatre Commission, the same organization that had provided invaluable sup-. port for the TBC in the early 1960s. Amália Zeitel, former president of the commission, explained in our interview that Antunes Filho's intention was to base the course on themes drawn from Brazilian Modernist writer Mário de Andrade's 1928 narrative *Macunaíma*. If the results were satisfactory, the experiment might lead to a staged adaptation of the work. After several months of classes, a new theatre company was born, initially called Grupo de Arte Pau-Brasil,[2] and the first stage adaptation of the classic entitled *Macunaíma* was about to be launched.

The group's initial production came to be an unprecedented theatrical phenomenon. The original version, with its running time of four and a half hours, and the subsequent three-hour version, were performed 876 times, beginning with the São Paulo opening on 15 September 1978 to the final presentation in Athens on 5 July 1987. The play toured to thirty Brazilian cities and to sixty-seven cities in seventeen foreign countries, including Venezuela, Mexico, Canada, the United States, Israel, Australia, and ten European nations. The production traveled to numerous international theatre festivals and accumulated several awards for the play and the director.

Critics, both Brazilian and foreign, have showered *Macunaíma* with accolades. Some examples: "A single production—*Macunaíma*—would suffice to declare the [1978] São Paulo theatre season exceptional. For the first time in eleven years (since the opening of *O Rei da Vela*), we witnessed an event whose impact was too overwhelming to be taken in at once, but upon leaving the theatre we knew it was bound to be a milestone in the annals of the Brazilian stage" (Michalski, *Teatro* 75). Mariângela Alves Lima evaluates the national and international significance of the production:

> It is at the very least curious that a hero so Brazilian, so Indian and so black and so white, is somehow able to carry on a dialogue with such a diversity of nationalities. . . . The hero's voyage represents not only a country but a civilization; it is the point where theatre assumes the task of translating the universality of the theme to a universal language. [The play] is not successful because it is *as good as* productions staged abroad, nor because it is *exotic.* It is a work that establishes its own form of communication because it places on stage the dreams, experi-

ences, and humor of spectators with vastly different origins.
(*Macunaíma,* 1984 program notes)

Foreign critics have compared Antunes Filho to such stage and
film directors as Robert Wilson, Peter Brook, Fellini, and Buñuel.
Following is a potpourri of quotes appearing in the 1984 program:
from New York, "a work that triumphs over length . . . and language . . . to transmit a rare theatrical excitement. [It is] a journey of
adventure, joy, and despair . . . like that of Peer Gynt"; from Washington, "*Macunaíma,* a spectacular epic comedy from Brazil, is the
most exciting theatrical event yet seen at the Kennedy Center Ter-
race Theater"; from Basel, "A colossal work, able to communicate
in a foreign language and keep the audience glued to its seats from
beginning to end. A grand spectacle, filled with evocative ideas,
overwhelming vitality"; from London, "The great virtue, apart from
the show's intrinsic merit, is to open our eyes to a vibrant new theatrical expression. I had no idea this sort of work—if indeed it is
typical—is taking place in the Third World"; from Madrid, "Ladies
and Gentlemen: *Macunaíma* is to the theatre what *One Hundred
Years of Solitude* is to the novel"; from Melbourne, "The impact of
Macunaíma puts it up with the great productions of Peter Brook and
Pina Bausch."[3] Post-1985 reviews are equally encomiastic: from
Montreal, "Pity those who did not go to the Monument National
Theatre on Tuesday or Wednesday to see *Macunaíma,* the most
beautiful theatrical spectacle—or should we say, the loveliest cele-
bration of inventiveness—we have yet seen in the Festival of the
Americas" (Lévesque, "merveilleux"); from the Baleares, "one of the
most important spectacles—in the broadest sense of the word—of
the last decade" (Rotger, "poderoso").

Nelson 2 Rodrigues

The company had undergone several changes by 1980: some members had left, and as a result of the success of the first production the
name had been changed to Grupo Macunaíma. Antunes Filho continued in his role as sole guiding force, and he initiated rehearsals for
a new work based on the plays of Nelson Rodrigues. Inspired by the
stagings of Robert Wilson, which he had seen during the 1970s, the
director also began experimenting with the concepts of Carl Jung
and Mircea Eliade. Antunes was interested in Jungian archetypes
for several reasons, one of which was to change the stereotype of
Nelson Rodrigues as an author of contemporary comedies of man-

ners. This attempt to change the playwright's image would incur the wrath of many critics and theatre artists, among them Teatro Oficina's José Celso, according to whom the director of Grupo Macunaíma was "refining and elaborating the colonial tradition installed in Brazil by the Teatro Brasileiro de Comédia. [Antunes] has translated Nelson Rodrigues to German and Italian, and the upshot has been to destroy his greatest strength: his humorous and sardonic side" (quoted in "vendaval," *Isto É*). José Celso's objection is based on the criticism leveled at the TBC by Augusto Boal and others, according to which that company had squelched Brazil's genuine "popular" theatre, of which the quintessential representative was the comedies of manners staged by Procópio Ferreira. The comedy of manners, however, had already become a worn-out formula, well before the establishment of the TBC. What Antunes was attempting to reveal were levels in Nelson Rodrigues beyond and beneath the comedic elements. Because he was applying the theories of Mircea Eliade, he decided to call the production *Nelson Rodrigues o Eterno Retorno* (Nelson Rodrigues the Eternal Return). He tested several of the playwright's works during the fifteen-month rehearsal period. The company settled initially on six plays: *A Falecida* (The Dead Woman), *Álbum de Família* (Family Album), *Os Sete Gatinhos* (The Seven Kittens), *Boca de Ouro* (Golden Mouth), *Beijo no Asfalto* (Kiss on the Asphalt), and *Toda Nudez Será Castigada* (All Nakedness Will Be Punished). It soon became apparent that the resulting production would have an unmanageably long running time, and the group began the painful process of cutting scenes and even plays that had been extensively rehearsed, "otherwise the performance would have lasted 15 hours. The process of cutting was a collective effort, and in the end the essence of Nelson's texts remained" (Zeitel, interview). The first plays to go were *Sete Gatinhos* and *Beijo no Asfalto*. The running time was now reduced to three hours.

The final result was an innovative production that reinforced the reputation the company had gained with *Macunaíma*. The original staging and the subsequent shorter version—including only *Álbum* and *Nudez*, it was retitled *Nelson 2 Rodrigues*—saw 235 performances, from the São Paulo opening on 6 May 1981, to the final presentation in Madrid on 13 March 1985. The two versions of *Nelson 2 Rodrigues* toured Brazil and three European countries: Germany, England, and Spain.

Critical reaction to the production has been, as in the case of *Macunaíma*, encomiastic. The Brazilian critics: "*Nelson 2 Rodrigues* celebrates . . . the capacity to speak beyond consciousness and establishes a dialogue between the stage and the deepest images in the spectator's unconscious"; "The poetry of the staging consists in its transformation of two plays into a sequence of scenes in which pathos intermingles with lyricism. . . . Horror and waltz, innocence lost and eternally dreamed of"; "The perfect scenic creation [producing] immense aesthetic pleasure."[4]

The foreign critics: a British critic compares *Nelson 2 Rodrigues* to "scenes from Balzac darkened and made murderous under the Brazilian sun" and states that the director's "superb stagecraft conveys ironies that need no translation" (Hudson, "Darkness"). According to a German critic, "the way in which Antunes Filho and his group enrich their 'poor theatre' with their refined, expressive, and imaginative style could serve as a model for German theatre."[5]

Romeu e Julieta (*Romeo and Juliet*)

In 1982, after the international tour of *Nelson 2 Rodrigues*, Grupo Macunaíma gained the support of the Serviço Social do Comércio (SESC), a private entity supported by the São Paulo business community whose purpose is to carry out diverse social and educational activities and to facilitate access to cultural events at little or no cost. SESC sponsors seminars, courses, and amateur theatre festivals. Antunes's company also gained use of the Anchieta Theatre in downtown São Paulo, one of many well-equipped cultural spaces maintained by SESC. Under the organization's sponsorship, Grupo Macunaíma has become part of the Centro de Pesquisa Teatral (CPT), or Center for Theatre Research, which in addition to staging plays, offers classes on acting, play writing, and design.

SESC would fund Grupo Macunaíma's third project, Shakespeare's *Romeo and Juliet* (*Romeu e Julieta*). Play rehearsals lasted nearly a year and a half, beginning in late 1982, and the final result was a stage production with a running time of an hour and forty minutes, which was performed 123 times. It toured Brazil, Spain, and Germany, opening in São Paulo on 26 April 1984, and closing in Munich on 9 June 1985.

Antunes Filho's conceptual basis for the staging was a passage from Roland Barthes's *Fragments d'un Discours Amoureux* (*Fragments of a Lover's Discourse*), quoted in the 1984 program: "The discourse of love is today an extremely lonely one. Perhaps such discourse is spoken by thousands of people (who knows?), but it has no defenders. It has been totally abandoned by neighboring languages, or ignored, scorned, or mocked by them; it has been excluded not only from power, but from its mechanisms (science, knowledge, art). Whenever the very power of a discourse condemns it to obsolescence, ostracizes it from the community, it is left only with the inconsequential, confined space of an affirmation." Leyla Perrone-Moisés (1984 program) defines the lover's discourse in this way: "In the final phase of his life, Barthes often used the adjective 'amorous' to refer to several personal practices: traveling, listening, teaching, but especially writing." For Barthes, the lover's discourse was a means to combat "the ferocious 'machines of thought'; the discourses of Certainty, Arrogance, and Triumph."

Inspired by Barthes's theories, Antunes Filho saw in Shakespeare's play a means to express a nondogmatic ideology, the lover's discourse, in opposition to the discourse of power. In the 1984 program the director explains the connection: "*Romeo and Juliet* is a subterranean song against stereotypes, against authoritarian rules and powers." More concretely, he explained to a São Paulo reporter why he utilized in the production the music of the Beatles: "'We linked the nostalgia for the loss of the Beatles to the nostalgia of *Romeo and Juliet*'" (Pereira, "dose tripla"). That is, "both Shakespeare and the Beatles began with a genre of youth—the impassioned poetry of love and sex—and leapt effortlessly into the full human comedy, as understood in their respective eras" (Okun, "To Be[atles]"). Several Beatles songs were heard during the production. The most evocative example was "Lucy in the Sky with Diamonds," played during Juliet's funeral.

The critics once again responded very positively: "Without scenery, the staging suggests ballrooms, narrow medieval streets, bed chambers, and forests, which only the magician Antunes is able to do with such simple ingredients" ("vendaval," *Isto É*); "Antunes works with such concentration, such emphasis on the fundamental meanings of the play, that the text, in his hands, reappears in its purest essence" ("Milagres"). Sábato Magaldi ("Romeu e Julieta") wrote—as he so often does—the definitive review:

> The poetry of the work just written, the truth of eternal sentiments, the beating pulse of characters who are our contemporaries, these are just a few of the emotions transmitted by *Romeo and Juliet*. . . . Antunes Filho has stripped Shakespeare's tragedy of the cold erudition the specialists have imposed on it and has recreated it in its essence. The audience receives no lessons, but is able to identify the evils that everywhere thwart human freedom to love and exist. . . . What forms the basis of the spectacle's magic? When one considers the various elements, what stands out, in my opinion, is the casting for the protagonists. I cannot imagine anyone with the charm, shape of the

face (like something out of a medieval painting), the purity, and the determination to compare with Giulia Gam in the role as Juliet. . . . Antunes's free-form adaptation is another decisive factor in the play's success. . . . Without betraying the sense and continuity of the story, he has managed to eliminate from the text everything not absolutely essential [and has maintained] the fundamental characteristics of the tragedy.

Along with *Romeo and Juliet,* in 1984 Grupo Macunaíma restaged *Nelson Rodrigues o Eterno Retorno* and retitled it *Nelson 2 Rodrigues.* The company also restaged *Macunaíma,* and linking the three productions it experimented with a repertory system, something almost unheard of in Brazil. Unfortunately, the experiment was not financially viable and was not repeated after 1984.

Augusto Matraga

The company's fourth production was performed 121 times, from its São Paulo opening on 6 May 1986 until its closing on 28 June 1987, in Freiburg, Germany. *Matraga* toured Brazil, Germany, Spain, France, and Canada.

Like the play that gave the company its name, *Augusto Matraga* is an adaptation of a Brazilian narrative classic, in this case the story "A hora e vez de Augusto Matraga" (The Hour and Time of Augusto Matraga), by João Guimarães Rosa, from his 1946 book *Sagarana.* The group began rehearsing an adaptation of the author's epic novel *Grande Sertão, Veredas,* but gave up that idea when it became clear that the running time would be excessive. Nevertheless, the research the director and actors conducted for the adaptation of the novel was utilized for *Augusto Matraga.* And for the first time one of Grupo Macunaíma's productions would include an established professional actor, Raul Cortez, in the role of the protagonist. The experiment, however, did not have very positive results. Owing to the many commitments of Cortez, an actor very much in demand for stage, film, and TV roles, the rehearsal period had to be very short, which compromised the production. The restaging in 1987, with a regular company member in the lead role, gave rise to a far more satisfactory production in terms of production values.

In great part due to the haste with which the original version of *Augusto Matraga* was staged, the Brazilian critics did not express their usual enthusiasm for the company's work: "Now, in *Augusto Matraga,* it is again Antunes Filho who shines. As to Guimarães Rosa, it is not yet the 'hour and the time' for him to shine brightly onstage" (Sérgio Conti, "Reflexos"). Foreign critics, who saw the second version, had a more positive view: "Antunes Filho's mise-en-scène is beautiful and inventive, and the acting is characterized by strong ensemble work and excellent physical preparation" (Léonardini, "western").

Ideology and Method

The application of Barthes's theories to *Romeu e Julieta* could be extended to all the group's projects. In an interview with Sábato Magaldi ("Consagração"), Antunes Filho explains that he is not interested in "'using theatre to proselytize. Which does not presuppose the absence of ideology. What it means is an ideology that is an organic part of the performance.'" This is based on the notion that "'we must put magic back into theatrical performance; this is essential for the Third World.'" He mentions, in that regard, García Márquez and Cortázar. And he defends the archetypal perspective: "'There are many who will say that the idea of collective unconscious will lead to a conservative view of history as endless repetition.'" The director insists, however, that "'surrealism and revolutionary African art [demonstrate] that magic appears only on the surface to be elitist.'" Freud and Jung, according to Antunes, ignited the bonfires of popular liberation. The magic motifs in *Macunaíma*, in his view, constitute an ideology of liberation and transformation; he does not mean revolutionary dogma, which suffers from the same rigidity as official ideologies. Antunes Filho's position is that of permanent opposition to the discourses of power; he embraces the discourses of love and youth: "'Young people wish for dialogue and they refuse to accept the imposition, the authoritarianism of those who speak in the name of truth and distort the means [and therefore] the end.'"

Barthes's concept of *discours amoureux*, which Antunes associates with young people, has influenced his rehearsal and acting methods. In our interview, Amália Zeitel described the company's approach: while working on *Macunaíma* "Antunes opted for working with young actors untainted with previous experience, with pure raw material." Rehearsals were long and arduous, and the discipline was rigorous. The actors were not paid, although meals and transportation were provided. The rehearsals for *Nelson 2 Rodrigues* operated in a similar fashion. The actors studied a wide variety of techniques—music, dance, martial arts, voice, acting methods—and there were reading assignments in a wide range of subjects. The rehearsal process, in short, constituted a school of the dramatic arts, probably the most complete and thorough of any such school in Brazil. Those who join the group receive an enormous benefit, "because it is a school where the actor receives without charge his courses and learns from Antunes's long experience." This is important to keep in mind because "there are so many schools of dramatic arts where you pay a tidy sum for mediocre classes" (Zeitel, interview).

On the downside, the company's dependence on inexperienced actors has meant that the company has been to some extent a revolving door, with less stability than stronger ensembles like Arena and Oficina, although they, too, experienced significant turnover of personnel. The tendency is exacerbated in Grupo Macunaíma, however, because Antunes Filho so totally dominates the company. All of this has given rise to a kind of *leyenda negra* surrounding Antunes's methods. The comments of Maitê Proença, an actress who worked on *Nelson 2 Rodrigues* but left the company before the play opened, summarize the anti-Antunes position: "'Working with Antunes is devastating. He requires that you give up your personal life [and] he tries to tear down the actor's personality'" ("Milagres da criação," *Veja*). In spite of such charges, there is a core of actors that has remained with the company since the beginning.

To place the director's tight control over the group in perspective, Antunes faces a general problem in Brazil today: young people who wish to become involved in theatre "lack any concept—ideological, existential, aesthetic—of continuity in their work." At the same time, "extreme individualism and the lack of a genuine collective spirit—the consequence, in part, of the education and training that prevailed during the years of the dictatorship—make group collaboration very difficult" (Michalski, *Teatro* 90). According to this perspective, to overcome the damage done during the era of authoritarianism, it is necessary to utilize a tightly disciplined approach when working with amateur actors in Brazil.

The Antunes Method has many staunch defenders: the "confidence the cast has in him may be the best indication that, in spite of the folklore that always places him in the role of the villain, Antunes is, first and foremost, a director with a highly unusual degree of competence" ("vendaval," *Isto É*). According to another actress who worked with the company, Salma Buzzar, "'There is simply no other way to obtain training as a theatre artist'" ("vendaval"). Grupo Macunaíma and the Center for Theatre Research offer unique opportunities: intensive training, both practical and theoretical, the opportunity to tour in Brazil and abroad; in short, those accepted into the program receive the equivalent of a scholarship for a first-rate theatre school.

The Grotowskian Influence

Foreign influences have been crucial to the development of modern Brazilian stagecraft: Os Comediantes and Ziembinski's Expressionism, TBC and the Italian directors, Arena and Brecht, Oficina and the international avant-garde. Grupo Macunaíma has established a paradigm for a unique form of *poor* theatre, which has had a marked influence on alternative troupes in Brazil attempting to break the commercial mold and to return to a social vision, lost during the darkest years of the military dictatorship. Grotowski's *Towards a Poor Theatre* outlines the abstract formulation and practical applications of the method he elaborated in his Polish Laboratory Theatre. The director-theoretician proposed first and foremost to overturn what he called *rich* theatre: a form of staging using "borrowed mechanisms" from movies and television and expensive scenic technology. The Polish Laboratory, on the other hand, was an actor-centered theatre in which the stage was redesigned architecturally for each performance to allow the performers to interact with the audience and in which there were no naturalistic sets or props, no recorded music or sophisticated lighting. The actor, through a complex system of *signs*,[6] continually created and recreated the meaning of text, costumes, set, and props. "By this use of controlled gesture the actor transforms the floor into a sea, a table into a confessional, a piece of iron into an animate partner, etc." (*Poor Theatre* 21). Grotowski's plays were filled with costumes made of torn bags, bathtubs serving as altars, bunkbeds becoming mountains, hammers used as "musical" instruments. "Each object must contribute not to the meaning but to the dynamic of the play; its value resides in its various uses" (Flaszen, "Akropolis" in Grotowski, *Poor Theatre* 75). Other tenets of the Grotowski system germane to my discussion are a return to mythical and ritual roots, the theatrical remaking of classical works, and the collective basis of stagecraft.

The Macunaíma company, under the firm guidance of Antunes Filho, has developed all its productions through a collective process, which has a special significance in the context of Brazil, for it bypasses sophisticated and expensive theatrical technology. This labor-intensive mode is appropriate to a Latin American theatrical milieu because it allows for what journalistic critics call "spectacular" or "epic" stagings through the utilization of human resources and creativity, without a great outlay of capital. "Raw materials" on stage signify a kind of nationalization of poor theatre; they are signs, without literal meaning, transformed variously into props, costumes, and sets according to context. While Grotowskian techniques have been adopted by European and American troupes to obtain the aesthetic result of avoiding the literalness of naturalistic sets, for Brazilian theatre they take on the social function of constantly reminding the audience of a reality characterized by few material resources for the many. The company's poor-theatre approach and its collective praxis also pertain to the search for a national language of the stage founded on the roots of Brazilian culture: myths, rituals, and variegated folkloric-popular modes. In order to examine the Grotowskian influence, I discuss below the productions of *Macunaíma* and *Augusto Matraga*. Chapter 6 is devoted entirely to *Nelson ? Rodrigues.*

Macunaíma[7]

Macunaíma, the play that gave the company its name, is the stage adaptation of a Brazilian classic, Mário de Andrade's 1928 narrative *rapsódia.*[8] Both the original text and staging draw heavily on traditional popular dances, songs, and oral narrative, and on Amerindian and Afro-Brazilian ritual. The production introduces the poor-theatre and collective techniques that have come to characterize all the group's work.

To understand how the rhapsody and the play transform popular culture, I refer to the theories of the Soviet critic Mikhail Bakhtin.[9] Bakhtin (1895–1975) is best known for his concept of *carnivalization*, with which he interprets Rabelais, and while other scholars have applied it to examples of contemporary literature, it more clearly defines *Macunaíma*. This is because Andrade's narrative takes in a universe still abundant in the folkloric modes that Bakhtin relates to Renaissance literature; in modern Europe and the United States the alternate and subversive world of carnival has little of the vitality it retains in Brazil. According to the Russian critic, there existed a vast medieval and Renaissance world of comic forms and modalities that mocked officialdom, both ecclesiastical and secular. This popular humor was especially prevalent during the time of carnival, which lasted—as it still does for the poorer classes in Brazil—for several months. Carnival, with its parodies of formal ceremonies, offered a vision of a life outside the spheres of power, a life of liberty and renovation. If the rituals of officialdom meant static cycles of nonchange, the carnivalesque philosophy was based on change itself. Carnival thus freed the people from the immutability of social hierarchy. During carnival, according to Bakhtin's utopian vision, the people were reborn into purely human relationships based on equality.

Mário de Andrade's narrative is filled with carnivalized burlesque forms and folkloric modes and the adaptation alters the rhapsody's verbal structures into visual images. In the production's most famous scene, a band of carnival dancers, or *bloco*, crosses the stage in slow motion, singing a samba, sotto voce and a cappella: "Hail Saint Anthony, patron saint of our military, which in 1888 was commissioned for its glorious service."[10] The verbal and visual parody mocks the Brazilian armed forces, whose "glorious service" has consisted of seizing power in several coups. The carnival band's "parade" across the stage and the actors' grotesque position and movement, the artificial smiles frozen on their faces, pillory the military parades—rituals that consecrate power—which Latin American generals are so fond of. The words of the samba ridicule the armed forces' "patriotic" mission.

Grupo Macunaíma recreates a popular festivity—the street carnival bands—to establish a unique collective stagecraft. That is, the company turns the *bloco* into a paradigm to carnivalize its entire performing style. Like the archaic universe described by Bakhtin, Antunes Filho and his actors have created a separate extraofficial world. Faithful to the rhapsodic structure of Mário de Andrade's text, the production includes innumerable variations on the *bloco* theme. There are bands of parrots, lice, and other fauna. There is a constant parade of statues, Indians performing ritual dances, folk dancers, groups of São Paulo workers. The play begins with a *bloco* performing a dance that suggests laborers tearing up a street with jackhammers. Their perfectly synchronized movements correspond to the rigidity they are subjected to by those who hold power. Soon, however, they metamorphose into a band of Indians performing a ritual dance; that is, the contemporary status quo is submerged in an extraofficial archaic world.

In addition to the *blocos*, the carnivalesque philosophy corresponds to the poor-theatre techniques. Carnival, according to Bakhtin, liberates humankind from all that is immutable. The objects and costumes created for *Macunaíma* represent the materialization of carnival's opposition to the static and completed forms of officialdom. In this regard, there are endless variations on uses for raw materials. A long strip of white cloth is transformed variously into a river, a shroud, an apartment, a jungle. Newsprint is used for costumes, masks, bonfires, food, parts of houses, miniature hot-air balloons; that is, newspapers, a literate product of the world of power—at least in much of Latin America—are broken down into a raw material, becoming, as it were, uncivilized. There is, however, one scene in which newspapers are portrayed—in carnivalesque par-

ody—within their official (i.e., civilized) context. When Macunaíma—the protagonist of the play—and his brothers leave the
jungle and arrive in the metropolis of São Paulo, they see a many-
legged monster that terrifies them. The monster is in fact a *bloco* of
city-dwellers, hiding behind their newspapers, moving as a single
body on their way to work. The urban beings, appendages of their
civilized newspapers, appear as giant insects to the barbarians of the
forest.

The production uses carnivalesque parody to annul the world of
power. Against the eternal cycle of repression, Grupo Macunaíma
counterposes the popular cycle of eternal change and holds the dark
solemnity of corrupt governments—military and civilian—up to
the light of carnival's corrosive humor. The implication is that renovation of Brazilian society must come from popular segments so far
absent from the spheres of power. And more concretely, the stage
adaptation of *Macunaíma* calls for a Brazilian theatrical renewal
based on the nation's deepest and most ancient roots. The company,
therefore, does not utilize carnival motifs in a mere formal way but
as a perception of liberation and transformation. As in the case of
Bakhtin's theories, that perception is festive and not dogmatic, contrary to official ideologies; there is no room for dogma in the universe of carnival.[11] *Macunaíma*, in short, "carnivalizes the present
because it is a hope for the future" (Holquist, in Bakhtin, *Rabelais*
xxii–xxiii).

Augusto Matraga[12]

The 1986–87 production of *Augusto Matraga*, like *Macunaíma*, is
an excellent example of the company's roots-based stagecraft. The
story and the play incorporate the mythology of the *sertão* (northeastern Brazilian backlands), with its abundance of folkloric traditions, religious fanaticism, and epic conflicts between good and evil,
banditry and sainthood.

Grupo Macunaíma's production fills the stage with an endless
stream of religious and mythical elements, making visual what
Guimarães Rosa's text only suggests. As the fourth line of the story
aridly states: "the procession entered, the prayer ended" ("A hora e
vez" 319). From this minimal verbal cue, Antunes Filho and his
company have constructed an elaborate procession that explodes
from offstage to begin the play.[13] The members of the procession are
dressed in traditional religious garb: angel, monk—in the guise of
Saint Francis of Assisi[14]—black-robed penitents with a cross, and
poor villagers, dressed in rags and carrying a litter with an image of

the Virgin and various and sundry offerings; the litter is brilliantly lit by candles. The procession winds about the stage in dreamlike slow motion, and then stops in one corner of the stage, where the participants kneel and begin a communal prayer, which is interrupted by laughter emitted by a puppet resembling the devil. This visual-auditory cue foreshadows one of the basic themes in the story: the conflict between good and evil, between god and the devil.

The group has created for the staging a visual frame that refers simultaneously to Christian liturgy, folkloric-popular culture, and the nature of everyday life and work in the *sertão*. The frame is the *presépio*, or Nativity scene, which has a ritual-mythic function within Catholic liturgy as an expression of the yearly celebration of Christ's birth. In the context of the short story and play, the protagonist Augusto Matraga in a sense is born (or reborn) in humble circumstances and in the arid environment of the *sertão*. In Brazil the *presépio* is much more: it is a popular folkloric tradition. In his novel *Gabriela, Cravo e Canela* (*Gabriela, Clove and Cinnamon*), Bahian writer Jorge Amado describes a spectacular *presépio* constructed over the years by two sisters and which comes to be considered communal property. The manger scene has been reduced to a small detail in the center of a universe filled with a great diversity of pictures of places and people cut out from magazines.

Grupo Macunaíma's theatrical *presépio*, like Jorge Amado's, presents not only the birth of "Christ"—that is, the protagonist's mystical awakening—but a vast array of scenes of life in the *sertão*. The play could be described as a Nativity scene in motion, a choreogaphed *presépio*, with a wide assortment of people and animals constantly flowing and racing across the stage indicating phases of life. Energy explodes from offstage to onstage throughout the production; there is a sense of great masses of people, such as migrating *retirantes* or bands of peasants fleeing the drought-stricken Northeast. Nativity scenes usually call to mind static images, but the Brazilian troupe does not frame its piece with a series of fixed tableaux. Rather, it has created a living *presépio* that moves constantly, not only across the stage but in the mind of the spectator across the whole expanse of the backlands.

On his voyages across the *sertão*/stage Augusto Matraga encounters herds of oxen—played by actors in stylized movement and posture—driven by *vaqueiros* (cowpunchers); women of the region sowing seeds (confetti), smoking their characteristic pipes, and carrying parcels and baskets on their heads; washerwomen singing at the river's edge; a woman giving birth; a lady, representative of the wealthy class, dressed in white with a parasol and riding a horse;

peasants plowing and reaping the harvest and stacking bundles of sugarcane; a man rowing a boat, reminiscent of Chinese circus pantomime; a blind *repentista*, or improvisational folk singer; the paradigmatic politician in white linen suit and sunglasses; a wandering religious sect; black-robed penitents; a mendicant leper, a deathlike figure covered with black rags; *cangaceiros*, or bandits. This great assemblage, created entirely through blocking, crosses the stage at many levels and angles and in varying patterns in a richly textured choreography.

One of the most impressive pieces of choreography in the *presépio* frame is the fight to the death between the bandit chieftain Joãozinho Bem-Bem[15] and Matraga. The two pull their knives, and the protagonist's donkey Jericó initiates the battle by stamping three times on the ground/stage, setting off a beating of hooves by the whole company of actors, who during the fight become a herd of cattle. The combatants are swallowed up by the herd, and the fight is dramatically suggested by the violent movement of the collective body, the occasional flash of a knife blade, and the dramatic pounding of hooves. When the herd parts, the battle is over; the audience has not really seen it but for that reason felt it even more intensely. The two men emerge from the fray mortally wounded, and the collective herd stampedes offstage. When Matraga and Bem-Bem fall dead, the donkey/actor enters the stage and picks up a black box and places it at Matraga's feet. The box, which had previously served as an ammunition case, now is transformed into a gravestone. Jericó moves off to the side, stops, and looks at the grave, while the lights dim slowly to blackout, ending the play.

The staging abounds with choreographed scenes from everyday life, many of which were described above; a further dimension is the collective labor which is the basis of existence in the *sertão* and which, therefore, often takes the form of renewal ceremony. The blocking that most clearly illustrates this ritual notion is a kind of wood-stacking dance. The collective body of actors carries bundles of wood across the stage and piles them in changing patterns. The repetition and the festive, danceclike movements are not naturalistic; rather, they correspond to collective ritual. Other ceremonial movement in the production is also accompanied by rhythmical patterns, which the actors create with a variety of objects, like the "musical" hammers in a Grotowski piece. For example, the mendicant leper beats out a rhythm with his tin cup. The most significant forms of rhythm are created by the beating of feet and "hooves," using the stage itself as an instrument, just as feet "play" the bare ground in Afro-Brazilian and Amerindian festivals; in the latter case, ceremonial music is linked directly to the earth and nature. In this way, the staging of *Augusto Matraga* has recaptured one dimension of the archaic roots of Brazilian culture. The ideology of roots also extends to the poor-theatre aesthetic applied to the production design.

The lack of a set suggests perfectly the *sertão* in its expansive barrenness and poverty. All props are brought on- and off-stage by the actors, and as in the case of the Grotowskian model, they may be multifunctional: one example is the transformation of a munitions case into a gravestone; another is a plain black scrim that represents a cave. And the objects themselves result from the company's theatricalization of the simple and natural materials and the generalized poverty of the Latin American environment, particularly such semifeudal regions as the *sertão*. To express this idea with an oxymoron, there is a wealth of poverty in the production: innumerable objects characteristic of the backlands correspond to the richness of craftsmanship, to the ingenious and manifold artisans' manipulation of limited local resources. One could say the same about the region's oral tradition: fecundity and imagination based on apparent simplicity. It is that popular linguistic material which Guimarães Rosa recasts in his prose. Antunes Filho, because he works in a visual medium, recreates the *sertão*'s craftsmanship. The raw materials appearing in the play are wood, stone, straw, iron, clay, and animal hides. The audience observes their transformation into inventively crafted objects. The *cangaceiros*'s characteristic clothing is prominently featured: the leather hat resembling a half-moon lying on its side, decorated with emblems, and the jacket, chaps, sandals, and saddlebags, also made of leather. Sackcloth is used for clothing and blankets. Visible in nearly every scene is a potpourri of utensils and other practical objects: wooden plates, boxes, carts, plow, stools, buckets, and tools, as well as clay vases and bottles, gourds, baskets, kerosene lamps, and cowbells. The raw materials of nature and cultivation are also presented directly: leaves, stones, bamboo sticks, coconut shells, bread, corn, cassava. The colors are earth tones of brown, black, and gray. Finally, the group incorporates a material dimension that links nature with its mythical re-creation in the human sphere: the elements of water, earth, and fire are utilized throughout *Augusto Matraga* in various ceremonies, such as the protagonists's rite of purification.

Conclusion

The São Paulo troupe has adopted many tenets of Grotowski's Polish Laboratory Theatre and recast them to establish a unique Brazilian poor-theatre paradigm. It is ironic that while poor, collective, and physical theatrical modes are considered by many in Europe and the United States to be passé, in the Latin American context they constitute an enduring legacy. But perhaps there is no irony here: the social transformation of Grotowski's methods is akin to what Latin American magic-realist writers have done with surrealism. Writers like Julio Cortázar and Gabriel García Márquez have taken a European mode based on abstract notions—the magic, as it were, like carnival, long absent from surrealist artists' lives—and have fitted it to a reality where the magic is still afoot.

Not all Laboratory Theater principles suit Grupo Macunaíma's purposes. In the first place, Grotowski never intended to establish a dogma but a flexible set of possibilities. In the second place, the foundation of his stagecraft was more spiritual than social. In the third place, the Laboratory's practice of architecturally redesigning the performing space for each production and playing to small, select audiences would be a luxury few if any theatres in Latin America—where state support is practically nonexistent—could afford. Finally, one of the Polish director's fundamental purposes, the forcible encounter between actors and audience, whether through participation or set design, has led frequently to disastrous results—Oficina's theatre of aggression is a good example—and has deservedly been abandoned for the most part. That is because so-called audience participation is based on a power relationship: the actors have all the control and the spectators are subjected to the actors' sphere of power, which turns the encounter into a form of repression. Grupo Macunaíma, on the other hand, seeks a collective encounter based on carnival's liberating spirit, where no one is physically forced to submit to anyone else's theatrical authority. The company's stagings symbolize, like Bakhtin's vision of a popular universe, the people's rebirth into a more human and equal condition.

6. *Nelson 2 Rodrigues*

The four-decade cycle of the modern Brazilian stage covered in this book begins and ends with epochal stagings of works by playwright Nelson Rodrigues (1912–1980). Chapters 1 and 2 examine the nation's entrance into the modern theatrical era via Os Comediantes's production of *Vestido de Noiva* (*Bridal Gown*), directed by Zbigniew Ziembinski. The most recent milestone in this cycle was Grupo Macunaíma's 1984 staging of Nelson Rodrigues's plays *Álbum de Família* (*Family Album*) and *Toda Nudez Será Castigada* (*All Nakedness Will Be Punished*), in a production entitled *Nelson 2 Rodrigues*. The playwright's strategic position is no coincidence; Nelson Rodrigues is the most revolutionary and challenging figure in Brazilian dramaturgy. While directors Zbigniew Ziembinski, José Renato, Augusto Boal, José Celso, and Antunes Filho and designers Tomás Santa Rosa, Hélio Eichbauer, and Flávio Império have been widely recognized for their pioneering work in Brazilian stagecraft, Nelson Rodrigues is the one modern dramatist whose name deserves placement alongside theirs. His specific stage directions and the very mythical and archetypal structure of his plays have excited the imaginations of a few exceptional directors and have led to stagings that have changed the course of Brazilian theatrical history.

There is a sharp irony here. Nelson Rodrigues shared with Ziembinski the responsibility for manifold changes wrought in Brazilian theatre. His creation of a new language of the stage and exploration of the forbidden zones of the psyche have influenced much of Brazilian dramaturgy. But he would receive no further acclaim as a playwright for decades. (His newspaper column, "Life as it is," continued to be very popular.) His 1945 play *Family Album*, which marks the beginning of the author's mythic cycle, enraged the public and won for him the censor's muzzle. Even when his works were not censored, they were always controversial. His exploration of sexual themes incensed arbiters of good taste and officialdom and brought down upon him charges of immorality and perversion. The TBC was too concerned with good taste to have staged his works, and Arena and Oficina would not consider them because he supported the military dictatorship.[1] In spite of those problems, Nelson Rodrigues continued to write and produce his plays. A few stagings were creative and intelligent, but most were failures. His work was too bold; the stage itself would not begin to catch up to his vision for decades.

Nelson Rodrigues responded to the success of *Bridal Gown* with the kind of audacity that would become his trademark: "'I went on to *Family Album*, which is an anti–*Bridal Gown*. Theatre is truly a laceration, an abscess; it doesn't have to be a liqueur-filled bonbon'" (quoted by Magaldi, in Rodrigues, *Teatro Completo I* 21). Although not as experimental in terms of its stagecraft as *Bridal Gown*, *Album*'s social and psychological vision is on the cutting edge. The author included it in a class of works he called his *unpleasant plays:* "'They are pestilent, fetid works, by themselves capable of producing typhus and malaria in the audience'" (quoted by Magaldi, in Rodrigues, *Teatro Completo II* 13). The playwright went much further than before in tearing away his characters' veils of self-censorship and in allowing brutal explosions of submerged emotion. "Unaccustomed to this shock treatment, the critics withdrew and the police organs banned [*Album*] for 22 years" (Magaldi, *Dramaturgia* 51). His former admirers now considered him obscene, perverse, sacrilegious, immoral, morbid, and literarily inept; he was accused of provoking scandal rather than creating art. His subsequent mythic plays, this *unpleasant theatre*, would suffer the same condemnation until the 1970s. "I believe the reactions against *Family Album* were due to moral rather than artistic judgment of his work, and to the application of aesthetic canons and codes unrelated to the author's designs. Ethical considerations were ruled by narrow-minded attitudes: fear and loathing in the face of incest. . . . If there had been a didactic clarification regarding the play's intentions, *Album*'s fate probably would have been different." (Magaldi, in Rodrigues, *Teatro Completo 2:* 14).

Finally, in 1981, Antunes Filho and his Grupo Macunaíma carried out a rescue operation and successfully staged *Family Album* as part of the production entitled *Nelson Rodrigues o Eterno Retorno*, restaged in 1984 as *Nelson 2 Rodrigues.*

Family Album: Text

The play, a terrifying journey through a murderous web of incestuous relationships, deals with a large landholding family in rural

Minas Gerais state, 1924. Family members include Jonas, the father, his wife Senhorinha, the children, Glória, Edmundo, Guilherme, and Nonô, and Senhorinha's sister Rute. The family photographs constitute the counterpoint to the tragedy. A social columnist, the Speaker, makes ludicrous comments on the pictures. The photos deal mostly with past action while the main plot takes place in the present. The story seems on the surface melodramatic, improbable. There is no police investigation of the many deaths, coincidences abound, emotional expression is apocalyptic, stilted, and naive. The play at times leaves the reader wondering if Nelson Rodrigues has written a parody of a melodrama with an incestuous bent, in which the romantic hero/heroine's beloved, for whom he/she pledges undying love and fealty, is his/her mother/father/daughter/son. A closer reading and an insightful staging, however, reveal something quite different and unexpected.

Family Album cannot be judged according to the realist canon, whose rules of cause and effect the work suspends while it carries the reader into a mythical and archetypal universe. In spite of a specific time and place, the real action of the play conforms to the characters' inner lives. Outside reality is merely situational. *Album* tears away social masks to reveal certain inner truths. Nelson Rodrigues presents the action in *Bridal Gown* from the perspective of Alaíde's hallucinations and memories, and this external projection of hidden zones of the unconscious—and in other plays his exposure of perversions and taboos—brings his work in close proximity to Expressionism. "His penchant for invading his characters' intimacy, freeing them from the censorship that disciplines social intercourse . . . gives rise to the shocking explorations of Olegário, Alaíde, Madame Clessy, Jonas" (Magaldi, *Dramaturgia* 40).

Nelson Rodrigues's characters overturn social and moral codes by revealing their deepest yearnings and by speaking directly from the unconscious. Dialogue in *Family Album* and other mythic plays is filled with expressions of forbidden sex, fear, and murderous desire. What would normally be repressed is shouted on the stage; there is no sublimation. A common procedure in presenting characters theatrically is to reveal their inner selves through the play of masks and social exchange. The Western realist-naturalist theatrical tradition, in fact, mirrors a social norm that demands psychological self-censorship. Nelson Rodrigues, however, ignored norms that would cloud the brittle clarity with which he vowed to display the human image onstage, and so he has presented his characters directly, from the inside out, without social masks and normative behavior. Some of his mythic plays (e.g., *Dorotéia*) carry this inside-out process so far that the characters seem not like real people but abstractions, symbols of emotions, as if they represented only the unconscious. "The zone of the conscious mind is discarded because it is part of [social] convention" (*Dramaturgia* 52). What is important here is that in the post-*Gown* mythic works the playwright's creatures lose contact with external reality as he attempts to bring out their inner selves, their essential truth, even if it means the sacrifice of the social being.

That is why the behavior of figures like Jonas at times strains credulity: there is no barrier between desire and act. If the characters in *Family Album* "obeyed social norms, they would certainly repress much of what is shouted on the stage. The incest would be sublimated . . ." (51). Instead, they confess openly the most horrible crimes that leap from the hidden recesses of unconscious urges. We learn, for example, that Jonas, after impregnating a deaf-mute, kicked her in the stomach and killed her. In some of their statements, the characters return to an infantile state of primordial desire, fear, and rage, piercing the shield of social convention. Tia Rute complains to her sister Senhorinha that her mother never cared for her and used to watch Senhorinha bathe: "WHY DIDN'T SHE EVER REMEMBER TO WATCH ME BATHE?" (*Album* 81). And all the members of *Album*'s family participate in a vortex of incestuous relationships. The principal reason for these actions and utterances is that the work suspends the realist-naturalist rules of cause and effect and carries the reader/spectator into a mythical and archetypal universe.

Although the setting of the play is clearly specified—a plantation in the state of Minas Gerais, early 1900s—the characters live in an atemporal space, outside of society, law, and history. Jonas's clan symbolizes the mythical, primordial family, *ab origine*. The play begins with the album photo depicting Jonas and Senhorinha's wedding in 1900. Both the marriage ritual and the date represent notions of beginning (birth, century). Jonas and Senhorinha exist "before History and Civilization" (Magaldi, in Rodrigues *Teatro Completo II* 15), and thus become a kind of Adam and Eve whose behavior obeys the myths of humankind, which persist in the archetypal dimensions of the collective unconscious.

Director Antunes Filho utilized Mircea Eliade's theories on the myth of the eternal return to inform his 1981 and 1984 stagings, hence the inclusion of the words *eterno retorno* in the first title. Antunes understands that *Album* in particular corresponds to Eliade's view of archaic or primitive societies, whose members perceive time in a cyclical manner. That is, Eliade explains those societies in terms of a metaphysical ontology according to which the things of this world have value only when they are part of a transcendent reality, which is revealed by symbols and rituals. Religious and ritual acts repeat the mythical examples or paradigms established by the gods and heroes *in illo tempore,* in the time of Creation; human acts in this way become divine and therefore legitimate. Those acts not included in the sacred and mythical categories are empty of meaning; they lack reality. On the other hand, all ritual repetitions of the original Creation suspend profane time and project humankind back to mythical time. The members of archaic societies thus live in a continuous and eternal present. In spite of the atemporal conception, primitive cultures uphold the notion of the periodicity of time, year, cycle; that is, life is regenerated periodically. Such regeneration leads to a new Creation, and rituals—antirituals, really—are conducted for the expulsion of demons, before and after the new year or cycle, during which the world of the living is invaded by the dead, and social norms are suspended. The antirituals may take the form of orgies and other behavioral excesses, which serve to annul the old year or cycle and constitute a form of purification, an eternal return to "pure" time, to the mythical moment of passage from Chaos to Cosmos. Finally, the concept of continuous regeneration is related to the cycles of nature: the seasons, the phases of the moon, the rising and setting sun, recurring natural catastrophes. Humankind also regenerates, appears, and disappears, in a grand cycle of eternal return. Degeneration and destruction are necessary for the beginning of the new cycles, just as death and the occasional sacrifice of individuals are necessary for the regeneration of humanity.

In *Family Album* Nelson Rodrigues has projected his characters back to the creation myths, to the time before time, and their behavior will correspond not to psychological and social realism but to mythical patterns. They will fulfill the implacable destiny of the eternal cycle. Their tragic, accursed fate is bound up in the familial myths of Electra and Oedipus. (The pregnant girl whose screams are heard throughout the play and who finally dies literally places a curse on the family.) At the same time, the characters are conscious of their mythical stature, which they use to justify their actions. Jonas believes that in his position as father, as a kind of biblical patriarch—*Family Album*'s structure is in many ways biblical—he deserves the sacred respect of his family. He sees himself as godlike and his behavior—the seduction and murder of young girls—beyond censure. (One may posit that Jonas's attitude represents all those who commit evil in the name of religion or ideology.) He surrounds his sexual desire for his daughter with a religious aura. He transforms—one might say dehumanizes—Glória into a "porcelain saint," an "angelic image." Jonas identifies all his victims with Glória, and when she dies he announces the end of desire in the world.

While the wedding, in 1900, begat the mythical world, it is Glória's return to the plantation that precipitates the main action of the play. The mere mention of her name brings a change over the other family members, for they imagine she represents what they are not: primordial innocence. But she also embodies the myth of Electra. Like the other characters, Glória insists on the purity of her feelings and imbues her incestuous love with religious meaning; she sees Jonas as a Christ-like figure.

Senhorinha burns with incestuous passion for her three sons, which she realized the moment each was born. That is, her incestuous feelings go back to the beginning of time and creation, symbolized by her sons' births. Her deepest love is for Nonô, and by seducing him she triggered Jonas's own pattern of sexual abuse and the long series of terrible events culminating in the violent death of most of the family members. Senhorinha's seduction of Nonô, the family's original sin, also gave rise to his madness, which in itself takes on a mythical aura, for he lives naked in the forest like a wild animal. That is, he is natural man, the noble savage, living in a state *ab origine,* before the advent of civilization. To put it another way, Nonô is Adam naked in the Garden, and Senhorinha wishes to be his Eve. So that she can be free to love him without restraint, she kills her husband.

The sons in turn embody the Oedipus myth. Incestuous feelings for Senhorinha lead them to patricidal fantasies and deadly sibling rivalry. Edmundo does not want his mother to see Nonô, the beautiful naked savage, for he intuits her incestuous love for his mad brother, and he describes to her a mythic time of Oedipal bliss, *ab origine:* "Heaven, before birth, was your womb" (*Album* 102). Incest, then, becomes a longing for paradise lost. Guilherme, on the other hand, castrates himself to purge his sexual desires. When he cannot overcome the family destiny, he transfers the incestuous obsession to his sister Glória, whom he imagines to be purity incarnate. In the end, upon discovering that she embodies the myth of Electra, he murders her to prevent her seduction by Jonas. All of the family's passions, whether lustful or murderous, are turned inward and fulfilled within its enclosed incestuous circle. Heloísa, whose husband had never known her sexually, laments that Edmundo was indifferent to all those outside his family: "He was unable to love, or to hate, anyone else" (*Album* 112). Edmundo's own words demonstrate the mythical nature of the family prison, when he explains his feeling that nothing exists in the world but his family, which is "the first and the only one" (*Album* 102).

While Jonas and Senhorinha's family life represents a creation myth, the play's action paradoxically takes place at the end of the mythic cycle, in the phase of chaos and destruction, before regeneration. Mircea Eliade describes this phase in the context of primitive societies as a time of orgies and unrestraint, the unleashing of demons. *Album* deals with Jonas's libertinage and the unleashing of the family's sex and death demons. According to Amália Zeitel, death in the play does not constitute crime against human life; it signifies ritual passage, the process of liberation toward rebirth, sacrifice leading to liberation. Nelson Rodrigues "defends man's right to be as he is and to have full power over his own acts and being." However, the "circumstances of man's life, when governed by himself, are disastrous." There is but one alternative: "Only rebirth and resurrection remain as a means of redemption, [leading to] an age of love" (Zeitel, program). Scrutiny of the playtext tends to support this view. At the end of the play, after the death of Jonas, the author writes, "Dona Senhorinha leaves to find Nonô and start a new life" (*Album* 119). To reinforce the mythical idea of eternal return, death leading to rebirth, "a new life," the playwright ends *Family Album* with a funeral prayer in Latin, an ancient ritual that perpetuates the eternal cycle of birth/death/rebirth.

"In Nelson Rodrigues the excavation takes us back to the archeological roots of the human being" (Zeitel, program), to the ancient myths, which persist in the instinctual repository that Jung calls the collective unconscious and which contains the archetypes.[2] Not only do *Family Album*'s characters project the "archeological roots" directly, they are themselves archetypal symbols of the collective unconscious.

Jonas and Senhorinha represent two archetypes upon which the entire Jungian system hinges: the animus, the father symbol, the man within the woman; and anima, which corresponds to the mother and provides feminine characteristics for the male personality. One's relationship to these archetypes is vital for psychological development; they can either abet growth and maturity or hinder them. In their positive function, they become agents of love and spirituality. In their negative forms, they may become death demons, as Jonas and Senhorinha do when they devastate the lives of their children. Glória imagines her father a Christ-like figure. A superficial conclusion would be that she projects on Jonas the animus's highest level, its spiritual dimension. A closer examination of the father-daughter relationship, however, reveals that the Christ-like image is only a false conception perpetrated by Jonas and naively embraced by Glória. She is entrapped by the negative animus, which keeps her pathologically tied to the father figure, unable to relate to the outside world, to people beyond the *huis clos* of the plantation. The negative anima crushes the young men's spirit. Edmundo attempts to break free of maternal bonds when he marries Heloísa, but he never makes love to her. His wife characterizes the negative anima as the "other woman," a haunting presence which prevents Edmundo from consummating the marriage. And so he returns home to annihilation in the anima's embrace. The internal mother, however, is not always identical to the external mother. When Jonas reveals Senhorinha's infidelity, Edmundo turns against her. His love for his mother is really a projection of the negative anima, which ties him to an impossible dream of maternal purity, to his vision of paradise within the womb. Edmundo and his father are also possessed by the anima, locked into archetypal infancy. Accusing Senhorinha of both infidelity and frigidity, Jonas makes this startling statement: "Women are not even females!" (*Album* 105). Jonas's oxymoron expresses an infantile anima manifestation in which the man views female sexuality as repugnant, because he projects his illusion of maternal purity on all women.

In spite of the fact that *Family Album*'s characters are immersed in a mythical and archetypal universe, the reader/spectator is not likely to be satisfied that notions of "archeological roots," renewal, liberation, and the search for an age of love are the only things the play is about or that they justify all the characters' acts. One is still left with problems of sexual abuse, incest, and brutal murder. Outside the mythic context, the characters' dark side must be considered. "It is man distant from social discipline, in the exercise of uncontrolled spontaneity, given over to the delirium which has abolished the convenience of reason. Only a single pretext was needed . . . for the protagonist to feel authorized to give vent to everything that he had repressed" (Magaldi, "Trajectory"). Among the dramatist's moral concerns is the notion that "uncontrolled spontaneity" may lead to death. Although civilization betrays authentic impulses by masking or sublimating them, its values allow the continuation of life (Magaldi, in Rodrigues, *Teatro Completo I* 20).

The incest taboo in the play is the predominant expression of "uncontrolled spontaneity." Whether the characters attempt to mask incestuous feelings with moral or religious claims or give free vent to them, the result is nearly always death and destruction. Guilherme, denying his true feelings for Glória, shoots her to "save" her from Jonas. Senhorinha once tried to drown Glória, and she kills Jonas to be free to fulfill her sexual desires for Nonô. Guilherme and Edmundo commit suicide. All efforts to leave the incestuous circle of the family come to grief: Glória transfers her love for Jonas to Tereza, and their lesbian encounter results in her expulsion from the boarding school and return to the plantation; Guilherme enters a monastery and castrates himself, yet he too goes back; Edmundo's failed marriage leads to his return. They are all sucked into the vortex of "uncontrolled spontaneity," and their world ends in a paroxysm of violent death. Outsiders are also dragged into the family's maelstrom of hatred and murder. Heloísa loses her husband Edmundo to suicide. An innocent man is falsely accused by Senhorinha and killed by Jonas. And the latter, abetted by Tia Rute, victimizes countless young girls. He is the corrupter, attracted to innocence and paradoxically its destroyer. The characters display neither moral concern nor remorse, only fulfillment of desire. Each views the other family members as sexual object or target of homicidal design.

Album's male characters are torn between obsession for sexuality and for innocence. Women who are not virgins are impure, unworthy. They must be punished for their libidinous urges. Guilherme: "Mother must be humiliated. She must atone, because she desired love, she married" (*Album* 86). Yet the men in the play desire the women only as sexual objects. And all the characters, including the women, dress their carnality in religious garb. Because Jonas made love to her, Tia Rute considers him a saint, and she prostrates and degrades herself before him. But the religious pretense furnishes the characters no moral guidelines.

The play also touches upon certain points of social reality. Nelson Rodrigues, in his real-life role as police reporter, associated sex with uncontrolled urges on the part of the mighty: "Power stimulates the desire for material satisfaction, including sex" (Magaldi, *Dramaturgia* 76). Jonas uses his high social station to abuse and even murder young girls with impunity, and the victims' families, from the lower classes, collaborate with him, debasing themselves totally. His actions transform sex into a social metaphor, the rape of the poorer classes in Brazil. Extremes of human behavior do not exist only in some distant mythical universe. While the sexual exploitation of young girls by the lord of the manor reflects the Brazilian patriarchal system, incest and sexual abuse of children are not exclusive to that nation; they are timely subjects in American society as well.

All Nakedness Will Be Punished: Text

Twenty years separated *Album* and *Nakedness*. Nelson Rodrigues had gone through his mythic phase and the Carioca tragedy series, which culminated in the 1965 *Toda Nudez Será Castigada*. Sábato Magaldi writes that the Carioca tragedy combines the archetypal dimensions of the mythic plays with the local color and concrete reality of Rio de Janeiro (Magaldi, *Dramaturgia* 63). The Carioca tragedies suffered a kinder fate than did the mythic plays. In general, their grounding in a concrete reality made them more palatable to the aesthetic standards of audiences and critics. Specifically, in regard to *All Nakedness Will Be Punished*, by 1965 the public had become more tolerant of previously taboo subjects. Finally, *Nudez* had its first success on the stage in 1967 (direction by Ziembinski) and was made into a 1973 movie (direction by Arnaldo Jabor) that received wide acclaim.[3] But the play was fixed definitively in the Brazilian dramatic firmament with Grupo Macunaíma's 1981 and 1984 productions.

Nakedness clearly has many parallels to *Family Album*. Sibling rivalry is a decisive factor in the play. Ostensibly because the protagonist Herculano, a Rio de Janeiro millionaire, did not save him from bankruptcy, his younger brother Patrício wants to destroy him. Indirectly, he seduces Herculano, using the prostitute Geni as his means. He later involves Herculano's son Serginho in what becomes a revenge plot of fratricide/patricide/matricide, for each seduction, as in *Album*, leads to the destruction of the object of incest. Although the incest is indirect or metaphorical—Patrício seduces his brother through Geni, who becomes Serginho's step-mother—its destructive intent is explicit. Patrício, for example, declares, "Geni, my brother is chaste, which is obscene. Your [naked] photograph will be a bullet in his head" (*Nudez* 31). Serginho resolves to seduce Geni only after she is married to Herculano, thus his symbolic patricide is also a fulfillment of his Oedipal complex, examined below.

It is clear then that morbid passions, fed by sex, destroy the lives of both Jonas and Herculano. The two plays include the theme of the great and potentially deadly power of sexual obsession. Although in *Nakedness* there is only one violent death, Geni's suicide, it informs the entire structure of the play. That is, a tape-recording she makes for Herculano before her suicide reveals the shocking news that she is now a dead woman, and her "voice from beyond" reveals terrible facts concerning the true story of their marriage, facts about which he is ignorant. The scenes that follow unfold in flashbacks.

From their very first encounter, death is Geni's link to Herculano.

His widowhood and her sense of impending doom awaken her initial interest. Presentiment of death is a recurring thread in the play, and it is central to their relationship: Geni insists that she will die of breast cancer, as did Herculano's wife and her own mother, although her prophecy ironically refers to her suicide. Herculano calls the beginning of their affair—he is drunk in the brothel where she works—"seventy-two hours of death." He has unleashed his sexual instincts, which, paradoxically, are for him fetid horror and death rather than life-force. While the protagonists are bound together in a fatal pas de deux, Serginho and the Aunts are equally obsessed with death. After his mother dies Serginho expects his father to commit suicide; when that does not happen he insists that Herculano dress always in mourning. Serginho himself makes daily visit to the cemetery. One of the Aunts dreams that Serginho has killed Herculano, another ironic prophecy because he contributes not to the death of his father, but to that of Geni, his step-mother/lover.

The power of the death-force in the play points to a general pathology afflicting all the characters. That is, the death fixation results from their denial of life-giving instincts. Herculano has fashioned his existence on the basis of instinctual repression. As long as he and the other family members played by the rules of that repressive structure, Herculano maintained control of all their lives. But enter Geni and the entire system collapses. Herculano unlocks his repressed instincts while continuing to uphold the old structure. That is the main conflict in the play, and it creates an untenable situation leading to a tragic outcome.

The death obsession is only one manifestation of the characters' pathological repression. Serginho particularly goes to absurd lengths to deny instinct. He refuses to remove his clothing for a medical examination and insists hysterically that his father remain eternally faithful to what has become his phantom mother. And when sexuality pushes at the restraints of the family's puritanical code, the forces of destiny are unleashed. In terms of their own life-denying moral system, the characters degrade themselves. The melodramatic scene in which Serginho espies Herculano and Geni naked in the garden leads to his drunkenness, arrest, and subsequent rape at the hands of the "Bolivian crook." Eventually, the incident activates his latent homosexuality, the root cause of his sexual phobia.

There is also a humorous side to this conflict. The old-fashioned Aunts are a parody of a social code that requires turning a blind eye to reality. The maiden aunts are so locked into traditional values that they go to absurd lengths to hold reality within their frame. For example, they convince themselves that Geni is a virgin bride. One of them solemnly swears that Serginho is "impotent like a saint."

Sexuality colors *Family Album* and *All Nakedness Will Be Punished*, although the latter play is less mythical and closer to social reality. In both works sexual obsession leads to tragedy. While in *Album* the key principle is "uncontrolled spontaneity," in *Nudez* it is the opposite problem of repression that destroys the lives of the main characters. The complex interplay between sexual phobia and desire takes them down a tortuous path that could lead to liberation or annihilation. It is this very ambivalence that tears Herculano apart. After his first wife's death he places a gun barrel in his mouth, which makes him think of "obscene penetration." This feeling of sexual nausea paradoxically saves him from suicide but later shatters his life. Repression leads to debasement, and yet this very degradation has the potential of liberating the characters from their puritanical obsessions: it awakens the dormant sexual feelings of both Herculano and Serginho. After the latter's rape, the doctor who examines him states, "this monstrosity was the point of departure for an entire life process, [a] resurrection" (*Nudez* 167). The potential "resurrection," however, fails due to their continual denial of instinct and to Patrício's machinations.

Patrício and Geni share responsibility for the tragedy because their use of sex to manipulate others has destructive consequences. Patrício, in his role as antagonist, uses sex as a weapon to avenge Herculano's lack of financial support: he preys upon his brother's vulnerability and uses Geni to tempt him; when he later brings together Geni and Serginho, it results in her suicide. It is a bitter irony that Geni is transformed by her love for Serginho, who uses her for his own devious ends. If she is prey to betrayal and manipulation, she also participated in Patrício's plots and is therefore to some extent a willing victim.

All the characters in *Nakedness* are victims on another level in that they are destroyed by their own primordial impulses: "playthings of the ancestral forces which act upon them . . . , they speak with the voice of the most legitimate human nature, but they squander this heroic exuberance in their rash gestures" (Zeitel, program). This means that what Nelson Rodrigues presents in *Nakedness*, as in *Album* and *Gown*, are the archetypal dimensions of the unconscious. He repeats the central notion that there is a thin veil of rationality covering the unconscious, irrationality, and madness. In the words of Herculano, "Geni, there is a fine line between us and madness" (*Nudez* 98). And as in many other Nelson Rodrigues plays, the archetypes of the collective unconscious figure significantly in the Carioca tragedy.

Serginho is in the clutches of the negative anima, which appears as his mother's ghost. After her death she continues to enter his room, and without her kiss he cannot sleep. The negative anima takes on the extreme form of death demon: Serginho insists that Herculano respond to his wife's demise with his own suicide and declares, "I think a family in full mourning is a lovely thing" (75). His mother's ghost ceases to visit him after his rape. That is, because all sexuality must be punished, the negative anima "chastises" him. The aunts are further negative anima symbols: they reinforce the notion that the body and instinct are evil (even putting talcum powder on the feet is obscene to them).

The *shadow*, an archetype of the same sex as the individual and which corresponds to repressed facets of the personality, plays an equally important role in *Nudez*. The "Bolivian crook," for example, is transformed into a shadow figure and has begun to take over Serginho's life, replacing the mother/anima and representing his repressed sexual instincts. Serginho, in the hospital after the rape, expresses hysterically his fear over the appearance of the shadow: "Do you realize he's on the loose? . . . 'He' is circling the hospital [and] he may be in the corridor" (156–157). According to Jung, to achieve inner harmony the individual must assimilate into the personality the repressed aspects the shadow represents. And indeed, Serginho casts out the negative anima/death demon and accepts his homosexuality when he runs off with the "Bolivian crook." The other characters are less successful in coming to terms with archetypal forces.

The archetypal linkage between Herculano and Geni is a powerful and deadly attraction. Geni becomes in her posthumous voice-over a ghost that haunts the play, another kind of death demon.[4] She claims that her mother had placed a curse on her when she was twelve years old, predicting her death from breast cancer. It is this death obsession that attracts her to Herculano and sets off the play's tragic events. That is, her mother becomes an unresolved shadow figure in her own life.

Herculano refuses to listen to archetypal messages from the unconscious about his own life; he attempts to thwart at every turn the shadow as truth-teller. He is obsessed with hiding certain truths from himself through language, dress, behavior, and rules of decorum. He is terrified of confronting his shadow self and unleashing what he believes are his inner demons. "Drunk, I might commit murder, incest" (37). What actually happens is much less melodramatic. During his two days of inebriation with Geni his shadow speaks: he admits that his late wife was a shrew, inferior to Geni. When Herculano sobers up and learns what he has revealed, he attempts to repress the shadow once again and denies everything hysterically, calling Geni a "public urinal" and his wife a "saint."

In his debauchery Herculano has become naked. He has fulfilled his erotic desires and bared his soul; thus the title of the play is revealed. In *Bridal Gown* there is a metaphorical tearing away of the veil to expose certain social and psychological truths, and in the Carioca tragedy all nakedness will be punished: the nakedness of the self-truth and instinct. Herculano has poured out to Geni all his true feelings about his wife, but instead of being purified by that nakedness of the soul, he attempts to cover up the truth once revealed, searching desperately for verbal fig leaves. And Serginho's subsequent discovery of his father and lover naked in the garden leads to his own nakedness: the revelation of his homosexuality. Is there then something biblical about the work? The garden scene does suggest a kind of post-Eden loss of innocence and shame before nakedness, but the biblical metaphor is not developed extensively as it is in mythical plays like *Album*. More important is the metaphor of "naked truth." Nelson Rodrigues brings many sexual truths out of the closet. There are references, for example, to the homosexual rape common in jails, sadomasochism, masturbation. Female sexuality is dealt with frankly in the play. Nelson Rodrigues is the first Brazilian playwright to state openly that it is natural for women to have the same sexual desires as men. But the naked truth will be punished and leads not to salvation in the play—except perhaps for Serginho—but to damnation. All *nudez* will be punished, by middle-class society and instinctual repression.

While the playwright persists in his criticism of social mores, he implies that there are certain moral and spiritual values worth upholding. Herculano, struggling toward an understanding of his own situation and the sexual violence committed against his son, states: "Yes, if God exists what matters is the soul, [and Serginho's] rape is but a . . . trifling detail" (136–137). Sex, he suggests, is not in itself significant enough to cause so much misery and consternation. The important thing is the "soul"—love. And so Nelson Rodrigues repeats one of his perennial themes, his belief in eternal love as a bulwark against life's miseries, with a concomitant view of love's fatality. That is, love is a path that leads beyond the limitations and adversities of everyday life. For that reason, because it seems to offer a kind of salvation, the search for eternal love may become obsessive and morbid, a path to murder and suicide.

Nelson 2 Rodrigues[5]

In the 1984 staging Antunes Filho has reduced the four works of the 1981 production to two and the three acts of *Album* and of *Nakedness* to one each. The director and his company have demonstrated clearly that built into Nelson Rodrigues's texts is a unique and most contemporary vision of stagecraft. Following the example of Grupo Macunaíma, it is now possible for critics who approach these texts to understand more clearly specific stage directions for attitude, gesture, movement, lighting, and sound, the importance of which is equal to that of his bold vision of society. Moreover, Antunes Filho has brought to light the playscripts' profound archetypal and mythical levels to inform the staging. He has preceded the critics in finding new keys to interpreting the playwright: the concepts of Mircea Eliade and Carl Jung. A close reading of Nelson Rodrigues's plays proves the validity of those discoveries, and to communicate them to audiences the director has created a total theatrical language comprised of a ritual-processional style of movement, cinematic visual imagery, a vast array of sound effects, and an acting method that aims to reproduce the language of the unconscious.

Family Album: Staging

The stage directions in *Family Album* indicate an acting style reminiscent of Expressionism: exteriorization of inner states and grotesque extremes of emotion verging on the melodramatic. The actor is instructed to use a "cruel expression" or the "maximum hysteria possible," with wildly fluctuating and abrupt changes in emotion. For example, one twenty-line stretch of *Album* (p. 60), describes Jonas's states as taciturn, suffering, startled, profoundly interested, violent, rageful, somber. All of this could lead simply to the overblown and false acting of melodrama and soap opera, and indeed there is a correlation, in the sense that Nelson Rodrigues consciously explored in his plays the many dimensions of kitsch, including those of melodrama. The acting style called for in *Album* is also derived from the Expressionist cinema (one could argue, for example, that Jonas was modeled after Nosferatu). Nelson Rodrigues's constant stream of directions regarding fluctuation in attitude and gesture also refers to the metamorphosis of dreams or schizophrenia, in which there is direct access to the unconscious.

Antunes's acting method is based on a collective approach of multiple role playing.[6] The thrust of this system is to go beyond the Stanislavskian concept of emotional memory and to allow the actor to manipulate unconscious forces onstage. To prepare for *O Eterno Retorno*, the company rehearsed for over a year, twelve hours a day, with subsequent lengthy rehearsals for the 1984 restaging. The actors were trained in a variety of performing techniques—movement, breathing, diction, dance, music—and in Oriental modes like tai-chi, yoga, and Zen meditation. The purpose of all this is to enable the actors to function in a state of total awareness in which there is a flow of external and internal—including unconscious—impulses the actor can respond to instantaneously and therefore control. The director explains: "In Brazilian theatre actors are intuitive and out of control. They scream and shout and run all over the stage and the result is chaos. I try to train my actors to make every movement count, to turn every gesture into a sign" ("vendaval," *Isto É*). The result is that the actors "play off" the melodrama to create a kind of Brechtian distance. Many of the performers successfully convey Antunes and Rodrigues's intentions, expressing an array and flux of emotions to create an oneiric climate. In the 1984 production, Actor Marcos Oliveira portrays Jonas as a Nosferatu-like figure, without accentuating the horror such a character evokes. Oliveira makes Jonas's monstrous behavior seem natural, and in fact manages to bring out an absurd, grotesque humor in his actions and statements.

The horror of the vampire myth is emphasized in other ways. Constant screams are heard from offstage during the production, the terror taking place just outside the spectator's field of vision. This auditory frame, too, is indicated in the stage directions: "a frightening, inhuman, animal shriek . . . a thick, heavy voice, of someone who has screamed and suffered unbearably" (*Album* 58–59). The cries suggest both the fear of Jonas's victims, the young girls in labor, perhaps dying, and the madness of his son, Nonô. Spectators are also reminded of the victims' screams in Nosferatu's castle. On another level, the incessant expression of unseen horror represents the primal scream, immersion into the unconscious and into the world of primitive myth.

Antunes adds several further elements to the auditory frame. *Family Album*, the first part of the program, begins with Nelson Rodrigues's voice, recorded shortly before his death (six months prior to the opening), telling the audience how he became a playwright.[7] Another recorded voice heard throughout is that of the Speaker, who announces and comments upon the album photos. This unseen character is a Greek chorus gone awry, a kind of stupid social columnist, or "public opinion" as the playwright calls him. He is "incapable of being moved by genuine feeling," and his comments, made in a commercial broadcasting voice, are "in hideously bad taste" (Magaldi, *Dramaturgia* 37). The Speaker transmits false information and glosses over the family's tragic circumstances. He speaks in a tone of hypocritical morality, and when he gives scriptural advice—"grow and multiply"—to Jonas and Senhorinha on their wedding day, he sounds merely salacious. His frivolous advice about etiquette—whether or not young ladies should drink soda from the bottle—contrasts absurdly with the family horrors. Thus, the Speaker—along with the photos—serves as a fiercely ironic counterpoint to the main action of the play, the form for a totally opposite content. While this device is a means for the playwright to manipulate the language of social convention, subverting it and exposing what it attempts to hide, the Speaker also "relaxes the tragic tension of the events" (*Dramaturgia* 37). Indeed, his comments unfailingly provoke audience laughter during the production.

The Speaker's remarks accompany the album pictures. The playwright was the first in Brazil with a distinct visual style that appeals to contemporary sensibility, which the photos exemplify vividly. The final scene in *Bridal Gown* predates the oneiric visual style of Robert Wilson, and the pictures in *Album* do so as well; Antunes Filho, an admirer of Wilson, uses them to rich and varied plastic effect. According to the stage directions, a photographer in the play's opening scene, who does not appear in *Nelson 2 Rodrigues*, sets the stage for the wedding photo: "With this scene, completely silent, it is possible to create the small ballet of a family photograph" (*Album* 55). The suggestions are enticing for the director—dancelike movement in silence to create an oneiric effect—and the possibilities are stretched to the limit by Antunes Filho, the only Brazilian stage director with a distinctive style, an *auteur* capable of "maximum visual perfection with minimum technical resources" ("vendaval," *Isto É*). The director has recreated the playwright's photographs with a compelling visual leitmotif based on processions.

The frequency and variety of processions characterize the importance of ritual and myth in Brazilian society. Many processions pertain to Catholic liturgy, some to folklore, and yet others to Afro-Brazilian religious tradition. In *Album*'s first procession, a line of nuns, illuminated by blue backlighting, files across the upstage area in slow motion, to the sound of a Chopin nocturne. The image suggests a timeless ritual, and the backlights create an oneiric effect by making the figures in the procession shadowlike. The choreography is synchronized and rigid, accentuated by the "cold" blue light. Although in the script the wedding photo opens the play, Antunes Filho has inverted the order of the initial scenes, and the procession of nuns leads to Glória's first appearance on the stage, a lesbian scene with another pupil (Tereza) in a Catholic boarding school. The segment ends with a young boy ringing a bell and summoning the members of the wedding for the first photo. The bell, linked to the religious/ritualistic character of both the Catholic school and the wedding, bridges the gap between the two scenes. The transition is reinforced by a religious piece by Handel, played over the loudspeakers.

For the wedding procession, the guests enter in formal dress, silently throw rice on Jonas and Senhorinha, and freeze downstage. The director dispenses here with the photographer indicated in the script, a comic, somewhat slapstick silent-movie figure, replacing him with the figure of the young boy. During the freeze the audience hears the comments of the Speaker, after which the actors break the album photo pose and rearrange the set to indicate the living room in Jonas's plantation, where the bulk of the central, present action will take place. During the scene change, the bride and groom perform an elegant waltz to the strains of "The Blue Danube," which is played in this and other scenes to indicate the delicate veneer masking the characters' hidden perversions. The guests enter the dance, but again freeze with the reappearance of the Speaker's voice. Subsequently, to the sound of a music box playing Mendelssohn's "Wedding March," the guests bid adieu to Jonas and Senhorinha, who are going on their honeymoon, but the nuptial celebration is shattered by a scream from the future—the mad son Nonô—the guests dance off stage, the bride and groom remain, the scream is heard again, and the first present time-frame scene begins.

Processionals accompany the third photo, Glória's Communion, and the funeral of Edmundo and Glória. The photograph is accompanied by a group of actors chanting in Latin ("Panis Angelicus"). Jonas gives Glória his "blessing," while upstage Edmundo and his mother Senhorinha embrace. The Communion procession dissolves when a group of young women leads Glória offstage, to the strains of Rossini's "Garza Ladra." Glória's "angelical" innocence contrasts ironically with the incestuous suggestion of mother and son locked in an embrace—and with the father's desire for his daughter—all of which underlines visually the Speaker's absurd commentary: "If Senhorinha is a devoted mother, Glória is an obedient and respectful daughter" (*Album* adaptation 11).

During the funeral of Glória and Edmundo, a line of veiled figures carries the coffins in slow motion, also to a Latin chant. Jonas and Senhorinha argue bitterly, she shoots him, and he falls, mortally wounded. His body abandoned centerstage, the funeral procession moves offstage and into an amber spot that cuts directly across the stage. The golden light symbolizes both the glory of heaven and the burning of hell. The veiled pallbearers lean slightly in a grotesque position, as if blown backward by the stream of light entering from the world beyond.[8] The ritual funeral procession, accompanied by a liturgical piece by Mozart, takes place near the end of the play and thus provides an apocalyptic end to the mythic cycle of Jonas's clan. The play itself, however, in Grupo Macunaíma's adaptation, ends with the beginning of a new cycle. For the last page of the album, the young boy—he replaces the photographer called for in the original script—resuscitates Jonas and prepares him for the last portrait. The other actors, to the sound of the Speaker's voice, remain upstage in a freeze. The photo scene completed, the boy leads Senhorinha, dressed in her bridal gown, to centerstage and places her beside Jonas and organizes the cast for the last waltz ("Blue Danube"). The resurrection of Jonas and the return to the first album portrait represent an eternal return, and the boy symbolically initiates a new cycle, the renewal of life, as he playfully pushes a baby carriage among the dancing couples while the lights slowly fade to black.

The director has based the ritual-processional elements in the play on the theories of Mircea Eliade, the most significant of which is the concept of the eternal return in archaic societies, where rituals serve to repeat Creation and time is made to imitate the cycles of nature. In Grupo Macunaíma's production of *Family Album*, the second and the seventh portraits are repetitions of the first, the photograph of the wedding, which represents the beginning, in its ritual function, and initiates the cosmos in which the characters are created and destroyed. The sacred processions in the play correspond to the rituals that repeat the eternal cycle—marriage, communion, burial—and they provide the visual frame for the mythical universe set forth by Nelson Rodrigues.

The staging reveals yet another perspective on the mythical dimensions of the work. The preceding chapter examined *Macunaíma* in the context of Mikhail Bakhtin's theories. The element of carnivalesque parody is also present in *Album*, for is not the mythical-processional aspect in some ways a travesty of official liturgy? In the first place, the "priest" who presides over the liturgy of the photo ceremonies ("grow and multiply") is the Speaker, a buffoon. Second, the pictures serve not merely to portray Jonas's world but to carnivalize it, because it is the sphere of power where rituals sanctify the status quo. On one level the photos recreate the past in order to consecrate the present. But given their carnivalesque treatment, the album pages constitute antirituals, burlesque mythical re-creations.

Their intention is thus subversive: instead of sanctifying the established order controlled by Jonas, they destroy it.

The director includes visual elements in the production not called for literally in the *Album* script but that are very effective. The first character to appear onstage, following the playwright's recorded story about his youth, is the young boy. He represents the playwright himself in his boyhood, and he appears throughout the production to direct the proceedings, a healthy and innocent counterpart to the madness and corruption surrounding him. As the vigorous and uncorrupted controller of the action, the puppeteer, he invites the other characters onto the stage and signals for lighting changes. In addition to arranging the photographs, he plays the role of Nonô, age nine, in one of the family pictures before the child's innocence is turned into madness. For the final photo, the boy, as life-force, resuscitates Jonas, death-force, and playfully organizes the entire ensemble for a last waltz. The play's final image, then, is one of exuberance and health, the moment of rebirth after death in the mythic cycle.

Other components of the visual frame are lighting, sets, and costumes. The lighting design is simple enough to be used for the three productions of the *rodízio* and for touring, yet flexible enough for special effects. It consists of white spots for general lighting, while colored gels are used for the oneiric sequences (e.g., the blue backlights and the amber light from the beyond). While the white lights establish clear and stark lines for realistic scenes, the colored "specials" blur those lines. The design provides an archetypal effect with a large circle of light utilized for the chapel scene with Edmundo and Glória, adding a candle to enhance the ritualistic atmosphere.[9] The circle of light represents what Jung calls a *mandala,* a pictorial symbol of the collective unconscious whose form is usually round, an inner refuge from external difficulties. Edmundo and Glória's mandala is the chapel light where they retreat from the madness and horror; but their escape attempt fails, and Edmundo murders Glória in the darkness *outside the illuminated circle.*

The set is minimal: a long table and chairs. According to Sábato Magaldi the table represents the mythical center, linking heaven and earth (Magaldi, *Dramaturgia* 176). For many scenes the stage is bare. With the stark and simple set, the director continues the aesthetic he established for his 1979 production of *Macunaíma.* That is, he utilizes simple and inexpensive materials to create a Brazilian form of the Grotowskian poor theatre. This aesthetic of poverty in the design mode is appropriate to Third World economic circumstances and allows the company to focus on the richness of imagination and creativity, of which there is an abundance in Brazil. Both the set and the period costumes are in black and white, and the simplicity, purity, and elegance counterbalance the play's psychological and emotional complexity.[10]

All Nakedness Will Be Punished: Staging

Grupo Macunaíma takes full advantage of the stage directions for *Nudez,* especially quick-cutting from one setting and time frame to another, related to cinematic technique. One scene may end in suspense while the next begins after the fact, after the violence has been committed, as when Herculano's brother Patrício gives him a bottle and a photo of the prostitute Geni naked to awaken the protagonist's dormant sexual instincts. In the next scene it is forty-eight hours later in a brothel, where Herculano sleeps off the effects of alcohol following his orgy with Geni. This cinematic jump-cutting provides a breathtaking pace and heightens the psychological tension and sexual violence that lurks always just beneath the surface of the characters' actions. The dialogue adds to these effects. Short, crisp, and crackling, it snaps back and forth like gun shots or sword thrusts between the characters, who try always to manipulate or destroy each other.

The set for *Nakedness,* like that for *Album,* is minimal, and lights are the principal means of setting the stage for the rapid-fire flashbacks and flash-forwards. In one scene change, for example, the lights cross-fade from Heculano and Geni, in one time and place, to the Aunts, in another time and place, and Herculano enters immediately into their now illuminated area. Such cross-fades are conventionally used within a single scene or setting, but Nelson Rodrigues—and Antunes—uses them to cut to new settings and time frames, forcing the audience to suspend its expectations based on theatrical illusion of reality and linear sequence of events. It is the lights, rather than the set, that define the scenic space. That is, instead of actors moving within a space delimited by a fixed set, space moves with the actors through the variations in lighting patterns. Because there are so many scene changes (over fifty), the conventional techniques of blackouts—used sparingly in the play—or other modes of time-lapse would mean an extremely cumbersome production. A more subtle purpose for the jump-cut/cross-fade technique is to indicate emotional change. That is, the rhythm of the light changes varies according to emotional climate, speeding up, for example, when the characters are panicked or hysterical. During most of the second act and about halfway through the third, lighting changes define Herculano's voyage through the universe of *Nudez*. They establish the mood, speed, and even purpose of his movement through space and time. In one sequence the lights are on Geni, who is speaking on a public phone outside the protagonist's house; he enters her illuminated space; cross-fade to an Aunt, he enters immediately; cross-fade to Patrício, enter Herculano; cross-fade to Geni, enter the protagonist; a blackout breaks the tension of the repeated pattern. The pace of this series of cross-fades quickens as Herculano becomes more desperate and increasingly loses control of his life; when the tension is at its peak, it is cut off by the blackout. The pattern is then repeated until the end of the act, where it is again broken by another lighting technique. Act III begins with the pattern but soon presents a new variation, illuminating Geni's voyage to indicate that her destiny is at stake as she becomes increasingly involved with the family. The last half of Act III presents an array of varying patterns to suggest the chaos into which the main character's world is collapsing. Other techniques create effects and establish moods for specific scenes. The lights are used to create imaginary distances: Geni and Herculano, on opposite sides of the stage, each in a different light, talk on the phone. The lighting also freezes time when Geni's taped voice is heard while Patrício and the Aunts are motionless. This suspension of time visually reinforces the production's mythic structure,[11] and—in conjunction with the voice of the dead woman, Geni, who has committed suicide—refers to the timelessness of death. In the last scene of *Nudez* the lights come up on an empty bed; Geni speaks her final words, and only the sound of the tape, now off the reel, is heard slapping as the lights dim. This image of stark loneliness and the finality of death is reminiscent of the final scene in *Bridal Gown*: Alaíde's tomb in the moonlight.

What holds all the jump-cutting together is the device of Geni's last words recorded just before her suicide, a cinematic voice-over. Like the dying Alaíde in *Gown*, whose inner voice functions as a kind of narrator, Geni's voice from the beyond provides the narrative glue for *All Nakedness Will Be Punished*. While the photographs and Speaker in *Album* provide a past-time frame for the present-time main action, Geni's recorded voice begins the flashbacks that constitute the central portion of the plot. The snippets of tape reveal Geni's secret thoughts and provide the protagonist a view of events kept hidden from him while they transpired (e.g., Geni's affair with Serginho). And the recording adds to the play's mythical dimensions, in that it establishes a cyclical time frame, from Geni's death (the first words on the tape) to the death of Herculano's first wife (the beginning of the main action) and back to Geni's death (the end of the play). *Nakedness* closes with the tape reel spinning endlessly, an eternal return.

Grupo Macunaíma incorporates most of the playwright's stage directions for lighting and use of Geni's recorded voice. Several other elements of the visual frame distinguish the staging. Its minimal set consists of a few small tables, a bed, a row of chairs. The only prop is the all-important tape machine; the actors pantomime other objects. Costumes are in 1940s style, which places the action in a period when social mores were more rigid in Brazil, when the events of the play would be more shocking. The male characters wear their hair slicked back with brilliantine and have thin moustaches painted on. The johns in the bordello wear suit and vest, with a carnation in the lapel. The color of their clothing is gray, which reflects the ambiguity of the characters. Herculano, Serginho, and the Aunts wear black, symbolizing both mourning and a rigid moral system. The young women in the bordello are dressed in slips, while Geni wears the costume of a street hooker. Her clothing is white, a parody of the purity of Herculano's universe. All the actors' faces are covered with white makeup, giving them a sickly cast to reflect their characters' obsessions and to create a distancing effect.[12]

Antunes Filho makes his most important contribution to the cinematic visual frame through blocking. At the beginning of the play, the entire cast enters the stage, sits on the row of chairs that extends across the stage, and remains for a few moments in that position staring at the audience, while the latter watches the actors. This device and others in the production constitute a form of metatheatre, because they call attention to the staging itself by establishing a distancing effect. The characters—at times all of them, sometimes only a few—seated on the row of chairs, are a continuing presence throughout the production, which creates variations on the metatheatrical effects. When Herculano speaks to Geni about Serginho, he walks to the chair where the actor playing his son is seated. This illustration, not "observed" by Geni, allows the spectators to enter the action because they see what the characters do not, but at the same time the effect distances the audience by breaking the illusion of reality. And there are many other moments in the play when the spectators observe seated actors who are "invisible" to the other characters. With this technique, the characters can also become immediate participants in whatever is happening onstage or they can separate themselves without the need for cumbersome entrances and exits. Combined with the cinematic lighting techniques, the blocking and the utilization of the row of chairs provide agility and flexibility for scene changes.

A number of auditory and visual devices reinforce the meta-theatrical design. The production begins with a recording of the playwright's voice, in which he defines himself as a romantic and a ridiculous sentimentalist. During this "interview" with Nelson Rodrigues, the stage lights come up on the young boy, who places a tape recorder on a table. When the playwright ends his monologue, the boy signals the entrance of the cast and exits. Once the characters are seated, the audience hears another recording, a melodramatic song from the 1940s, an auditory illustration of Nelson Rodrigues's words and a musical preface to the play's tragic love story and its various kitsch dimensions.[13] In addition to the characters from the playscript, the first scene includes four girls, in states of partial undress—a visual reference to the title—by suggestion prostitutes from Geni's bordello, as well as four anonymous men, by implication johns. This image, repeated throughout the production, places all the characters, with their sexual obsessions, *within the brothel*. The childlike prostitutes, seated in the row of chairs facing the audience, function as a silent, watchful, and accusing Greek chorus. When they fix their gaze upon the spectators, the latter, too, are drawn into the play, into the whorehouse, and they also become johns. The visual reference to the bordello successfully conveys the play's themes, since the plot deals with the relationship of a proper upper-class man—Herculano, the protagonist—and a prostitute. The anonymous young women, whose presence has transformed the stage into a brothel, represent the classes that are exploited by patriarchal society. The alienation technique turned inside out—the audience is not distanced but brought metaphorically into the whorehouse—turns not only the men in the audience into the prostitutes' johns, into exploiters, but the women into passive onlookers. The spectators, along with the characters in the play, thus come to be accomplices in a system that, while punishing the open expression of sexuality—the play's "nakedness"—traffics in human bodies.

The atmosphere of the bordello persists as the following scenes unfold in the presence of the young women. When Patrício shows Herculano the photo of Geni naked, one of the four anonymous men gets out of his chair and flirts with the audience, reinforcing the metatheatrical audience participation. The four johns and the prostitutes then dance a tango. The tango theme is repeated in varying patterns throughout the production. The most striking variation is a john dancing a lone tango, interrupted with freezes, in the upstage area, under the blue backlights. He may move when other tango dancers or actors in a dialogue scene are in a freeze, or he may freeze when others are dancing or speaking. During Herculano and Geni's wedding a group of women—the young prostitutes in another guise—dance a tango with the guests. The women carry flowers and are dressed seminude in black-tie costumes to parody the decorum and formality of the occasion. Near the end of the play the same group of women carries Geni's coffin onstage. As they kneel to pray, the lone tango dancer can be seen in the background.

The tango establishes multifaceted effects and symbolism. It reinforces the forties motif suggested by the costumes, and its kitsch dimension parodies the solemnity and rigidity of Herculano's universe. It is the theme of the brothel—the mood of steamy sexuality—that constantly intrudes on the protagonist's ordered and puritanical system. The Tango-man represents the heart of the lonely dancer, a poignant visual image—reinforced by the row of silent prostitutes—of the characters' loneliness and separation and of their failure to create bonds of love. Like the processions in *Album,* the tango has a mythic function. With its stylized movements and freezes, it is a recurring ritual, an antiritual really. The dance creates a sense of timelessness in its projection back to another period and parodies liturgical rituals of renewal, for it takes place in the sterile environment of the brothel, where sex does not recreate life or express love, and it mocks the wedding ritual. The brothel therefore constitutes a travesty of a sacred place; it is an antitemple where an anti–Passion Play takes place, and the victim sacrificed is a prostitute, Geni. Extending the metaphor of the bordello, one could say that the chairs correspond to the waiting room where the customers await their turn. That is, when they exit from the stage they symbolically enter the prostitutes' cubicles where they will participate in a sterile ritual.

The final image in the production synthesizes the themes and motifs examined in this chapter. After Patrício's revelation that Serginho has run off with his homosexual lover, the four girls, still dressed in black-tie, enter carrying a coffin, which they place on the now bare stage—the chairs have been removed from the wedding-dance scene. Geni climbs into the coffin and lies down, disappearing from view. The young women kneel at the four corners of the coffin, and Geni's arm rises up. Herculano enters and caresses Geni's arm, crying, as the lights fade to black and the Tango-man continues his solitary dance upstage. During this final scene, the melodramatic song that opens the play is once again heard, and the cycle of destruction thus comes to a close.

Notes

1. Rio Theatre in the 1940s: Os Comediantes

1. All quotes appearing in *The Modern Brazilian Stage* originally in Portuguese, French, or Spanish are my translations. A few translations that are not my own appear in chapter 5.

2. *Deus lhe pague* is a beggar's phrase meaning literally "may God pay you."

3. Another irony in this regard is discussed in chapter 3: some members of Teatro de Arena and Teatro Oficina would attack their precursor, the Teatro Brasileiro de Comédia, for destroying the popular companies of Procópio Ferreira et al. whose staple, even in the 1950s, was still the comedy of manners.

4. After his work with Os Comediantes, Ziembinski spent seven years with the TBC and later co-founded the Teatro Cacilda Becker. "'If you ask me what I brought to Brazilian theatre, I truly believe I brought concern for the text . . . acting methods . . . costumes . . . lighting'" (*Nosso Século 49* 91).

3. São Paulo Theatre in the 1950s and 1960s: TBC, Arena, Oficina

1. The EAD would later become associated with the University of São Paulo and is currently housed in the School of Communications and Arts, Escola de Comunicações e Artes, or ECA. The ECA and EAD have together produced distinguished actors, directors, playwrights, designers, TV producers, filmmakers, critics, and professors.

2. The GUT was sponsored by the University of São Paulo. At the time of the TBC's founding, the GUT had done two productions of plays by Brazilian authors. In the TBC theatre space the GUT presented Jean Anouilh's *Thieves' Carnival* (*O Baile dos Ladrões*).

3. Abílio Pereira de Almeida (1906–1972): His themes included the sexual excesses of São Paulo high society and the corrupting power of money. "A good observer . . . who handled theatrical dialogue well, Abílio never reached his full potential because he did not have the necessary literary . . . background. Although a pathfinder in that he was São Paulo's first dramatist [to reach a wide public], he fell into the trap of sensationalism, which made

a considerable profit for him but doomed him to watch from afar the promised land of the new dramaturgy" (Almeida Prado, *História* 551).

4. Without too much exaggeration, one could say that the post–World War II depression that created Italian neorealism also created the TBC; that is, economic problems gave rise to a group of emigré directors, from which Brazilian theatre benefited. Moreover, Italian directors, technicians, and producers put Brazilian cinema on the map with the establishment of the São Paulo "Hollywood," the Vera Cruz Studios (1949–1959).

5. Other Celi stagings included Kesserling's *Arsenic and Old Lace* (*Arsênico e Alfazema*), Patrick Hamilton's *Luz de Gás* (*Angel Street*, retitled *Gaslight* for the cinema). Other foreign directors brought in by Zampari included Luciano Salce, Flamínio Bollini, Ruggero Jacobbi, Mauro Francini, as well as set designer Gianni Ratto, from Italy; Alberto D'Aversa, from Argentina; and Os Comediantes's Ziembinski, from Poland.

6. João Bethencourt would later be identified with the "new dramaturgy" of the late sixties and early seventies, which included playwrights Leilah Assunção, Isabel Câmara, Consuelo de Castro, José Vicente, and Antônio Bivar.

7. The works of Jorge Andrade (1922–1984), one of modern Brazil's most highly considered playwrights, focus on rural São Paulo themes, particularly the decadent coffee aristocracy. Among his most notable works are *A Moratória* (The Moratorium), *Vereda da Salvação* (Path of Salvation), *Os Ossos do Barão* (The Baron's Bones), and *Milagre na Cela* (Miracle in the Cell).

8. Dias Gomes, who for the last two decades has written for television, carved out a niche for himself as a non-Marxist engagé playwright in the 1960s. His best-known works, besides the 1960 *Pagador*, are *O Santo Inquérito* (The Holy Inquest), 1960, about the inquisition in northeastern Brazil in the eighteenth century; *A Revolução dos Beatos* (The Revolution of the Blessed), 1962, which deals with the career of Father Cícero, religious leader and protorevolutionary in the *sertão*, or arid Northeast; *A Invasão* (The Invasion), 1962, in which homeless slum dwellers occupy a building; *O Berço do Herói* (The Cradle of the Hero), 1965, banned by the censors; *Dr. Getúlio, Sua Vida e Sua Glória* (Dr. Getúlio, His Life and His Glory), 1968, which tells the story of a Rio samba group whose theme for the upcoming carnival parade is the dictator Vargas in his role as "father of the poor" and anti-imperialist hero.

9. Silveira Sampaio's works were very popular during the 1950s; his farces were staged by many groups, including the TBC and Arena. His plays ranged from updated comedy of manners (e.g., *A Garçonnière de meu Marido* [My Husband's Mistress's Love Nest])to political satire (e.g., *Pharaoh*).

10. Another irony here: Boal has almost universally received the credit as the father of Arena's Brazilian dramaturgy phase (and he has promoted himself as such in his many writings). Actually, though, José Renato and Gianfrancesco Guarnieri were responsible—the latter by writing and the former by selecting and directing *Black-Tie*—for sending the company in its new direction.

11. *Black-Tie*'s original title was to be *O Cruzeiro lá no Alto* (The Southern Cross on High).

12. *Black-Tie* was made into an award-winning movie in 1982, with Guarnieri himself in the lead role. Gianfrancesco Guarnieri, born in Italy in 1934, has distinguished himself as one of Brazil's leading actors—stage, film, and TV—and playwrights. His engagé works were staged by various groups in the 1960s and 1970s, and they continue to be a staple of amateur companies. His best-known plays are *Black-Tie*, *Gimba* (1959), *Arena Conta Zumbi* (1965, with Augusto Boal), *Arena Conta Tiradentes* (1966, with Augusto Boal), and *Ponto de Partida* (Point of Departure, 1976).

13. Oduvaldo Vianna Filho (1936–1974), a playwright and actor, in 1956 joined Teatro de Arena, which produced his early plays *bilbao*, *Via Copacabana* and *Chapetuba, Futebol Clube*. In 1964 he co-founded the Rio de Janeiro Teatro Opinião, which along with Arena and Oficina was on the cutting edge of engagé theatre in the 1960s. He co-authored two of the company's most important productions, *Show Opinião* (1964)—a musical piece about the samba—and *Se Correr o Bicho Pega, Se Ficar o Bicho Come* (If You Run the Beast Will Catch You, If You Stay the Beast Will Eat You, 1965). The "beast" of the title is a veiled reference to the military dictatorship that took over the government in 1964. Vianninha, as he affectionately came to be known, spent the last ten years of his life working as an actor and writing for TV, cinema, and the theatre. His plays, however, were almost always censored, and so they were staged only after his death from cancer in 1974. Several of his posthumous plays have been highly successful. The most important of these was *Rasga Coração* (Heart Stopping) (1974), staged in 1979—it ran until 1981—by Arena founder José Renato. It featured former TPE and Oficina member Raul Cortez, one of Brazil's most acclaimed actors, in the lead role. Vianninha's dramaturgical production was immense, in spite of his short life. Along with Gianfrancesco Guarnieri, he established a legacy of well-crafted plays that communicated engagé social consciousness through a unique Brazilian fusion of Brechtian technique and high-powered emotion. For further information see Carmelinda Guimarães, *Um Ato de Resistência: O Teatro de Oduvaldo Vianna Filho*, São Paulo: MG Editores, 1984.

14. "Plínio Marcos (1935), former circus clown, has written plays of great intensity, bringing to the stage the reality of the lower depths of Rio and São Paulo's urban subproletariat" (Cacciaglia, *Pequena História* 268). There are many ways to characterize the playwright's career: enfant terrible, because he has managed to offend nearly everyone; *autor maldito*, "accursed author," because his works represent the voice of the oppressed and have nearly all been banned at one time or another. Among his better-known works are *Dois Perdidos numa Noite Suja* (Two Lost Souls on a Dirty Night, 1966); *Navalha na Carne* (Knife in the Flesh, 1967); and *Poeta da Vila* (1976), about the life of seminal pop composer Noel Rosa.

15. Paulo José and Juca de Oliveira have both gone on to fruitful acting careers. Flávio Império would become Brazil's leading theatrical designer, as

well as a renowned painter. Following is a description of his set and lighting design for Fauzi Arap's 1977 play *Um Ponto de Luz* (A Point of Light), which the playwright based on his experience with Jungian psychotherapy: the stage was a wide-open semithrust, and the walls of the set, beginning about four rows up into the audience, were covered with a hanging scrim cut in geometric patterns: circles, ovals, parabolas. The scrim had openings downstage right and left for entrances and exits. Part of the scrim swept up toward the audience in a shape suggesting wings, and when the eye took in the entire set it resembled a giant bird and created the sensation of flight, all of which related to the Jungian concept of transcendence. The back two-thirds of the scrim wrapped around the sides and back of the stage, closing off the downstage area. The form of the performing space itself, because of the scrim, was nearly round—the set contained few straight lines—and in its center was a raised square platform, on top of which was superimposed another platform, round, indicating the mandala, or center of the psyche in the context of Jungian psychology. To create different settings, various architectural forms suggesting walls, verandas, rooms, and so forth, were silently lowered to and raised from the stage by invisible cables; they seemed to flow like the rest of the set, again connoting flight and transcendence. The lighting, with constantly shifting colors, angles, and intensities, created a dreamlike atmosphere. Império died of AIDS in 1986.

16. Director Carlos Diegues made a 1986 film, *Quilombo*, on the same subject.

17. Peixoto did stage an acclaimed revival of *Zumbi* in 1976.

18. Barbara Garson's play is a thinly disguised allegory, based on *Macbeth*, that implicates Lyndon B. Johnson in the assassination of John F. Kennedy.

19. Boal's best-known theoretical writings are *Teatro do Oprimido* (Theatre of the Oppressed) and *Técnicas Latinoamericanas de Teatro Popular* (Latin American Popular Theatre Techniques).

20. Inácio Loyola Brandão has become one of Brazil's most renowned prose writers.

21. The title in Portuguese means literally "life printed on a dollar," which is the subtitle of the original play.

22. Abujamra would go on to become one of Brazil's most innovative directors, and he continues to be active at the present time.

23. Fernando Peixoto became one of Oficina's leaders as translator, director, and actor. Currently, he is one of Brazil's most prominent theatre scholars.

24. The last revival was directed in 1990 by Renato Borghi, former Oficina member. Borghi is still an active director and playwright, having achieved great success in 1987 with his play *O Lobo do Ray-Ban*, starring another former Oficina member and currently one of Brazil's leading actors of stage, screen, and TV Raul Cortez.

25. Chico Buarque de Hollanda has been, from the late 1960s until this day, one of Brazil's most highly regarded popular composers. In his music, he has combined samba and carnival motifs with social consciousness. In

theatre, he has collaborated, as composer and co-author, on many original Brazilian musicals. The most successful of these, *A Ópera do Malandro,* based on Brecht's *Three Penny Opera,* was made into a movie in 1985.

26. The title in Portuguese means literally "black power." The translator was Francisco Martins.

27. AI5, as the state-of-siege decree was commonly known, was not repealed until June 1978.

28. The translators were Elizabeth Kander, Fernando Peixoto, and Renato Borghi.

29. *Don Juan* was translated by Peixoto, Celso, and Guarnieri.

30. Julian Beck died of cancer in 1987.

31. The Argentine Grupo Lobos was a five-member vegetarian communal troupe that performed nonverbal and highly disciplined physical theatre. While in São Paulo it presented its piece *Casa, 1 Hora y 1/4.*

32. The Living Theatre's third stop after Rio de Janeiro was the eighteenth-century colonial capital Ouro Preto, where it performed in the streets its one Brazilian piece, *As Pernas de Caim* (The Legs of Cain); some reports list the title as *O Legado de Caim* (The Legacy of Cain). Soon after, the group members were arrested for possession of marijuana—several people claimed the charges were trumped-up—and expelled from the country.

33. This and the following quotes in the paragraph are from Almeida, "Don José."

4. *The Candle King*

1. Yan Michalski, Rio de Janeiro's foremost theatre critic, died of cancer in 1990.

2. The self-deprecatory term *tupiniquim* refers to Brazilian provincialism.

3. The title parodies the *Frente Única,* a São Paulo political coalition of the 1930s, "established by traditional politicians" (Magaldi, diss. 107).

4. My observations on the staging are based on many sources, including José Celso's film version of the play, notes by the director and designer and other primary materials located in the São Paulo Municipal Ministry of Culture theatre archives and in the library of the University of São Paulo School of Communications and Arts, *O Rei da Vela* programs and flyers, conversations with the director and other participants, photographs, reviews, and other bibliography cited in this chapter.

5. According to Maria Eugênia Boaventura, Oswald de Andrade's inspiration for Anthropophagy was Tarsila Amaral's painting entitled *Abaporu.* The painter considered Anthropophagic the work she produced from 1928 to 1930. She described in her words the principal characteristics of her paintings from this period: "'aggressiveness of the heavy line, figures with enormous feet, bulbous and swollen plants, strange creatures which a naturalist could never classify'" (*Vanguarda* 130).

Notes to Pages 98–121

6. In his dissertation, "O Teatro de Oswald de Andrade," Sábato Magaldi took up seven pages just to list the cuts censors made in the text.

7. Nelson Pereira dos Santos's film *Como Era Gostoso o Meu Francês* (*How Tasty Was My Little Frenchman*) brought the Anthropophagic idea back to its source by telling the story of an Indian tribe that took in, coddled and fattened, and finally devoured a shipwrecked French explorer.

5. Theatre in the 1970s and 1980s: Grupo Macunaíma

1. Guerra directed the 1983 film *Eréndira*, the adaptation of a Gabriel García Márquez story.

2. The company's original name was based on another work of the Modernist canon, Oswald de Andrade's manifesto and collection of poems entitled *Pau-Brasil*, a reference to the dye-producing brazilwood that the Portuguese colonizers exploited and that gave the nation its name.

3. The 1979–1984 quotes, in order of their appearance, came originally from the following sources: Gerald Rabkin, *Soho Weekly News*, 21 June 1979; Don Shirley, *Washington Post*, 8 June 1979; Siegmar Gassert, *Basler Zeitung*, 9 June 1980; Michael Coveney, *Financial Times*, 6 August 1981; Ignácio Amestoy Eguiguren, *Diario 16*, 15 April 1982; John Larkin, *Sunday Press*, 18 March 1984. The quotes from French and Spanish are my own translations. I based the translation of the quote from *Basler Zeitung* on the Portuguese translation appearing in the program.

4. The quotes appearing here are from the following sources: Mariângela Alves Lima, 1984 program notes; Jefferson del Rios, "As Sombras de Nelson Rodrigues," *Folha de São Paulo*, 11 May 1984; Clóvis Garcia, "Nelson Rodrigues numa grande concepção teatral," *O Estado de São Paulo*, 30 May 1984.

5. Thomas Thieringer, *Suddeutsche Zeitung*, 23 June 1982, Munich. This quote appears in the 1984 program in Portuguese.

6. The Grotowskian *sign* refers to the gestural elements the actor creates through intense physical and vocal training to compose his/her role; it means the actor's elimination of the distance between outer and inner impulse. But I use the term in the sense that Roland Barthes uses it: a "healthy sign" is flexible in that it calls attention to its own arbitrary nature; it is not fixed by ideology; it is "unnatural." I utilize the term to refer to a single word (e.g., *popular*) or a cultural mode (e.g., *carnival*) that changes meaning in varying contexts.

7. My analysis of *Macunaíma* is based on several viewings of the play from 1980 to 1984, the working script, videotaped scenes, and conversations with company members.

8. Mário de Andrade called his *Macunaíma* a "rhapsody" rather than a novel because he based it on variations of preexisting texts, both popular and erudite, and on the rhapsodic principle of the suite, widely used in Brazilian popular and improvisational folk music. See Gilda de Mello e Souza, *O Tupi e o Alaúde*.

9. I have utilized for this section of my analysis Bakhtin's *Rabelais and His World*.

10. *Macunaíma*, theatrical adaptation by Jacques Thieriot and Grupo Pau-Brasil—the company's original name—1979. Carnival sambas typically deal with historical subjects and are frequently parodic. The *blocos*, or bands of carnival revelers dancing in the streets, represent the genuinely popular dimension of the yearly festival. While even carnival has been usurped to consecrate officialdom—I refer here to the lavish Rio parades with their expensive floats and costumes—the *blocos*, which persist in Rio but are more characteristic of cities like Bahia and Recife, are spontaneous and unorganized celebrations where nothing is sacred and all can join.

11. In this regard, it should be noted that Bakhtin's theories turn upside down the socialist-realist categories of the Stalinist era (Michael Holquist, prologue to *Rabelais and His World*, xvii).

12. *Augusto Matraga*, presented by Grupo de Teatro Macunaíma, directed and adapted by Antunes Filho, Teatro Anchieta, São Paulo, 1986–87. The observations and interpretation of the stage production are based on my own viewings, the playscript, and interviews with Antunes Filho.

13. The myriad processional forms in Brazil demonstrate the importance its people give to ritual and myth. Many processions belong to Catholic liturgy, some are folkloric, others pertain to Indian and Afro-Brazilian religious tradition and are part of the carnivalesque tradition.

14. Saint Francis is considered a local patron saint—the São Francisco River is named after him—and in the folklore of the region he is said to have traveled through the *sertão*.

15. *Bem-Bem* is a pun: the literal meaning is "good-good," while the sound refers to gunshots ("bang-bang").

6. *Nelson 2 Rodrigues*

1. Teatro de Arena founder José Renato gave his perspective on the matter in our interview when I asked him why Arena, the "home" of the Brazilian playwright, never staged Nelson Rodrigues: "There was a sort of taboo surrounding him in São Paulo. He was successful in Rio but not in São Paulo, where only a few of his works were known and those were considered to be of poor quality. And people were not at all fond of what they perceived as his 'Expressionism.'"

2. The Jungian analysis is based on Jolande Jacobi's *Complexo, Arquétipo, Símbolo*, Elie G. Humbert's *Jung*, and my conversations with the Brazilian psychoanalyst Antônio Galvão Bueno.

3. In addition to *Nakedness*, there have been many screen adaptations of Nelson Rodrigues's works.

4. The protagonist of *Bridal Gown*, Alaíde, takes on a similar ghostlike function.

5. The observations in this section are based on several viewings of *Nelson 2 Rodrigues* in São Paulo's Teatro Anchieta, in May and June of

1984, the adapted script, videotaped scenes, interviews with Antunes Filho, and other sources cited.

6. Multiple role playing has had a practical purpose as well. In 1984 Grupo Macunaíma instituted the *rodízio* system, which meant three plays in repertory alternating on different evenings. The productions were *Nelson 2 Rodrigues, Macunaíma,* and *Romeu e Julieta.* The actors in the system not only played many roles in each work, but those with major roles in one production had minor ones in another. The system provided training and flexibility in varied acting styles and characterization. With the *rodízio,* the company attempted something taken for granted in the United States but almost unheard-of in Brazil: encouraging the public to purchase tickets ahead of time, potentially a significant financial advantage for the theatre, a kind of capital investment in its future (theatres are always financially strapped in Brazil). As Antunes explained the system, "'from the point of view of the box office it's good because the success of one play helps that of the others, and from the spiritual point of view it's great, because it makes the actors more flexible'" (quoted in "vendaval," *Isto É*). But the repertory experiment did not prove to be financially viable and was discontinued after 1984.

7. In the recording, Rodrigues relates an anecdote from his boyhood about how he became a playwright. He discusses a grade-school assignment for which he wrote a prize-winning story about adultery and murder. *Nudez* also begins with a recording of the playwright's voice, in which he calls himself a romantic sentimentalist who believes in eternal love.

8. In the original script the characters in the funeral procession are four black men carrying torches, barefoot and naked from the waist up. Antunes replaces them with the veiled figures. The director, however, does follow one aspect of the stage directions here, which state: "This is a scene from which one should derive the maximum visual effect" (*Album* 114).

9. The ritual climate is also reinforced by an oratorio, Keetman's *Recitative.*

10. Antunes has left out of the production an Expressionist device in the original script, a huge portrait of Jonas in the chapel, which depicts him with a cruel and bestial face (his guise as Nosferatu), yet at the same time he is Christ-like (Glória's vision of him).

11. Time in the mythical conception does not move forward, it merely repeats that which existed in the beginning, it is suspended.

12. I use the concept of distancing in the Brechtian sense of an effect that produces "alienation" or "estrangement" and that counteracts empathy. Realist theatre attempts to create an illusion of reality by which the audience will suspend disbelief and identify the characters as real people and not as actors. Distancing effects, on the other hand, overturn illusion and empathy and remind the audience that they are seeing a play, not reality. The purpose, in theory, is to lead the spectators to reflect on the ideas presented rather than to become lost in the emotion.

13. Amália Zeitel (interview) explained the kitsch elements in the production this way: "All the research we did into kitsch revealed the archetypal aspect of nostalgia, the flavor of our culture's vulgar, poor, longing-for-the-

past dimension. In *Album de Família*, for example, the actors' costumes were turn-of-the-century, where the action begins, and they do not change during the performance in spite of the passage of time. It is as if someone were narrating the life of his children, telling how they grew up, but in his imagination nothing has changed. In the case of *Toda Nudez*, the presence of the girls on the stage, with their dolls and braids, represents the childhood traumas of the prostitute Geni; that is, she has remained a little girl, with no possibility of growing up and experiencing the pleasure of maturity."

Bibliography

I. Drama and Fiction
A. Published Works
   Amado, Jorge. *Gabriela, Cravo e Canela*. Lisbon: Publicações Europa-América, 1978.
   Andrade, Mário de. *Macunaíma*. São Paulo: Martins, 1973.
   Andrade, Oswald de. *O Rei da Vela*. São Paulo: Difusão Européia do Livro, 1967.
   Guarnieri, Gianfrancesco. *Eles Não Usam Black-Tie*. São Paulo: Brasiliense, 1966.
   Guarnieri, Gianfrancesco, and Augusto Boal. *Arena Conta Tiradentes*. São Paulo: Sagarana, 1967.
   Guarnieri, Gianfrancesco, Augusto Boal, and Edu Lobo. *Arena Conta Zumbi*. *Revista de Teatro*, no. 378. Rio de Janeiro: Sociedade Brasileira de Autores Teatrais, November–December, 1970.
   Guimarães Rosa, João. "A hora e vez de Augusto Matraga." *Sagarana*. 11th ed. Rio de Janeiro: José Olympio Editora, 1969.
   Jarry, Alfred. *Tout Ubu*. Paris: Éditions Fasquelle, 1968.
   Rodrigues, Nelson. *Álbum de Família*. In *Teatro Completo*, vol. 2. Edited by Sábato Magaldi. Rio de Janeiro: Nova Fronteira. 1981.
   ———. *Toda Nudez Será Castigada*. Rio de Janeiro: Distribuidora Record, n.d.
   ———. *Vestido de Noiva*. In *Teatro Completo*, vol. 1. Edited by Sábato Magaldi. Rio de Janeiro: Nova Fronteira, 1981.
B. Unpublished Works
   Andrade, Mário de. *Macunaíma*. Theatrical adaptation by Jacques Thicriot and Grupo Pau-Brasil, 1979.
   Gracias, Señor. Collective creation by Teatro Oficina, 1971.
   Guimarães Rosa, João. *Augusto Matraga*. 1986 adaptation by Antunes Filho.
   Rodrigues, Nelson. *Álbum de Família* and *Toda Nudez Será Castigada*. 1984 adaptation by Antunes Filho and Grupo Macunaíma.
II. Critical Books and Articles
   Alcântara Machado, Antônio de. "Terra Roxa e Outras Terras." Quoted

by Décio de Almeida Prado in "O Teatro," in *O Modernismo*, edited by Affonso Ávila, pp. 139–152. São Paulo: Editora Perspectiva, 1975.

Almeida, Hamilton. "Don José de la mancha." Interview with José Celso, *Revista Bondinho* (São Paulo), 13 May 1972.

Almeida Prado, Décio de. *Apresentação do Teatro Brasileiro Moderno.* São Paulo: Martins Editora, 1956.

———. "Dois Grupos Amadores." *O Estado de São Paulo*, 2 November 1958.

———. "A encenação de 'O Rei da Vela.'" *O Estado de São Paulo*, 20 October 1967.

———. "O Teatro." In *O Modernismo*, edited by Affonso Ávila, pp. 139–152. São Paulo: Editora Perspectiva, 1975.

———. "Teatro: 1930–1980." In *O Brasil Republicano*, edited by Boris Fausto, pp. 528–589. Vol. 4 of *História Geral da Civilização Brasileira.* São Paulo: Difel, 1984.

———. *O Teatro Brasileiro Moderno.* São Paulo: Editora Perspectiva, 1988.

———. *Teatro em Progresso.* São Paulo: Martins Editora, 1964.

Arte em Revista. No. 2 (May–August 1979). São Paulo: Editora Kairós.

Bakhtin, Mikhail. *Rabelais and His World.* Translated by Hélène Iswolsky. Bloomington: Indiana University Press, 1984.

Benedikt, Michael, and George E. Wellwarth, ed. and trans. *Modern French Theatre.* New York: Dutton, 1966.

Boal, Augusto. "Tentativa de Análise do Desenvolvimento do Teatro Brasileiro." *Arte em Revista*, no. 6 (October 1981), pp. 8–11. São Paulo: Editora Kairós.

Boaventura, Maria Eugênia. *A Vanguarda Antropofágica.* São Paulo: Editora Ática, 1985.

Brandão, Roberto. "Os Comediantes Profissionais." *Diário Carioca* (Rio de Janeiro), 23 December 1945. Quoted in *Dionysos*, no. 22, pp. 95–98.

Burns, E. Bradford. *A History of Brazil.* New York: Columbia University Press, 1970.

Cacciaglia, Mario. *Pequena História do Teatro no Brasil.* Translated by Carla de Queiroz. São Paulo: Editora da Universidade de São Paulo, 1986.

Campos, Augusto de. *Balanço da Bossa.* São Paulo: Editora Perspectiva, 1974.

Celso Martínez Correa, José. "O Rei da Vela: Manifesto do Oficina." In Oswald de Andrade, *O Rei da Vela*, pp. 45–52. São Paulo: Difusão Européia do Livro, 1967.

Del Rios, Jefferson. "As Sombras de Nelson Rodrigues." *Folha de São Paulo*, 11 May 1984.

Depoimentos II. Rio de Janeiro: Serviço Nacional de Teatro, 1977.

Depoimentos IV. Rio de Janeiro: Serviço Nacional de Teatro, 1978.

Dionysos. No. 22. Special issue on Os Comediantes. Rio de Janeiro: Serviço Nacional de Teatro, Ministério de Educação e Cultura, December 1975.

Dionysos. No. 23. Special issue on Teatro do Estudante do Brasil. Rio de Janeiro: Serviço Nacional de Teatro. Ministério de Educação Cultura, September 1978.

Dionysos. No. 25. Special issue on the TBC. Rio de Janeiro: Serviço Nacional de Teatro, Ministério de Educação e Cultura, September 1980.

Dionysos. No. 26. Special issue on Teatro Oficina. Rio de Janeiro: Serviço Nacional de Teatro, Ministério de Educação e Cultura, January 1982.

Doria, Gustavo. "Os Comediantes," *Dionysos,* no. 22, pp. 5–30.

———. *Moderno Teatro Brasileiro.* Rio de Janeiro: Serviço Nacional de Teatro, 1975.

Eliade, Mircea. *Le Mythe de L'Eternel Retour: Archétypes et Répétition.* Paris: Libraire Gallimard, 1949.

———. *Mythes, Rêves et Mystères.* Paris: Libraire Gallimard, 1957.

———. *The Sacred and the Profane.* Translated by Willard R. Trask. New York: Harper & Row, 1961.

Favaretto, Celso F. *Tropicália: Alegoria, Alegria.* São Paulo: Editora Kairós, 1979.

Figueiredo, Guilherme. "'Vestido de Noiva,' de Nelson Rodrigues, no Municipal pelos Comediantes." *Correio da Manhã* (Rio), 26 June 1948. Quoted in *Dionysos,* no. 22, pp. 109–112.

Flaszen, Ludwik. "Akropolis: Treatment of the Text." In Jerzy Grotowski, *Towards a Poor Theatre,* pp. 61–79. New York: Simon and Schuster, 1968.

Folha de São Paulo. "'O Rei da Vela' provoca reações." 4 October 1967.

Furtado, Celso. *O Brasil Pós-"Milagre."* Rio de Janeiro: Editora Paz e Terra, 1982.

George, David. *Grupo Macunaíma: Carnavalização e Mito.* São Paulo: Editora Perspectiva and Editora da Universidade de São Paulo, 1990.

———. "Nelson 2 Rodrigues." *The Latin American Theatre Review* (Spring 1988): 79–93.

———. "Os Comediantes and *Bridal Gown.*" *The Latin American Theatre Review* (Fall 1987): 29–41.

———. *Teatro e Antropofagia.* São Paulo: Editora Global, 1985.

———. "Towards a Poor Theatre in Brazil." *Theatre Research International* 14 (2): 152–164. Oxford University Press, 1989.

Gonçalves, Martim. "O Rei da Vela." *O Globo* (Rio), 6 October 1967.

Grotowski, Jerzy. *Towards a Poor Theatre.* New York: Simon and Schuster, 1968.

Guimarães, Carmelinda. *Um Ato de Resistência: O Teatro de Oduvaldo Vianna Filho.* São Paulo: MG Editores, 1984.

Guzik, Alberto. "Crônica de um Sonho: O Teatro Brasileiro de Comédia." Master's thesis, Escola de Comunicações e Artes, Universidade de São Paulo, 1982.

Helena, Regina. "Um rei (de velas) no Oficina." *A Gazeta* (São Paulo). 3 October 1967.

Heliodora, Bárbara. "O Hamlet de 1948." *Dionysos*, no. 23, pp. 41–44.

———. "Influências Estrangeiras no Teatro Brasileiro." *Cultura* 1 (Brasília), (1971).

Hudson, Christopher. "Darkness in Brazil." *The Standard* (London), 9 August 1982.

Humbert, Elie G. *Jung*. Translated by Marianne Ligeti. São Paulo: Summus, 1985.

Isto É. "O vendaval Antunes." São Paulo: 25 April 1984, pp. 43–47.

Jacobbi, Ruggero. "Teatro de Arena." *Folha da Noite* (São Paulo), 11 March 1953.

Jacobi, Jolande. *Complexo, Arquétipo, Símbolo*. Translated by Margit Martincic. São Paulo: Editora Cultrix, 1986.

Jafa, Van. "O Rei da Vela." *Correio da Manhã* (Rio), 26 November 1967.

Johnson, Randal. "Nelson Rodrigues As Filmed by Arnaldo Jabor." *Latin American Theatre Review* 16 (Fall 1982): 15–28.

Lemos, Tite. "A guinada de José Celso." Interview with José Celso. In *Revista da Civilização Brasileira*, pp. 115–130. Caderno Especial no. 2. "Teatro e realidade brasileira," July 1968.

Léonardini, Jean-Pierre. "Un western libre penseur." *L'Humanité* (Paris), 6 April 1987.

Lévesque, Robert. "Macunaíma: Ces merveilleux Brésiliens et leur drôle de machine." *Le Devoir* (Montreal), 29 May 1987.

Lins, Álvaro. "Algumas Notas Sobre 'Os Comediantes.'" *Correio da Manhã* (Rio), 2 January 1944. Quoted in *Dionysos*, no. 22, pp. 61–68.

Luiz, Macksen. "O Espetáculo Coletivo do Oficina." *Jornal do Brasil* (Rio), 1 February 1972.

Magaldi, Sábato. "Antunes Filho: A Consagração." *O Estado de São Paulo*, 3 September 1981.

———. *Nelson Rodrigues: Dramaturgia e Encenações*. São Paulo: Editora Perspectiva and Editora da Universidade de São Paulo, 1987.

———. *Um Palco Brasileiro: O Arena de São Paulo*. São Paulo: Brasiliense, 1984.

———. *Panorama do Teatro Brasileiro*. 2d ed. Rio de Janeiro: Serviço Nacional de Teatro, 1979.

———. "Romeu e Julieta, em uma recriação superlativa de Antunes Filho." *O Estado de São Paulo*, 17 April 1984.

———. "Surge o TBC." *Dionysos*, no. 25, pp. 43–58.

———. "O Teatro de Oswald de Andrade." Ph.D. diss., Escola de Comunicações e Artes, University of São Paulo, 1976.

———. "Teatro: Marco Zero." In Oswald de Andrade, *O Rei da Vela*, pp. 7–16. São Paulo: Difusão Européia do Livro, 1967.

———, and Maria Tereza Vargas, "Cem anos de teatro em São Paulo." Special supplement. *O estado de São Paulo*, 17 January 1976.

Mello e Souza, Gilda de. *O Tupi e o Alaúde: Uma Interpretação de Macunaíma*. São Paulo: Livraria Duas Cidades, 1979.

Mendonça, Paulo. "O Rei da Vela—I." *Folha de São Paulo*, 3 October 1967.

Mesquita, Alfredo. "Nota sobre a visita de 'Os Comediantes' a São Paulo." *O Jornal* (São Paulo), 23 July 1944. Quoted in *Dionysos*, no. 22, pp. 85–95.

———. "Origens do teatro paulista." *Dionysos*, no. 25, pp. 33–42.

Michalski, Yan. "Considerações em torno do Rei (II)." *Jornal do Brasil* (Rio), 17 January 1968.

———. "O Rei da Raiva." *Jornal do Brasil* (Rio), 16 February 1971.

———. *O Teatro sob Pressão: Uma Frente de Resistência*. Rio de Janeiro: Jorge Zahar Editor, 1985.

———. "A Vela Volta a Reinar." *Jornal do Brasil* (Rio), 31 January 1971.

Mostaço, Edelcio. *Teatro e Política: Arena, Oficina e Opinião*. São Paulo: Proposta Editorial, 1982.

Nosso Século. No. 49. São Paulo: Abril Cultural, 1980.

Nosso Século. No. 54. São Paulo: Abril Cultural, 1982.

Nunes, Benedito. Introduction to *Do Pau-Brasil à antropofagia e às utopias: Manifesto Antropófago*. Vol. 6 of *As Obras Completas de Oswald de Andrade*. Rio de Janeiro: Civilização Brasileira, 1972.

Pacheco, Mattos. "Teatro de Arena." *Ultima Hora* (São Paulo), 28 April 1953.

Paiva, Marcelo. *Feliz Ano Velho*. São Paulo: Brasiliense, 1982.

Peixoto, Fernando. "A fascinante e imprevisível trajetória do Oficina." *Dionysos*, no. 26, pp. 29–114.

———. "O Teatro Oficina." *Ciclo de Conferências Sobre o Teatro Paulista*. Teatro da Aliança Francesa. São Paulo, 16 and 23 May 1977.

———. "Zampari, Ruggero, semente, ossos." *Dionysos*, no. 25, pp. 59–64.

Pereira, Edmar. "Antunes Filho em dose tripla." *Jornal da Tarde* (São Paulo), 26 April 1984.

Rodrigues, Nelson. "O ensaio geral." *Dionysos*, no. 22, pp. 51–53.

Rodrigues, Teresa Cristina. "O segundo incêndio do Oficina: 'O Rei da Vela.'" *Jornal do Brasil* (Rio), 20 October 1967.

Rosenfeld, Anatol. "Living Theatre e Grupo Lobos." *Palco e Platéia* (São Paulo), August 1970, pp. 43–49.

Rotger, Francisco. "El poderoso influjo de la imaginación, la 'primera dama' de la escena." *El Día* (Baleares), 19 April 1987.

Sérgio Conti, Mário. "Reflexos do assombro." *Veja*, 14 May 1986.

Sérgio da Silva, Armando. "A irreverência do teatro paulista." *Le Théâtre sous le Contrainte*, pp. 187–210. Actes du Colloque International realisé à Aix-en-Provence, les 4 et 5 décembre 1985, Aix-en-Provence: Publications Diffusion, Université de Provence, 1988.

———. *Oficina: Do Teatro ao Te-ato*. São Paulo: Editora Perspectiva, 1981.

Silveira, Miroel. "'Esta Noite É Nossa' Pelo Teatro de Arena." *Folha da Tarde* (São Paulo), 23 April 1953.

Singer, Paul. "O Brasil no Contexto do Capital Internacional, 1888–

1930." In *Estrutura de Poder e Economia,* edited by Sérgio Buarque de
Hollanda, pp. 363–389. Vol. 3 of *História Geral da Civilização Brasileira.* Rio de Janeiro: Difusão Editorial, 1977.

Skidmore, Thomas E. *Politics in Brazil.* New York: Oxford University
Press, 1970.

———. *The Politics of Military Rule in Brazil, 1964–85.* New York: Oxford University Press, 1988.

Sokel, Walter H. *The Writer in Extremis.* Palo Alto: Stanford University
Press, 1959.

Última Hora. "Que há com O Rei da Vela." São Paulo, 13 October 1968.

Veja. "Milagres da criação." 25 April 1984, pp. 107.

———. "Setting Fire to Lambada." Translated and reprinted in *World
Press Review* (June 1990).

Wirth, John D. *The Politics of Brazilian Development.* Palo Alto: Stanford University Press, 1970.

III. Program Notes

Alves Lima, Mariângela. "A fábula do peregrino." Program notes for
Macunaíma, Grupo Macunaíma, 1984.

Barthes, Roland. *Fragments d'un Discours Amoureux.* Quoted in the
1984 program for *Romeu e Julieta.*

Dort, Bernard. "Uma comédia em transe." Quoted in the 1969 program
for *O Rei da Vela.*

Magaldi, Sábato. "Trajectory and Unity of a Work." Program notes for
Nelson 2 Rodrigues, 1984.

Okun, Milton. "To Be(atles) or Not to Be(atles)." Program notes for
Romeu e Julieta, 1984.

Perrone-Moisés, Leyla. "Amor e Poder." Program notes for *Romeu e
Julieta,* 1984.

Zeitel, Amália. "Nelson Rodrigues, a Vital Author." Program notes for
Nelson 2 Rodrigues, 1984.

IV. Personal Interviews

Almeida Prado, Décio de, 27 September 1983, São Paulo.

Celso Martínez Correa, José, March 1980, July 1982, June 1984, São
Paulo.

Filho, Antunes, March 1984, January 1987, and January 1988. São Paulo.

Guarnieri, Gianfrancesco, 24 August 1977, São Paulo.

Império, Flávio, 7 September 1977, São Paulo.

Queiroz Telles, Carlos, 29 August 1977, São Paulo.

Renato, José, 10 August 1977, Rio de Janeiro.

Zeitel, Amália, 10 April 1983, São Paulo.

Index